THE CLASSICS
OF WESTERN
SPIRITUALITY

D1286538

THE CLASSICS OF WESTERN SPIRITUALITY
A Library of the Great Spiritual Masters

Margaret Ebner
MAJOR WORKS

TRANSLATED AND EDITED BY
LEONARD P. HINDSLEY

INTRODUCED BY
MARGOT SCHMIDT AND LEONARD P. HINDSLEY

PREFACE BY
RICHARD WOODS, O.P.

PAULIST PRESS
NEW YORK • MAHWAH

Cover art: The cover design is based upon a painting representing Margaret Ebner, of which there are numerous versions to be seen at the Monastery of Maria Medingen. The original was painted on the back of the choir stall of the subprioress and is one of an entire series of portraits of Dominican saints and blesseds painted on each choir stall ranging from St. Dominic to Venerable Jerome Savonarola pictured in flames! The symbolic portrait dates from 1720 and is based upon the tomb effigy of 1353. Margaret is portrayed in the habit of her order bearing the crucifix which she always had with her—the same crucifix located on the altar in the Margaret Chapel at the monastery today. The crucifix represents Margaret's acceptance of the sufferings of Christ into her own life. She even wondered how anyone could be said to be following Christ without accepting suffering in imitation of the Savior. Also symbolically portrayed with Margaret is her statue of the Child Jesus which is still preserved in the museum at Maria Medingen. While the Crucified Savior represented salvific suffering, the Infant Jesus represented joy for Margaret. It was common for each Dominican nun to have a statue of the Infant Jesus in her monastic cell. For Margaret this statue was not only a means of meditation upon the infancy, but also a mode of revelation from the Child through prayer. The presence of the crucifix and the statue speak powerfully of a spirituality that is centered on Christ and as such is a spirituality both of suffering and of joy. Even during her greatest periods of illness, Margaret attests that she felt interior joy because of the presence of Christ to her. This deep and interior relationship with Christ is represented in the portrait by the open book of *Revelations* wherein Margaret reveals to us her life hidden in Christ. She wrote that she had truly received from him "what no eye has seen nor ear heard what God has prepared for those who love him" (1 Cor 2:9).

Library of Congress Cataloging-in-Publication Data

Ebner, Margaret, ca. 1291–1351
    [Offenbarungen. English]
    Major works/Margaret Ebner; translated and edited by Leonard P. Hindsley; introduced by Margot Schmidt and Leonard P. Hindsley; preface by Richard Woods.
        p.   cm.—(The Classics of Western spirituality)
    Also includes Margaret's Pater Noster, translated from the Middle High German (4 p.).
    Includes bibliographical references and indexes.
    ISBN 0-8091-0462-8: (cloth)—ISBN 0-8091-3397-0 (pbk.)
    1. Ebner, Margaret, ca. 1291–1351. 2. Dominican sisters—Germany—Biography. 3. Women mystics—Germany—Biography. 4. Spiritual life—Middle Ages, 600–1500. I. Hindsley, Leonard Patrick, 1950–.
    II. Ebner, Margaret, ca. 1291–1351. Pater Noster. English. 1993. III. Title. IV. Series.
BV5095.E2A3   1993
271'.97202—dc20
[B]
             92-46650
             CIP

Published by Paulist Press
997 Macarthur Boulevard
Mahwah, New Jersey 07430

Printed and bound in the
United States of America

Contents

Editor and Translator of this Volume
Co-Author of the Introduction
LEONARD P. HINDSLEY is associate professor of humanities and
assistant dean of undergraduate students at Providence College. He
also serves as editor of *Providence: Studies in Western Civilization.*
He studied at LaSalle University and the University of Fribourg. He
earned the Ph.D. in Germanic languages and literatures at Rutgers
University in 1980, after which he received a licentiate in sacred
theology from the Pontifical Faculty of the Immaculate Conception
in Washington, D.C.

Co-Author of the Introduction
MARGOT SCHMIDT is professor of medieval spirituality at the
University of Eichstätt. She is the editor of a new series of medieval
texts entitled *Mystik in Geschichte und Gegenwart.* In that series she
produced two volumes with translations of the works of Richard of
Biberach and another volume of papers read at the Conference
"Theologia Mystica" at Weingarten in November 1985. She has
written extensively on women mystics, especially on Hildegard of
Bingen, Mechthild of Magdeburg, and Margaret Ebner.

Author of the Preface
RICHARD WOODS, O.P., is associate professor of spiritual theology in the Institute of Pastoral Studies, Loyola University of Chi-
cago, and adjunct associate professor in psychiatry at Loyola University Medical School. Former editor of *Spirituality Today,* he is the
author of *Christian Spirituality: God's Presence Through the Ages, Eckhart's Way,* and other books and articles.

DEDICATION

To Mary and John

Gloria haec est omnibus sanctis ejus

Foreword

Various works of great names among the German mystics, such as Meister Eckhart, John Tauler, and Henry Suso, have appeared in the Classics of Western Spirituality Series. These Dominicans were remembered, if not always appreciated, throughout history because of their great influence on many later figures. The mystic Dominican nuns, such as Christina Ebner and Adelheid Langmann, were less well remembered, in part because they generally recorded their experiences using the medium of their own Middle High German dialects. Within one hundred years these vernacular texts began to be difficult to understand for the ordinary reader. For a long time these works remained obscure, hidden like the lives of these nuns. Margaret Ebner's major works, presented in this volume, have never before been translated into English. It is hoped that this translation will make Margaret Ebner more widely known in the English-speaking world, thus giving her the praise that is her due among mystics of the fourteenth century.

I would like to thank Fr. Benedict Ashley, O.P., who first encouraged me to pursue a study of Margaret Ebner while on a brief walk at River Forest.

Thanks must also be given to Fr. Gabriel O'Donnell, O.P., for his care and advice as director of my S.T.L. thesis on the spirituality of Margaret Ebner. Thanks also to Fr. Boniface Ramsey, O.P., for his time in reading through portions of the translation at that stage.

It is difficult to express adequately my debt of thanks to the Franciscan Sisters of Maria Medingen, especially to Sr. Kolonata, Sr. Ingeborg, Sr. Dagmar, and Sr. Clarice, who were so kind and generous to me during my research time in the archives of Maria Medingen.

Thanks also to Professor Charles Duffy and to Sr. Mary of the Assumption of the Monastery of the Mother of God in West Springfield, who kindly read the manuscript at various stages and made useful suggestions. Special thanks go to Fr. Nicholas Ingham, O.P., for his thoughtful corrections and suggestions in the final stages of work, and also to Bernard McGinn, the editor of this series, for his invaluable assistance.

Preface

The twentieth century is likely to be remembered as the second era during which the Western church discovered women—or perhaps more accurately, the second period in which the creative presence and leadership of women were clearly revealed in the church.

During the High Middle Ages, beginning with religious women such as Hrotsvit, the incomparable Hildegard of Bingen, and a generation of twelfth-century Cistercian nuns, religious women successfully defied the most powerful and austere monastic orders in Christendom to secure their identity and independence. In the thirteenth and fourteenth centuries communities of lay women likewise emerged as a powerful and sometimes threatening presence in a religious world dominated for centuries by men.

The Dominican nuns of the period, particularly those in southern Germany and northern Switzerland, represent the epitome of spiritual liberation, combining the mystical enthusiasm of the Béguines and the deep learning of their Cistercian and Benedictine predecessors as well as that of their own Order.

They lived in a turbulent era, one disturbingly like our own, and thus instructive for understanding many of the religious tensions of the twentieth century, including the struggle of multitudes of religious women to discover or create an appropriate place and ministry as fully adult members of the People of God. For many reasons, of all the many hundreds of Dominican women the record of whose lives and many of whose writings have survived, Margaret Ebner is an excellent choice to be both guide and exemplar.

At first glance, however, women and men today seem to have very little in common with the mystical nuns of fourteenth-century Germany. They were, after all, *nuns*—cloistered women removed in fact and intention from the ordinary social world. Moreover, they are remote from us in time and geographically distant. And if thousands of such women once filled German monasteries, today their numbers are inexorably diminishing.

Second, their spirituality appears alien, in many respects opposed to the kind of religious life that women in the church today want, need, and are creating. Margaret's acceptance and even quest for suffering in imitation and love of the crucified Christ, like her devotion to the Infant Jesus and the "poor souls," is an aspect of medieval spirituality largely repugnant to our modern "healthy-minded" sensibilities. While of clinical interest to students of religion, ecstatic rapture, visions, the stigmata, and other mystical phenomena represent ideal or even desirable goals of spiritual development for few Christians today.

Above all, the nuns' apparently unquestioning submission to religious authority, their cheerful and absolute obedience to superiors or male spiritual directors, and their meticulous observance of the minutiae of the monastic rule hardly seem appealing in terms of contemporary spiritual liberation.

But at second glance, fourteenth-century nuns such as Margaret Ebner have a great deal to tell us about the struggle for and meaning of liberation then and today. Even their attitude toward inescapable suffering has increasing significance to Christians in central Africa, Latin America, and southeast Asia, as well as the economically and politically blighted areas of the First World. Observed more closely, their approach to authority, obedience, and observance takes on a surprisingly creative hue.

As detailed in the comprehensive introduction by Margot Schmidt and Leonard Hindsley, during the long struggle between Emperor Louis of Bavaria and popes John XXII and Benedict XII, Margaret Ebner personally, and her monastery collectively, supported the emperor, while the Dominican order as a whole, and Margaret's own confessor, supported the pope. Moreover, the nuns were able to resist interdiction even though the convent of Maria Medingen had been under direct papal jurisdiction since its founding. Sometime afterward, the monastery found itself in defiance of the local bishop, again exercising a spiritual autonomy (some might say anarchy) that Margaret found completely consonant with her devotion to God, Christ, and the church.

Intellectual liberation was no less a feature of the nuns' lives. In the tradition of Hildegard of Bingen and Mechthild of Magdeburg, next to being mystics the German Dominican nuns were above all students. They read, wrote, and discussed theology. Among the precious gifts sent to Maria Medingen by Margaret's adviser, the secular priest Henry of Nördlingen, was a manuscript copy of the

Summma Theologiae. He also sent a copy of his translation of Mech-thild's *The Flowing Light of the Godhead,* Henry Suso's *Horologium sapientiae,* and other books.

Obtaining and copying manuscripts was a principal work of the monasteries. Some applicants were refused admission because they lacked the requisite abilities to flourish there—particularly skill in reading and writing. The Dominican provincial, Hermann of Min-den, stipulated around 1290 that their spiritual mentors should them-selves be learned. And thus began the association between scholarly mystics—Eckhart, Suso, Tauler, and Henry of Nördlingen among them—and the hundreds of German Dominican nuns, a relationship that would permanently transform the spiritual and literary landscape of Europe.

Through sometimes reciprocal spiritual guidance and the sup-port of their brethren and secular priests such as Henry of Nördlingen, the nuns likewise achieved a freedom of spirit that sur-passed the liberty sought by the schismatic and heretical groups that proliferated during this period.

Preaching and radical poverty, the twin fonts of the *vita apos-tolica,* were the encompassing ideal of Albigensians, Béguines, the Fraticelli, and Spiritual Franciscans, as well as the Conventual Fran-ciscans, Dominicans, and other mendicants of the thirteenth and fourteenth centuries. While the nuns of the fourteenth century did not minister publicly, they were far from isolating themselves from the world. Many of them engaged in extensive exhortation through letters and other writings. They provided counsel to ordinary lay people as well as to kings, bishops, and priests. In 1350 Emperor Charles IV sought the advice of Margaret's contemporary Christina Ebner. Margaret herself advised noblewomen and the abbot of Kais-heim, among others. From the establishment of the first convents by St. Dominic himself, the nuns cultivated true poverty of body, mind, and spirit. Theirs was a life of gospel simplicity, one reduced to bare essentials, particularly devoid of the ostentation and refinement in-creasingly characteristic of the urban culture burgeoning in the pros-perous world of medieval Europe.

But if the fourteenth century was an era grown opulent and indulgent from increased trade and commercial enterprise, it was also an epoch of violence and bloodshed. Papal and Imperial armies clashed repeatedly, rivals battled for the Imperial and lesser thrones, free-booting ex-crusaders terrorized the countryside, peasant rebellion and civil strife exploded with unprecedented fury, and the Hundred Years' War between England and France erupted intermittently. But most frightening of all, beginning in 1347 the worst epidemic in Western history carried off as much as half the population of Europe during the following fifty years. Sudden and often unprovided death was an ever-present reality, a dominant motif that altered art, literature, music, and spirituality for centuries.

In this respect, perhaps the nuns' greatest liberation was to be able, quite literally, to sing and laugh in the face of death. Despite the genuine sorrow she felt at the death of several of her friends, Margaret's attitude was one of supreme confidence in the mercy of God, one which was often rewarded by some kind of experience of assurance that the deceased individual had entered into eternal peace. When the Black Death reached Germany in 1348, Margaret expressed the same compassionate but peaceful concern for its victims as she did for all those entrusted to her prayers.

An era of increasing formalism and clericalism in the church, the fourteenth century was also one which exalted courtly love—idealistic, romantic, and ultimately adulterous. Not surprisingly, by the end of the period, coldness and cynicism prevailed. Thus, achieving sincere and equal friendship with other women and men represents a third triumph of spiritual liberation in the lives of the German Dominican nuns. The mystical, largely literary partnerships of the nuns and their spiritual advisers, such as Elsbeth Stagel and Henry Suso, and particularly that between Margaret and Henry of Nördlingen, disclose an alternative of impressive depth, sensitivity, and—significantly—parity.

All this may seem far from Margaret Ebner's reflections on experiences of grace during her life. But it would be all too easy to miss amid her descriptions of unusual and bewildering phenomena and apparently quaint devotions the simple lucidity and depth of her faith, the strength of her friendships human and divine, and her sincerity and fidelity in the face of great suffering, illness, and death. By placing her "revelations" in the context of the times and exploring their hidden riches, Leonard Hindsley and Margot Schmidt have rendered a great and lasting service to students of spiritual literature. They have also indirectly illuminated aspects of our own time by means of what Barbara Tuchman described as "a distant mirror."

Additionally, in providing the first English edition of the *Revelations* and *Pater Noster* of Blessed Margaret Ebner, Father Hindsley has introduced us to a woman whose experiences, themes, and profundity of spirit make her a worthy companion of her later contemporaries, St. Catherine of Siena, Julian of Norwich, and the ecstatic Margery Kempe.

Questions concerning the place and authority of women in today's church and that of the future will increasingly require the ability to discern fundamental matters from symbolic or peripheral ones. I do not think that the major issues will really revolve around the redistribution of rank, power, and wealth, but rather, the emergence and recognition of new paradigms of spirituality.

In this respect, women are manifestly surpassing men in the church today as they did in the Middle Ages insofar as growing rich and exercising control have never been their major objectives. Theirs has been another route and a deeper issue: moral and spiritual autonomy, that is, the art and right of self-determination within the limits of the Gospel obedience which obliges all Christians to the law of Love.

Attaining adulthood in the City of God offers a deeper and broader objective than achieving political power, canonical status, or security. It is analogous to and coupled with the struggle for liberation of third-world churches among first-world churches. It is, moreover, allied to the quest for liberation of all peoples everywhere in the name of God who, as revealed in the human person of Jesus Christ, is the truth who sets us free. This was Margaret Ebner's way and life.

Introduction

The biography of a saint or a blessed is always an account of the life of God acting in and through a believer, as well as an account of how that individual chose to live the Gospel life of charity. This is especially evident in the autobiography of a saint or blessed that covers the entire adult life and experiences of that individual with God and neighbors. The spiritual autobiography of Blessed Margaret Ebner is one such account of the mysterious action of God calling a beloved daughter to conversion and to the fullness of Gospel life, a life of love for God and neighbor and service to others.

A considerable amount of scholarly and popular work has been accomplished in order to make known the lives and works of Dominican friars of the Later Middle Ages, such as Meister Eckhart, John Tauler and Henry Suso, but relatively little has been done to make known the lives and writings of Dominican nuns who were their contemporaries and friends. This translation and commentary will help to introduce one of these nuns—Margaret Ebner—to the English-speaking world. Parts One and Two of this Introduction provide necessary and useful information concerning the life and times of Margaret by a presentation of her family background, her monastery, her friends, and the political circumstances of that age. Part Three presents an exposition of some of the elements of her spirituality in terms of her conversion to a deeper spiritual life. The body of the text is a complete translation of her spiritual autobiography, *Die Offenbarungen* or *Revelations,* and also of her *Pater Noster,* which was her personal prayer of private devotion. This English translation is based on the manuscript of 1353, still extant in the archives of the Monastery of Maria Medingen and on other subsequent versions found there and in the British Museum. The critical edition done by Philipp Strauch in 1882, reprinted in 1962, was also consulted.[1] Reference was also made to the incomplete Modern German translations of Hieronymus Wilms, O.P., and Josef Prestel, and to the Latin translation used in preparation for the beatification process of Margaret Ebner in 1979.[2]

INTRODUCTION

PART ONE

1.1. Primary Sources

Thanks to the spiritual friendship between the secular priest, Henry of Nördlingen, and the mystically-graced Dominican nun, Margaret Ebner, her writings, the *Revelations,* and the collection of letters from Henry to Margaret have been preserved for us. This testimony to an exceptional relationship between the Dominican Blessed and her Father Confessor not only gives us cultural-historical insight into centuries past, but is also a notable portrayal of the mutual striving of two courageous souls to overcome daily adversities by the power of the spirit and of grace.

According to Philipp Strauch, the editor of the critical text of Margaret's book, the *Revelations* and her *Pater Noster* have come to us as transcriptions on a parchment manuscript of 1353, preserved in the archives of the Monastery of Maria Medingen (=*M*).[3] The original is no longer extant. In Medingen three further copies exist from the years 1676, 1687, and 1728. Other copies of the oldest Manuscript *M* are found in Berlin, ms. 179, dated around 1470,[4] and in London at the British Museum, Cod. Add 11430, from the sixteenth century.[5] This manuscript also contains letters to Margaret from Henry of Nördlingen and other contemporaries. The transcription of the paper manuscript Cod 3, 40, 43 in Marburg, Fürstliche Oettingen-Wallerstein'sche library from the year 1735, appears to derive from the original manuscript.[6]

For the process of beatification initiated in 1686, Prior Anton Holdermann of Obermedlingen composed a Latin translation of the *Revelations* in 1744 in order to promote the cause. He sent this translation to the Dominican Generalate in Rome to be examined. After lengthy delays and renewed attempts over many centuries, the veneration of Margaret Ebner was officially recognized by Rome on 24 February 1979, when her cult was ratified and she was officially given the title "Blessed."

Margaret Ebner would never have undertaken the task of writing her *Revelations* for posterity, and indeed thought herself incapable of composing such a document, had it not been for the insistence of her spiritual director, Henry of Nördlingen. Having served in that role for twelve years and having guided Margaret along the path to spiritual perfection by timely advice and having helped her to discern the action of God's grace in the daily events of her life, he requested that she record all the revelations and experiences that God had given her. She resisted this suggestion, for she hoped that he would compose the desired biography since he possessed detailed knowledge of her life and relationship with Christ. Wisely, he refused. However, it is quite probable that he did read and edit the final manuscript some time after her death.[7] And so, during the Advent of 1344, she began to dictate and to write down her experiences. The content of the *Revelations* covers the years 1312 to 1348.

The literary worth of the *Revelations* has been variously evaluated by scholars. Ludwig Zoepf judged the text to be an honorable record of the grace given by God, but thought the account was often reported in a very dry style.[8] He maintained that Margaret's limited literary ability made endless repetitions necessary. Also, few real images were employed in the work.[9] Philipp Strauch agreed with the paucity of images and complained of the monotony despite several instances of the use of rhyme and assonance.[10]

Margaret's language and style are simple and unpretentious. Frequently she made grammatical errors, especially in the use of verb tenses. Occasionally it seems as if she merely copied the contents of one of her letters to Henry of Nördlingen without adapting it to the circumstances. It must be remembered that her goal was never the production of a work whose greatness would rest upon its literary worth. Rather, she wrote and dictated in a straightforward, conversational manner all she could recall concerning her spiritual life, all that seemed important or significant to her. Thus we read reports of numerous experiences of conversion, of gifts of God's grace received through various channels, of relationships with sisters in the monastery, with Henry of Nördlingen, with the emperor, with superiors, with long-dead saints, and souls suffering in purgatory. She related her desires with regard to mystical experiences and offered an account of those given to her. However, both Karl Bihlmeyer and Ludwig Zoepf took note of her literary independence. She did not imitate the contemporary style of biography, and therefore her book is free of the excesses and exaggerations commonly found in standard *Vitae* of the period.[11]

The value of the *Revelations* lies in the woman it reveals. Her character is disclosed to us by a process of conversion during a difficult era in church history, and by her account of a loving relationship with God and the consequences such a great love entailed for her. As Hieronymus Wilms correctly asserted, the true value of the *Revelations* rests on Margaret Ebner herself. She was, in the fullest sense, a mystic blessed by God, and therefore her writings have continuing value.[12]

A complete translation of her major works is of great importance for the history of medieval spirituality. It reveals the inner life and thought of a nun who was considered to be holy even during her lifetime, while offering a glimpse into the life of a woman who was an important member of a great spiritual movement—the Friends of God. This new and complete translation affords insight into the lives of cloistered Dominican nuns of the Middle Ages—how they related to each other in community and how they viewed their role in society. Margaret was the first Dominican nun to write such a document about her spiritual experiences.

1.2 The Life of Margaret Ebner

The sources for Margaret's life are the text of her *Revelations*, produced under unique circumstances, and the surviving collection of letters from Henry. However, these comprise no biography in the modern sense with a continuous presentation of external events, but rather give only scant information, which mainly portrays and illustrates the events of her interior life. It is upon these sources that the various "Lives" written since the seventeenth century are based. The "Description of Her Life" by Sebastian Schlettstetter (1662) and another by Eustachius Eysenhuet (1688), both manuscripts preserved in the monastery of Maria Medingen, contain excerpts from the *Revelations* as evidence of her virtue.[13] From these sources and from historical research Margaret's external life may be summarized as follows.

Margaret was born around 1291 at Donauwörth into a patrician family whose origins are documented as early as 1239. At about fifteen years of age, in 1305, she entered the monastery of Dominican nuns at Maria Medingen near Dillingen on the Danube as a choirsister. According to Eysenhuet, this occurred with the approval of her parents. One of Margaret's aunts already belonged to the convent and other close relatives seemed to have followed her there. Two of her close relations, Agnes Münzmeisterin (1351–53), perhaps her sister-in-law, and Elizabeth of Höchstetten (1364–70) were each elected prioress of the monastery. Thus there were evidently strong ties between Maria Medingen and the upper levels of society from the Imperial Free City of Donauwörth in the fourteenth century.[14]

The name Ebner (MHG *ebenaere*) means "arbiter, referee, judge" (MHG *ebenen* = to make smooth, to level, to settle appeals), so that Margaret probably belonged to a judicial family of Donauwörth.[15] Johannes Traber compiled fifty excerpts from title documents in which members of the Ebner family of Donauwörth were named during the years 1245–1391.[16] The good reputation and wealth of the family were due to foreign trade, to their lands, and not least of all to the profitable office of magistrate, which the German kings granted mainly to the patrician families of Donauwörth. As such, members of the Ebner family frequently controlled the destiny of the city. Anton Michael Seitz sees Hartmann, Margaret's brother, among the documented councilors of the city. In her *Revelations* and in the letters of Henry of Nördlingen, it is simply stated that she had a brother.[17] In her book Margaret wrote once of her "geschwistertig" (brothers and sisters), so that it is likely that she had a sister whose name and fate remain unknown to us.

The monastery was founded in 1246 by Hartmann IV, Count of Dillingen, and in the same year the care of the nuns was given to the Order of Preachers. Medingen was numbered among the more than sixty-five monasteries of nuns in Upper Germany that were entrusted to the spiritual care of the Dominican friars in the fourteenth century. The monastery at Medingen had already grown to number more than seventy nuns by 1260, when it was decided to make a new foundation, a daughter house in nearby Obermedlingen.

On 6 February 1312, "the feast of SS. Vedastus and Amandus," as Margaret expressly wrote in retrospect, she was overcome by a mysterious, severe illness, which led to physical breakdown and caused her continuing physical suffering until 1325. After intermittent periods of recovery, the illness would overcome her anew with violent physical pain as well as spiritual-religious emotions. She endured this illness up to her death. But at the same time interior consolations, happiness, and enlightenment increased, so that despite the meticulous description of all her painful conditions, Margaret shines forth as a character of great veracity and increasing spiritual power and ability to love; this brought about a deep inner peace, which was seen as the cause of blessings for her immediate circle of friends and far beyond.

Due to the instability caused by war, she spent the years 1324–25 outside the monastery at home with her family safe behind the fortified walls of Donauwörth. The background for this began in 1301, when King Albrecht I wrested the city of Werd (Donauwörth) from Bavaria and made it an Imperial Free City. When Duke Louis IV of Bavaria was elected German Emperor in 1314, he endeavored to reappropriate the city to his family. In Werd a rebellion arose against this attempt, but the majority of the citizens favored Louis. Louis frequently remained in the city, even staying four weeks in 1323. There, in the following year, he gathered together an army for the march to Burgau, a fortification defended for the Austrians by Burkhard of Ellerbach, who was later relieved by Duke Leopold of Austria. Being forced to retreat, Emperor Louis turned back toward Donauwörth about the middle of January 1325. This retreat brought "distress and trouble" to Medingen. Margaret alluded to this time of conflict in the *Revelations* when she wrote that she "had to go out of the monastery to her mother," accompanied by a lay sister, just as later during the Schmalkaldic War (1546–47) the entire community of the monastery had to flee.[18] The special connection between Louis the Bavarian and the city of Donauwörth may be the basis for Margaret's great interest in him, and may also explain why she later took up the cause of Emperor Louis in the dispute with the pope, unlike her spiritual director, Henry of Nördlingen. During this time she may even have met the emperor.[19]

After 1325 Margaret endured many years of sickness during which she was confined to her bed and required the constant care of another sister. As a new trial she suffered the death of her faithful care-giving sister, who had been her support in difficult times. This loss overwhelmed her with great sadness out of which she wrote, "I could not pay attention to anyone else, and those who were previously dear to me, I did not want to see."[20] The death of her companion strengthened her conviction to live in a state of yet greater withdrawal. While she mourned the death of her friend, the fateful meeting with the secular priest Henry of Nördlingen took place on

"St. Narcissus Day" (29 October 1332). Perhaps he had been summoned by the superior to help Margaret overcome her depression, for she "saw no one and went nowhere." When Henry came to Medingen for the first time, according to Margaret's own account, she hesitated to see him, admitting, "I did it unwillingly." Obviously this visit immediately established a mutual understanding, since Margaret later commented briefly on this first meeting with the words, "but when I came I heard his truthful teachings gladly." From that moment on a lifelong spiritual friendship grew, which brought her inner stability. In Henry she had found the spiritual partner "from whose words and life I always received powerful consolation," as she later noted. Margaret first met Henry when she was forty-one years old.

By supporting the pope at Avignon Henry became the ecclesiastical-political opponent of Louis the Bavarian, making it necessary for Henry to leave his Swabian homeland in 1338. For about ten years he lived mainly in Basel, where he worked as preacher and confessor and led a circle of Friends of God, whom he made known to Margaret. In this way a lively exchange of letters between Henry and Margaret became the means of exchange of thought. The fruit of this correspondence was Margaret's little book—the *Revelations*. At Henry's desire she began her writing in 1344, but sometimes dictated to Elsbeth of Scheppach, the future prioress of the monastery. Margaret's writings contain experiences of her inner life retrospective to 1312, expressing a bridal and passion mysticism coordinated to the liturgy of the church year. Of her first twenty years of life she has nothing to report, since up till then she had lived without any true "awareness of herself." Margaret's *Revelations* end with the year 1348. When, after his exile, Henry finally left Alsace and returned to Swabia at the beginning of 1350, the land was being ravaged by the plague. It is uncertain whether Henry and Margaret were ever reunited before she died around the age of sixty on 20 June 1351.

Because of her reputation for sanctity, a tomb effigy was erected to her honor in the Chapter room soon after her death. Only Margaret was entombed there; the usual burial place for the sisters would have been under the cloister walk. Soon thereafter the Chapter room was converted into a chapel for her veneration. Documented evidence for the great reverence Margaret enjoyed immediately after her death is quite clear. On 12 March 1353, not even two years after her death, Sister Adelheid of Nördlingen bequeathed one pound Haller perpetual rent from the "Austrian hide of land" for the "light in the chapel of blessed Margaret Ebner." She specified it should never be used for anything else, no matter into whatever need the monastery might fall.[21] On 4 July 1391 the prioress, Wulfit of Katzenstein, bought a hide of land at Weilerstettin for 111 pounds in Augsburg pence from a citizen of Augsburg "for the chapel at Medingen in the monastery where the blessed sister Margaret Ebner lies buried." Yet further evidence is given by a notable document dated 14 September 1428. For thirty florins Peter Pfeill, citizen of Dillingen, sold a perpetual rent of two florins on his house in his native city near to the lower gate at Dillingen to two nuns of Medingen, Margaretha of Renshofen and Margareta of Ramungen, with the stipulation that after the decease of both nuns this rent should fall "to the chapel situated in the cloister of the monastery of Medingen where Master Henry der Säldner and Ann (?) rest in peace near to Blessed Ebner." About this Johannes Traber noted, "This Master Henry der Säldner may well be Henry of Nördlingen, who after his death may have found a resting place by the side of his revered Margaret Ebner. Henry's surname was previously unknown. Perhaps this document will prompt further new research on Henry's life and work."[22]

According to A. M. Seitz, it is certain that the ancient male line of the Donauwörth Ebner family died out around 1400 (see Appendix, Figure 1). On the basis of numerous documents that attest to this distinguished Ebner family from 1239 onward, it is certain that the family possessed an armorial seal (see Appendix, Figure 2).[23] The round seal, which contains a three-cornered shield, bears the inscription: "+S(igillum) Hartmanni. Ebnerii." The shield displays an eagle's claw from left to right. The document to which this seal was attached is dated 18 July 1328. According to Seitz, this escutcheon may also be the personal shield of Margaret Ebner, since it is demonstrably the coat-of-arms of her brother Hartmann.

In memory of Margaret Ebner the North Swabian community of Mödingen (= Medingen) in the district of Dillingen has adopted the eagle's claw, the heraldic symbol of the Donauwörth Ebners, as its official insignia in order to emphasize the close ties between the monastery and village over the last seven hundred years (see Appendix, Figure 3). The heraldic symbol of the community of Schäfstall on the Danube, where the patrician Ebner family of Donauwörth had privileges and estates even earlier, also shows the eagle's claw of the Ebners, reminiscent of their connection in the Middle Ages (see Appendix, Figure 4).

1.3 The History of the Monastery of Maria Medingen

The Monastery of Maria Medingen near Dillingen looks back on a history of seven hundred years, having been founded in 1246 by Count Hartmann IV of Dillingen and Kyburg. Dedicated to the Virgin Mary, it was closely connected to the history of the surrounding area. According to an old topographical description of the community of Medingen, this place received its name from an old wood-carved statue of the Mother of God in a chapel on a large "Maad" or meadow ("Mary of the Meadow" or Maria Medingen), where pious women called Béguines made their devotions at that time.[24] Therefore, the later foundation of a monastery of Dominican nuns was merely the affiliation of a previously existing community of sisters, occasionally located elsewhere, who had already lived as penitents under the Rule of St. Augustine before being incorporated into the Order of St. Dominic. Another possibility for the placename derives from a curative spring (*mederi* = to cure). In fact there is such a spring in the cloister garden, "which flows with a great quantity of ochre in it." However, according to recent research it contains a quantity of minerals too small to be of curative value. In reality, the village of Medingen had already existed for centuries. In the course of time the spelling of the placename alternated among Mädingen, Mödingen, and Medingen.

Count Hartmann IV was descended from an ancient and distinguished Alemmanic noble family, which by plausible supposition had already been entrusted with the title of count in Brenzgau in the Carolingian period. The family acquired valuable possessions along the Danube and established the family seat at Dillingen, from which they took their name. Again and again, Hartmann appeared in the retinue of the emperor. From the Hohenstaufen emperors he received the office of Marshall of Swabia, the imperial advocacy over the city of Ulm, and acted as protector of various monasteries. "He was bound by the closest ties of relationship to the dukes of Bavaria, the Markgraves of Vohburg, the counts of Görz and Tyrol, and the

Landgrave of Thuringia, the counts of Württemberg, Helfenstein, Zollern, and the Markgrave of Burgau." He was praised as a "faithful vassal of the Emperor, obedient son of the Church, good husband and virtuous father of his children." Of his four sons only the youngest survived him—Hartmann, later the Bishop of Augsburg. The first prioress of Maria Medingen was Maria Sophia (1246–80), Countess of Dillingen-Kyburg, the sister of the founder and aunt of Bishop Hartmann of Augsburg.[25] The founder secured the tax-free status of the monastery, and like their father, the three sons who predeceased him endowed Maria Medingen with further property for its support.

It is noteworthy that already in the foundation document of 1246 the right of free election was guaranteed to the monastery. This included not only the right to elect and remove the prioress and monastery officials, but also to choose the priest for their spiritual care. It stipulated that he should be a "suitable priest" who should be presented to the Bishop of Augsburg by the prioress.[26] This provision is reminiscent of Hildegard of Bingen, who secured the same right in the statutes for her new monastic foundation at Rubertsberg in 1151, proof that from the twelfth century onward monasteries of nuns were concerned with their independence. By his letter of 8 February 1246, Pope Innocent IV placed the Monastery of Maria Medingen under his protection and confirmed these same privileges: "Namely, the church itself will be established with its possessions: the manor in Dale, the possessions at Dillingen, at Dorfusch, Wittislingen and Schabringen with meadows, vineyards, fields, woods, hunting rights in forest and field, with streams and mills and with all immunities and privileges."[27]

On 13 March 1246, Pope Innocent placed the monastery under the care of the provincial of the German province of the Order of Friars Preachers. A papal bull addressed to the sisters on the same date granted their earnest request, which had been delivered to the Holy See through the influence of the Count of Montfort, to be placed under the guidance of the Friars Preachers. On their own initiative the sisters had asked that the monastery be placed under the care of the Order instead of the bishop and had found in the Count their advocate in this matter. The connection of the Count of Montfort to the monastery is not clear, but he did use his influence under similar circumstances for the Dominican monastery of St. Katherine in Augsburg at the same time. Even before 1246 there were close ties between Maria Medingen and the Monastery of St. Katherine in Augsburg, a connection which in the course of its history would be of special significance. The nuns of St. Katherine housed the nuns of Medingen temporarily during the difficult times of the Reformation. As a result of the return to the Catholic faith of Duke Wolfgang Wilhelm, Count Palatine of Neuburg, nuns from St. Katherine were able to reestablish the monastery of Medingen in 1616, after it had been left vacant for ten years.[28]

The Dominican nuns of Medingen came from the higher levels of society, from families of counts, officeholders, and recognized patrician families. During the time of Margaret Ebner, one such patrician woman was Elsbeth Scheppach, from a notable governing family. Elsbeth was not only Margaret's scribe, but also later her prioress. In addition to the Ebners, women from other patrician families—notably the Münzmeisters and Höchstettens—also entered the convent.

For the choirsisters the divine office according to the rite of the Dominican Order was the principal duty. The choirsisters also had the right and duty of electing the prioress. The most responsible office in the monastery was the *procuratrix*, who had the task of overseeing the temporal needs of the community. At the time of Margaret Ebner, Elsbeth Scheppach had this duty before she was elected prioress. Margaret had the title of "mistress of construction" (*Baumeisterin*). An important activity of the monastery was conducting a scriptorium in which manuscripts were copied. The oldest extant evidence of these manuscripts is the writing of Margaret Ebner in 1353. This is still contained in the Monastery of Maria Medingen, along with a few other examples of their work. How much of their work has been lost is impossible to ascertain. Even the numerous office books and hymnals cannot be found. The monastery must have possessed scholarly texts also, for in his letters Henry of Nördlingen reported the purchase and transcription of the *Summa Theologiae* by St. Thomas Aquinas. In 1345 he wrote to Margaret, "With great earnestness, I wish you to acquire the three parts of the *Summa* of St. Thomas of the Preachers . . . which is for sale in Augsburg."[29] The *Little Book of Eternal Wisdom* by Henry Suso was also known and used by the sisters—a sign of a zealous spiritual life in the monastery. After an interval during the Thirty Years War (1618–48) the monastery thrived once again until the storm of secularization broke over the monastery in 1802–3 bringing about its end. The neighboring Franciscan nuns of Dillingen took over the monastery buildings in 1843 and founded a school for girls which exists to the present time. Friedrich Zoepfl noted that the closing of the Dominican monastery came about "without any tact whatsoever," when the civil authorites appeared in person on the eve of the patronal feast (14 August 1802).[30] The newly elected prioress, Aloisa Miltner, and her successor, Alberta Stark, repeatedly petitioned the authorites for permission to receive novices, even promising to be "useful" by establishing a school for girls. Permission was never granted. The Franciscan nuns housed the Dominicans until the last sister, M. Katharina Holzmann, died in 1862. The Franciscans of Dillingen still care for Margaret Ebner's legacy and her tomb in the Margaret Chapel.

1.4 Political Circumstances

The Roman Imperium of the German kings was always the starting point for ever new disputes between pope and emperor. This was especially the case at the time of the investiture of the German king with the imperial crown, his coronation signifying the approval of the pope. Beginning with the crowning of Charlemagne by Pope Leo III, on 25 December 800, the imperial dignity was a hybrid creation that contained within itself the root of conflict. At the time of the crusades in the twelfth century, the papacy understood the institution of the imperial dignity as defending the church, and the granting of the imperial crown as a free act of the pope, which enhanced the dignity of the king but did not increase his ruling power. The struggle between the popes and the Hohenstaufen emperors was a highpoint in the conflict between papacy and empire. The increase in the papal claims, combined with the powerlessness of the German kings, ultimately had the effect of promoting the development of the idea of imperial absolutism in the following years. Especially after 1309 when the popes began to reside in Avignon and the ruler of France sought to influence the papal court and its relations to the German princes, relations became very strained. Under Emperor Henry VII (1308–13) the tension was already so marked that Pope Clement V (1305–14) threatened him with ex-communication. Since the pope died shortly after the king, the conflict was put to rest temporarily. It flared up anew in connection with the dispute over the German throne at the beginning of the fourteenth century.

At the disputed election of 25 November 1314, Frederick the Handsome of Hapsburg and Louis the Bavarian were both chosen to be king. Each sought papal approval for his election. At first, Pope John XXII (1316–34) endeavored to remain neutral by putting off his decision on the double election, announcing that the imperial throne would remain vacant for the time being. After the victory over his opponent at Mühldorf on 28 September 1322, Louis tilted the balance of power against the opposing party. In 1326 the German princes came to an agreement—Frederick should rule over Germany; Louis should rule over Italy and be granted the imperial crown. A few days after this agreement Leopold of Austria died, and Louis's opponents were robbed of their leader. All those forces which were in dispute with the papal curia were given encouragement and Louis unleashed them. His physician, Marsilius of Padua, developed a system of thought in which the imperial dignity was independent of papal authority. The Franciscans William of Ockham and Michael of Cesena defended this teaching with learned argumentation, establishing the independence of secular power from spiritual. Thus the claim of the popes to exercise the right of approval for the election of the emperor was contested and undermined, a claim with which individual German princes agreed more and more.[31]

1.4.1. The Struggle of Louis the Bavarian and the Pope/ The Interdict

Since Louis did not accede to the pope's wishes, John XXII declared the imperial office vacant and initiated a series of actions against him. The basis of the pope's complaint was the fact that Louis had exercised the power to rule without waiting for papal confirmation. He declared the king's removal from office and excommunicated him in 1324. In retaliation, Louis strengthened the rights of the empire and accused the pope of heresy because of his position in the dispute over mendicant poverty. He also called for a general council. Both sides were irreconcilably deadlocked until 1327, when John XXII declared forfeit all imperial fiefs, even Louis's hereditary holding, Bavaria. In return, Louis removed John XXII from office and named Nicholas V as anti-pope (Nicholas V soon submitted himself to John XXII). In 1328, when Louis had himself crowned emperor by Cardinal Colonna in Rome, the pope declared the coronation invalid and condemned him as a heretic. Simultaneously, interdict was imposed on Germany. At the Imperial Diet in Frankfurt on 6 August 1338, Louis proclaimed the independence of the imperial dignity and declared the papal edict invalid. He demanded that acts of public worship be resumed by the clergy under penalty of exile, threatening the removal of their privileges and lands if they did not comply.

The letter exchange between Henry of Nördlingen and Margaret Ebner began during this time of the dispute between pope and emperor. The Imperial Edict forced Henry, who took the side of the pope, to leave the country, while Margaret openly held an unequivocal position in favor of Emperor Louis during this time of confusion. This essential difference in opinion in no way interrupted their twenty-year long spiritual friendship.

It is amazing how Margaret, with the meticulously detailed presentation of her interior life, also took note of the external political circumstances, made sense of them, and took a position on them. In her visions and prayers the king/emperor Louis the Bavarian played a large role. Despite the papal judgment, she felt herself to be unshakeably bound to Louis. Since there could have been no greater contrast than that between the fragile, unknown Dominican nun and the *Furor Teutonicus*, the powerful German king and emperor who defied the papal interdict by his imperial decree, Ludwig Zoepf was rather perplexed in the face of the "not fully explicable sympathy" of Margaret for Louis and by the motive for her devotion.[32] Margaret was fully aware of the difficulties of this ecclesiastical-political disagreement when she described the time of interdict as the "great disorder of the church."[33] She also saw it as "confusion of the church."[34] This had dire consequences for monasteries, since the regular care of souls became practically impossible. She complained about the lack of the reception of the Eucharist, but at the same time she emphasized that "our Order has not submitted to the (papal)

22

commands, as others have done. Although our monastery was still bound by the law, we were permitted to act according to our consciences here."[35] It seems that the solution to this dilemma was left to the conscience of the individual. Despite the interdict, Margaret received the sacraments because of her ardent yearning for the Eucharist. She believed that whatever one did out of such great love, God would compensate for it. She wrote, "Lord, if you let me do something wrong here, then you must do penance for me."[36] The response of the Lord assured her, "Whoever desires me in true love, I will never renounce out of true love."[37] In order to support the reality of divine authority based on the certitude of her received grace in opposition to human authority, she stated, "I speak in the truth, who is my Lord Jesus Christ, that the grace of God has never decreased in me because of this."[38] This inner freedom on the basis of divine inspiration determined her special connection to Louis, because she believed that he had been entrusted to her by God above all other men.[39] She held this conviction, even though by her own account she stated that Louis was "the cause of that confusion." No reproach was lodged against him. In her efforts to read the will of God in this unfortunate matter, she realized in general only that it "was caused by the sins and weakness of men."[40]

After Margaret had made her opinion in the matter of the interdict known to the pro-papal Henry, the very prudent priest responded in letter XXXIII, "I dare not prevent such a thoughtful, strong and honorable desire in God and for God in you nor in any friend of God."[41] He recommended that she read the story of Esther and King Ahasuerus, which was frequently interpreted as a type of the relationship between the believing soul and Christ (Est 15:10f). Ahasuerus said to Esther, "Fear not, I am your brother." Henry continued the scriptural dialogue equating Christ with Ahasuerus and Margaret with Queen Esther. "The commands were given and made for those who are subject to me, but you reign with me. Esther (Margaret) desired to eat with the king . . . therefore, you who have been raised above the people, since to you is given by the loving mercy of your dear brother and also your powerful king, Jesus Christ, you have been granted the privilege to reign with him, who has so often touched you with the scepter of his holy cross and long ago gave you free authority in heaven, earth and purgatory, ask him, you dear Esther, to eat with you."[42] By this answer Henry justified

Margaret's freedom from the law on the basis of her inner experience of salvation, a noteworthy position since he stood on the opposite side of the conflict.

It is known that Louis placed Maria Medingen under his own protection and thereby upheld the special character of the relations of the monastery to the emperor. On 21 September 1330, he not only confirmed the privileges of the imperial charter of his predecessors, by which Henry VII had placed the monastery under the protection of the empire on 18 July 1309, thereby removing any other protection (namely that of the Count of Dillingen and the Bishop of Augsburg), but Louis went even further in his favors. On 16 October 1330, he granted to the prioress jurisdiction in the area of her possessions, raising them to the status of a manor (Hofmark), an expression of his personal favor and perhaps also of his high regard for the monastery.[43] It is not known on what his attitude is based, but just before this time the beginning of Margaret's writings gave testimony to her great sympathy for the life and fate of Louis. Accordingly, Zoepf presumed "reasons from personal experience" for Margaret's ardently loyal attitude.[44]

Whatever unknown external causes may explain her connection to Louis—a possible meeting during her stay in Donauwörth remains pure speculation—her own words testified to her thoughts and affection. She followed a command of God in being an invisible guardian angel to defend Louis's salvation and his honor. "I considered him to have been given me by God. Then I had special grace and the inclination to pray for all his affairs and desires."[45] Of Louis's increasingly difficult situation in his own land during the year 1324–25, engendered by the pursuit of Duke Leopold and the unfortunate experience of the siege at Burgau, Ludwig Zoepf opined that Margaret's attitude was "a sign of the most beautiful fidelity and of the deepest sense of justice." The sign referred to Margaret's seeing the greatness of Louis just then in a dream and hearing the words of Psalm 71:11, "All the kings of the earth will adore him, all the nations will serve him."[46] Although she had seen him "in great sorrow," at the same time she recognized in the dream how the Lord "grasped the same man beneath his arms and spoke to him, saying he would never forsake him, neither here nor in the life to come."[47] God favored Louis, and she considered her own prayer for him to have the function of protecting him. "At the same time it was revealed to me that he (Louis) would not have lived so long without my prayers," and "that he would return safe and sound from Lombardy."[48]

Margaret perceived God's steadfast protection from the mouth of Christ, who justified Louis's own salvation "because he bears love for me about which no one knows, but I myself."[49] In 1346, on the occasion of the election of the anti-king Charles IV of the house of Luxemburg, Margaret perceived the same answer with the consoling assurance of divine assistance for Louis. She was also given the task by God to make this known to her emperor, who was in dire straits at that time. Margaret shrank back from delivering the message out of modesty, not wanting Louis to discover that it was she who protected him by her prayers. She commented tersely, "I failed to do it out of fear that he would know that it was I."[50] Soon thereafter, it was made known to her by the perception of "great delight and joy" that Louis would overcome his enemies. The almost immediate news of his death clarified the previous revelation as an indication that he had overcome the interior enemies of his soul and therefore had had a good death.[51] The sudden death of the emperor while under papal excommunication motivated Henry of Nördlingen, "the friend of Our Lord and my friend," who was just then visiting Margaret while returning to Basel from Bamberg, to exhort her to pray for the deceased emperor "with great earnestness." Henry was greatly concerned by "what God had accomplished with him in such a short time which he had at his death."[52] An emperor cursed by the pope could scarcely stand before the throne of God. Margaret had another means of knowledge at her disposal. The Child Jesus, especially revered by her, told her, "I have given him the pledge of eternal life." Margaret persisted, wanting to know "how he had deserved this?" The Child answered, "He loved me and besides, human judgment is often mistaken."[53] She was filled with great and perduring joy when, at the reception of communion two days later, she was assured by the voice of the Lord, "Praise me for the sake of my marvels which I worked in him during the brief period of time at his death."[54] On the first month's anniversary of his death, at her request, Margaret received a further revelation from Christ about Louis. "He bore me in his heart; therefore I have surrounded him with my mercy and I will never release him from it until I have prepared him for eternal life."[55] Margaret was convinced of the deep piety of the emperor, which would assure him of the mercy of God, despite all human weakness.

Such an informed contemporary as Marino Sandro believed that no one had reigned so well as Emperor Louis. Among other things, his promotion of religious life, especially by the foundation of the Monastery of Ettal, testified to his piety.[56] Margaret did not stand alone in her assessment of Emperor Louis. Her high opinion of the deceased was also shown by the fact that she regarded his death as a loss for everyone, which was also in agreement with the opinion of a "true friend of God," later confirmed for her by God. "The emperor should have lived longer, . . . but it happened due to the sins of men."[57] A final message about the soul of Louis came one year after his death on the basis of a prayer in which she learned from God that "he was in great suffering (in purgatory), but the degree of his punishment will not deprive him of eternal life for much longer."[58]

Roswitha Schneider calls Margaret Ebner a "messenger of divine mercy," since she protected the honor and orthodoxy of the excommunicated emperor up to his death and held him in high regard ever after.[59] Even after the election of Charles IV, Louis remained the true ruler for her. Her spiritual independence is also shown in her assessment of the ecclesiastical-political tensions between emperor and pope. In this regard she parted ways with her spiritual friend, Henry of Nördlingen. This difference did not jeopardize their friendship, even though it was not simply a superficial difference of opinion. In a letter of 1347–48 he chastised her somewhat indignantly because she had called Charles IV "his" king. With firmness he wrote, "You should not call the new king, *my* king, but rather the *Christian* king."[60] After the election of Charles IV and his papal approval in the fall of 1346, Margaret still remained faithful to Louis the Bavarian.

Margaret, who otherwise was in need of protection herself and who needed so much the counsel and the presence of her spiritual friend, persisted in her loyalty and imperturbable faith in Louis, who was upheld by the hand of God in this divisive public dispute. Aside from her firm belief in the saving mercy of God, her noble bearing probably sprang from the deeper insight that neither side was entirely free from lack of moderation in this terrible struggle for power. The selflessness and tenderness of her relations with others and with God is illustrated by her report that around 1330 the imperial regalia ("*daz hochwirdig hailgtum des riches*") had been kept at the Monastery of Maria Medingen and therefore that out-of-the-way monastery temporarily stood at the center of political-temporal events. Nothing would have been more natural than to gaze on the crown, scepter, and coronation mantle of the emperor. But an inner divine voice impelled Margaret not to take delight in this and not to direct her "great yearning" to such treasures. Instead she hastened to the tabernacle in the sisters' choir in order to contemplate Christ "rather than the emperor."[61] This form of asceticism may appear foreign to us today but it does reveal concentration of thought and purity of heart, as well as purposeful striving to come ever closer to God. Every deviation on the way of spiritual progress had to be subsequently eliminated, even when that deviation was merely the symbol of the emperor entrusted to her.

PART TWO

2.1 Henry of Nördlingen and the Friends of God

A completely different circumstance bound Margaret to Henry of Nördlingen, one by which her sufferings were transformed at times into human happiness. Their unforeseen meeting developed into a continuing spiritual friendship of twenty years. About this meeting there is something of the "noblesse of medieval friendship," whose goal in spiritual terms was the "work of love" of God.[62]

Almost nothing is known about the life of the secular priest Henry of Nördlingen prior to his meeting with Margaret Ebner. The years after her death are also obscure, and so neither the year of his birth nor of his death are certain. Only the two decades of his acquaintanceship with Margaret from 1332 to 1351 shed any light on his character. According to Strauch he was attested to be an "*honestus vir*" of "*magnae discretionis.*" Henry came from a family of imperial ministers.[63] When he met Margaret at Medingen for the first time on 29 October 1332, he had already worked for a considerable time as spiritual advisor to the surrounding monasteries of Cistercian nuns at Oberschönenfeld, Niederschönenfeld, and Zimmern im Ries, as well as to the Cistercian monks of Kaisheim. He was known as a "Friend of God." It seems that he had earlier had contact with Medingen as teacher at the school. In his fourth letter he sent greetings by way of

INTRODUCTION

Margaret to "your young school teacher, my dear pupil and friend."[64] From her first meeting with Henry in October 1332, she characterized him as "God's true friend."

The designation "Friends of God" is a phrase derived from Sacred Scripture, used in the Old Testament as well as in the New Testament. Jesus names as his friends those in whom he had confided, those he had chosen, and those he had sent forth (Jn 15:13–17). The biblical understanding of friendship with God was joined by the Fathers of the Church to philosophical reflection on friendship with others, based on friendship with God. Building on the interpretations of Ambrose and Augustine, Aelred of Rievaulx in his twelfth century work *On Spiritual Friendship* developed the idea of ascent from human friendship to friendship with Christ and thus to friendship with God as a high level of perfection. During the ordination ceremony, with hands extended over the newly ordained priest, the bishop prays the words of the Lord, "I no longer call you servants, but my friends" (Jn 15:15). The term "friend of God" as translation of *amicus Dei* has yet other biblical support in Psalm 139:17 and James 2:23.[65] Already in German literature of the twelfth and thirteenth centuries the term designated evangelists, apostles, Old Testament figures such as Moses, and also saints and pious individuals. In Mechthild of Magdeburg's *The Flowing Light of the Godhead* in the thirteenth century, the use of "chosen friend of God" was already familiar. According to W. Oehl, the German mystics of the fourteenth century defined this concept in more rigorous terms to express their striving toward the ideal of a living, interior Christianity by contrast to the merely external Christianity of most of their contemporaries. Tauler, Ruusbroec, Mark of Lindau (d. 1392), Otto of Passau (close of the fourteenth century), and yet others sought once again to define the essence and meaning of the "friends of God" as the supporting pillars of Christendom, that is, the church. For the religious movement of the Friends of God in the thirteenth and fourteenth century this tradition cannot be ignored.

The designation Friend of God was applied to Christians of every class, occupation, race, and gender in the fourteenth century. It designated individuals who led a more intense religious life characterized by active love of neighbor and contemplative prayer leading even to a mystical relationship with God. Occasionally, outside the monasteries, they gathered into groups under the direction of a priest.[66] One of their leaders was John Tauler. According to him, the Friends of God were "the pillars on which Christendom (the Church) rests, which if we did not have them, it would go very badly for us, you should know that."[67] Contrary to this conception was the fantastic idea of a "friend of God" who transcended the entire church in holiness and closeness to God, who, although a member of the laity, could lead the faithful and could even contravene the pope. This idea was formulated with inventive vitality by a Strasbourg author who wrote sixteen tracts under the name of the mysterious Friend of God in Oberland. This literature of the Friends of God had a wide circulation beyond Strasbourg until it was eventually unmasked as literary fiction.[68]

Through his connection with Margaret Ebner, Henry of Nördlingen became the mouthpiece for the Friends of God in Upper Germany (that is, along the upper reaches of the Rhine). Because of the conflict between the pope and the emperor and the consequent interdict, Henry, being a papal sympathizer, had to leave his Swabian homeland in 1338. Indirectly, as well as through the agency of Tauler (who had also been driven away by the imperial prohibition), he found a new sphere of activity in Basel. There, for ten years he assembled and led a circle of Friends of God in addition to carrying out his expected ministerial activities. Among these Friends of God the miraculous element of apostolic times was continued. The Dominican nun, Christina Ebner, from the monastery of Engelthal near Nüremberg, praised Henry's "fiery tongue." In Basel people swarmed to his preaching, as described in his letters.

The personal conversation between Henry and Margaret begun in 1332 continued by means of the famous exchange of letters during this time. Of Margaret's letters only one is extant. Fifty-six came from Henry. Henry's character is discernable from the letters. Margaret recorded his request that she write an account of the graces she had received in the *Revelations*. "I was asked by the true friend of God . . . that I write for him what God had given me."[69] At the conclusion of the letter of 1339, he underscored his request with the wish of Tauler and other Friends of God. "Also our dear father, Tauler, and other friends of God wish that you would write something to us about what our dearest Jesus has given you, especially about the present condition of the Church and about the friends of God who suffer much under these circumstances. Write something in addition about what God has given to you."[70] Henry, therefore, was the initiator of Margaret's writing. In her book she never called him by name. She referred to him as "the dear friend of God," the "worthy friend of God," but above all as "the true friend of God," and "the most faithful friend of Our Lord and my friend." According to these references, the question of truth is the criterion and basis of their friendship. Both recognized the importance of truth for their dialogue—Margaret in her *Revelations*, Henry by his experiences with and through Margaret. At the same time each recognized the truth of God in the other.

2.1.1 The Question of Truth and the Letter Exchange

Just as she was convinced that God in Christ is the Truth, Margaret was also certain that Henry had been given to her by God as an "angel in the light of truth."[71] She designated him as the "true friend of God" who had been sent to her in the monastery by God.[72] She let him know this in her only extant letter, in which she wrote that she knew that God's love "reigns in you powerfully with the efficacious power of his Godhead, which shines forth in truth from your whole life, as well as from your words, which give true witness to the honor of God."[73] In Henry she saw the representative of Christ, because divine Truth was acting in him. For her, Henry was the receiver and distributor of the truth that he had received from Christ. In this regard she wrote to him, "perfect light of truth, that gently flows forth from you to all to whom you give yourself out of love and goodness."[74] On the other hand, Henry wanted knowledge of her received truth and encouraged her to open herself up to its reception, in order that he himself might take part in it, because he wished "that He (God) truly open his mouth and speak the inner tone of his eternal word in your heart according to the most pure truth and the deepest, sweetest movement that has ever grasped the heart of his chosen ones."[75] For Henry, Margaret became a source of strength and a reflection of the original image of Christ, because the image of Christ "has never shown forth to me with such gentleness and humility and never in the complete truth of a faithful follower of the inner and outer life of Jesus Christ in such an interior, holy, peaceful and deep way in any other human being, as in your presence."[76] Henry proclaimed to her, "Your sweet, fiery and true words turn and direct my entire life to God."[77] For his own progress and that of the others, he pressed her to devote her heart and her voice "to eternal truth." As its "debtor" she is obligated to render an account, "a special witness for eternal truth" in her writings, so that from her heart Henry "may understand everything in new truth."

During the years of exile, the assurance of Margaret's "total and constant friendship in the truth" was the strongest human support and consolation for Henry. With every line from her came not only the fragrance of his earthly homeland, but also from her "glowing words" came "a holy fragrance and a divine taste." Therefore he praised her, "You, my heart's blossoming consolation in God."[78]

There is no better criterion for the authenticity of any human being than that individual's attitude toward truth. The old question naturally arises, "What is truth?" The truth spoken of here is religious truth, that of faith, which revealed itself as yet a greater truth for Henry in the special graces of Margaret. In accordance with this belief both friends justified and formed their lives with the goal to give God greater honor. From this conviction Henry wished Margaret "light to acknowledge the truth, fire to love the truth, and power to live the truth," and by this triplet of light, fire, and power he imaged the aspired-for trinitarian likeness in humans of knowledge, love, and action corresponding to the divine processions of the Trinity.[79]

Margaret's perceptiveness was as strong as her love for truth. Because of its demands she tested her relationship with Henry. A vision brought clarification to her searching question, which she reported as if giving minutes of a meeting using exact and sensible terms: "He wanted me to cooperate with him in faith. I said, 'I shall gladly cooperate provided that you intend only the honor of God by it.' He answered that he meant it in no other way. I have always found that to be true."[80]

2.1.2.   Henry—*Spiritus Rector* and Friend

The letters show the development Margaret and Henry experienced in their mutual relationship because of the demands of truth. At first, Henry had taken the lead as the spiritual advisor, filled with

the importance of his spiritual office, which he conscientiously fulfilled. In the course of time he became a deeply compassionate friend
in the most varied of situations. Eventually, he communicated his
own inner self ever more clearly, until finally at a third level he
sought her counsel, being greatly amazed at the richness of grace
given to her with the accompanying prophetic pronouncements.
These three levels of relationship were mirrored even in Henry's
forms of address. As *spiritus rector* he addressed her as "Margaret,
daughter," "Chosen daughter of God," "Child, Margaret," "my
chosen child," and "well-beloved child of God." On her part, she
recognized in him the God-sent "powerful teacher," the "faithful,
truthful teacher of Our Lord," the most ardently awaited confidant,
who alone knew about her inner condition and became for her a
"powerful consolation," so that he was her consolation and support
during the time of the "great suffering" and the "powerful grace."
During every visit Henry was the "faithful physician," who be-
stowed the various consolations with which the christological meaning of this title resonates. Later, however, it was Henry who called
her the "faithful physician of his wounded heart." She felt orphaned
when he was away. His occasional visits—there were only eight
during the entire time—were always times of spiritual refreshment
and strengthening for Margaret. In his presence she felt spiritually as
well as physically so light that she believed she levitated.[81]

After the second visit in the year 1334, Margaret wrote in her
Revelations, "The yearning arose within me to speak about all my
concerns with him."[82] And this was the case even though she had
initially not wanted to receive him at all because of her state of
depression. But now she perceived that "an inner joy of true sweetness lay in his words."[83] In her only extant letter she wrote that she
needed and yearned for his presence.

While Henry made known his own weaknesses, he also tried to
make her waiting more bearable on a religious as well as on a human
basis. In God she will find him again. But for him it was also
the same.

> I, too, am very weak. I also fear that I would not be safe with you
> in our homeland; I would have to be there in secret and I have
> been advised against that. Therefore ask God by the abundance
> of his freely given gifts, with which he alone can satisfy your

longings, that he represent me to you and replace my presence with his own holy face, with which he may smile upon you, so that you will have no need of me nor of any other creature.[84]

Occasionally, Henry was shocked by the deep reverence that she demonstrated for him, and believed he must place her love on a more realistic level, as when he gently, but also self-critically, declared to her:

One thing you have written me against which I must contend with your serene truth, so that you could not complain about my absence in your inner life. My heart's most faithful Beloved in God, when then will your Beloved Jesus forgive me, if you cannot pray to him for it interiorly? I ask you to set things right again with regard to him and me. I would like to commend this to him and to you.[85]

Against her yearning for his personal presence he quoted the words of Christ, "It is good that I go away from you."[86] In the purification from the pain of parting her life will gain spiritual power. But he warned her also against excessive asceticism. She should strengthen herself physically so that she will be that much better able to endure all suffering and be able to accept it more peacefully.

It is noteworthy how Henry, in his role as spiritual director, interspersed his letters with lengthy quotes from Mechthild of Magdeburg's *The Flowing Light of the Godhead*. With these quotes he hoped to manifest understanding, support, and encouragement for Margaret's situation, which was characterized by inner experiences that she did not always understand immediately. Without specifically citing his source he quoted from *The Flowing Light of the Godhead*, Book I, Chapter 22, showing the paradox of mystical ecstasy in antitheses with the introduction:

Now note further, the friends of God (namely Mechthild of Magdeburg) tell and describe these for us, that the bride becomes drunk in seeing the noble face. "In the greatest strength she loses herself. In the most beautiful light she is blind. In the deepest blindness she sees most clearly. In the greatest clearness she is both dead and alive. The longer she is dead, the more happily she lives. The less she becomes, the more she will experience. The more she fears herself, [the more flows to her.] The richer she becomes, the more she is in need. The deeper she lives (in God), the more receptive is she. [The more she yearns,] the more desirous she becomes. The deeper her wounds, the more violently she rages. The more tender God is to her, the higher will she be lifted up. The more beautifully she shines from the vision of God, the closer she comes to him. The more she applies herself, the gentler she rests. [The more she receives], the more she grasps. The deeper her silence, the louder her cries. [The weaker she becomes], the greater miracle she works with his strength by her might. The more his delight in her grows, the more beautiful her wedding. The more narrow the bed of love, the more interior the embrace. The sweeter the kiss of the mouth, the more loving the gaze. The more painful the parting, the more he endows her. The more she spends, the more she has. The humbler the leave-taking, the quicker he returns. The hotter she remains, the quicker she produces sparks. The more she burns, the more beautiful she shines. The more God's praise is spread, the greater remains her yearning."[87]

With these antitheses and paradoxes Henry clearly recognized the meaning of love-ecstasy as revelation of God's glory, which he wanted to confirm for Margaret Ebner. By means of this recognition he also wished to infer that the momentary ecstasy of love was only the basis for a yet greater yearning. The revelation of the love of God or its intensification could never lead to any diminishment of human yearning on earth, since the interior condition of love consisted in constant movement toward God. For a life lived by the love of God, in whatever form, there is no absolute negation or annihilation; rather such recourse to God's love is sanctification paradoxically revealed in ever-increasing yearning.

Dependent on Mechthild's style and content, Henry of Nördlingen explained Margaret's specific grace of the "binding silence" with the antithesis, "the fuller, the more quiet."[88] He did this in order to make sense out of her occasional periods of forced silence, which he interpreted as a sign of the following of Christ "into imprisonment according to the will of his Father," as he wrote to her, "in order to bring forth in you the divine image without hindrance on the part of any creature." He characterized this as a form of total divine indwelling.[89]

Thankful for Henry's help and trusting in him Margaret wrote to him, "I shall wait for you, because I prefer to fulfill all my wishes according to your advice and your teachings."[90] In this process of spiritual direction the *spiritus rector* began to change almost unnoticed into a spiritual friend. This change is also reflected by a change in forms of address: "most beloved friend of my heart," "the chosen joy of my heart," "the most interior good of my soul that I have on earth," "my faithfulness in God," and "my faithful power in God," "my most faithful heart of my heart and faithful soul of my soul," "the one whom I hold dear in God."

Imperceptibly their friendship grew by a process of mutual give-and-take. Only the constant partings were painful, about which Henry wrote to Margaret:

> Therefore know that your sorrowful face, your yearning glance, your tortured appearance, your tearful eyes and your painful going cut me to the heart and moved me truly in a unique way and caused me pain, as I went away from you. My heart would rejoice if I knew that your dear Jesus had so transformed you, since your sorrow is also mine, and your joy is mine as well.[91]

Each became like daily bread of spiritual nourishment for the other. From Henry's letters we learn how gladly he wrote to Margaret or heard from her. "When I read something from you or when I write to you with a recollected heart, then as usual a gentle flowing fountain springs up in my heart."[92] And Margaret assured him "that I always perceive consolation and divine power from you."[93] Henry asserted, "God knows, how gladly I would like to be with you always." And further he professed, "I would prefer to be with you, my consolation in God, and I trust in him that it will soon happen."[94]

2.1.3 Margaret's Transformation into Prophetess

Much to his surprise, Henry came to recognize a change in Margaret. She was no longer the prisoner of her sorrows, and he recognized in this change "a sign of heavenly life," with the result that she then became truly "the consolation of his heart." He expressed his wonderment in Letter XXXVII.

> This miraculous change and development, which has happened to you, is a sign of the heavenly life, since all sorrow, however divine that would be, has an end and joy and peace are yours in abundance. Thus by inner delight for you sorrow has become not-sorrow and you indeed suffer your loving desire, my heart's divine consolation. I thank . . . God for all his works of love which he works in you and will work eternally.[95]

Margaret became more and more the graced one, preferred by God, upon whom Henry gazed in wonder. When he had received the first part of the writings he had requested, he answered in 1345 from Strasbourg, "What shall I write to you? Your prophetic voice makes me speechless. Therefore, instead of any speech, I thank God for the heavenly treasure which he has granted to us through you and will grant us even more."[96]

Indeed Henry had once wished that Margaret climb the "mountain of highest perfection" and experience in vision the "supernatural peace" so that Christ might speak to her heart with the "sound filled with love of his eternal word," so that she would receive from God, whatever benefited her.[97] In the meantime he knew that she had surpassed him long ago by her inner experiences, so that to him her entire being signified "a holy model, a clear mirror, a well-graced way to all divine truth."[98] He himself suffered all too frequently from inner aridity. He characterized the outer success of his preaching with the ironic comparison that he came forth like a piper whose melody others understood better how to dance to than he himself. Margaret might help him so that he "might be able to master the steps of the dance of a true life to the sweet piping" of Christ.[99] She consoled him and wished for her teacher and friend the "high flight of the eagle of the apostle John," who soared up to the heart of Christ. Thus might Henry leave behind the "creeping pace" of all hardships and might lose the "unawareness of the perception of divine grace."[100] Extremely tender-hearted, she continued, "these graces have been perceived by me and by all those who have sought them in you." By this she hinted at his indispensable counsel, which first revealed to her the total extent of her visions and made possible her familiarity with inner experiences. Here there was no trace of embarrassment. Strengthened by his knowledge of her spiritual power and her inner wealth, he leaned on her. "I place upon you the heavy part of all my sorrows, because to the degree you have more love than I, to that degree you can bear more than I."[101] He saw in Margaret the "sweet fruit of the Holy Spirit" in the sense of a burning power of love and addressed her as "the true rule of my life and the sweet memory of my heart in which my thoughts find nourishment and divine teaching and grace."[102] Now Henry is the pupil.

Looking back to the first meeting with Margaret, he recognized the superpersonal character of her graced status and of her friendship for him. It was pure grace, he wrote to her, that "God sent you to me once. Him I trust, . . . that he wants to grant me and the whole church a special blessing by you and from you."[103] He also attributed to her a prophetic mission to give a "special witness for Eternal Truth" whose "debtor" she is, so that other insights could be gained which lead beyond knowledge and the ability achieved by natural means.[104] He clarifies her prophetic mission using the symbolically rich images from *The Flowing Light of the Godhead:*

> I and all created things must withdraw from you, however gladly we would wish to go with you! We are not let in . . . when interiorly with your royal and beloved Jesus Christ you gain entrance into the wine cellar, where chaste breasts will be filled to overflowing, so that they will not be mine only, but rather will become the source of good nourishment for the whole church.[105]

From various places in *The Flowing Light of the Godhead* Henry connected different images in a new way. The image of the wine cellar taken from the language of the Song of Songs symbolized intoxication in God, and the bridal relationship of the soul to God was the strongest image of union. Along with this series of images expressing Margaret's individual and personal connection to God, Henry understood her as the nurturing mother of all souls, whose spiritual office consisted in strengthening the faith of all Christians with the "overflowing milk of her teaching." Mechthild of Magdeburg applied this image to the Virgin Mary and the church, which with "her pure, immaculate milk," namely the unpolluted faith, had already nourished the teachers and prophets of the Old Testament as well as the apostles and martyrs. The "suckling breasts" as streams of salvation, which for Mechthild of Magdeburg flowed out from Mary and the church, were attributed by Henry to Margaret as the God-possessed prophetess of his grace. Henry connected Margaret's spiritual maternity with that of Mary and transferred her saving power as nourishing mother of the faith of all souls and of the church to Margaret. Concerning her spiritual motherhood, he wrote: "Prepare the soil of your heart and bear for you and for us the savior . . . without pain, as happened with Mary."[106] Finally, he reserved a place for Margaret next to the mother of God as a symbol of the restoration of original dignity and salvation.

The almost unnoticed yet important Marian piety in Henry's letters marked his spiritual direction. For Margaret's true nature and greatest works he called upon the "powerful Mother of God," because Mary was the first to be blessed and was filled with the spirit by taking up the "Eternal Word" so that she was completely illumined in his splendor.[107] Mary, as the Mother of God, had the deepest interior relationship to Christ, from which sprang her power to save as mediatrix of grace, her prophetic gift by which she was mistress over evil. As "pure vessel" of the love of Christ, she is teacher of the faith.[108] Henry saw Margaret in her "new grace" as imitator of Mary in these same ways. Like the Mother of God, he gave Margaret the name "faithful bearer of the sins of the world."[109] Using an eschatological meaning, he gave her the Marian titles that appeared in *The Flowing Light of the Godhead*. "You are a conqueror of the devil," "a mirror of the inner vision," and a "glowing crystal vessel of the love of Christ."[110] Since, for Henry, Margaret was the perfect guide to God, he wrote to her using the phrase. "You who have borne my heart in God." He designated her as "God's and Mary's blessed imitator moving from the earthly to the heavenly, from the transient to the eternal."[111] Thus, he understood his friendship with Margaret as based in God by way of Mary.

Henry wondered about this great blessing and wrote of Margaret, "there you stand in graced nobility raised above the heavens," and, "Lady, exalted indeed and revered above all, how your mouth is so closely joined to the mouth of God . . . divine union with all human nature."[112] She was the "highborn daughter of the heavenly king." He was convinced that God "wants to grant Christianity and himself a special blessing through you and from you," because Christ has "over-refined her," so that Henry became an "unequal friend" to her.[113] For him she became the "penetrating truth of God . . . in me."[114] Henry was convinced that Margaret's speech and writing were inspired, since John the Evangelist, God's author, is also "her author." He believed in a special calling for Margaret and raised his personal friendship above the merely personal in order to guide Margaret in the task of prophecy for all.

Henry brought Margaret into contact with the world of the Friends of God in Basel and Strasbourg. He did this chiefly by supplying Margaret and the whole monastery with spiritual writings. Above all, from Basel he sent her *The Flowing Light of the Godhead* by Mechthild of Magdeburg, which had been translated by his own initiative from the unfamiliar Middle Low German into High German. He called it a "heavenly song" and the "most moving fruit of love, which I have ever read in the German language." Margaret should read it with desire and with an attentive heart. Further, through his initiative the *Horologium sapientiae* by Henry Suso was procured for Maria Medingen, and also works by St. Thomas Aquinas and other spiritual writings, so that Margaret came into contact with Suso, Tauler, and their circle of friends. In his letters Henry called Tauler "our father and Margaret's faithful apostle." Above all, because of his role as spiritual director, Henry was the main cause for the writing of Margaret's *Revelations.* The letters make clear how he directed her to the circles of the Friends of God in Basel and in Strasbourg, where she found ready acceptance. He spoke of "the holy inheritor of spiritual company, of which there are many in Basel."[115] His friends became Margaret's friends.

How highly Henry values friendship as a path to God was shown by a letter of 1346–47 sent from Basel in which he enumerated some of his friends, such as the Countess of Falkenstein in the Dominican monastery of Klingenthal in Basel, Lord Henry of Rheinfelden, a knight at Pfaffenhofen, and a knight from Landsberg with his divinely enlightened lady. He closed this enumeration with the words, "I cannot name all of them for you." The cultivation of friendship was a great concern for him, since he was convinced that his friends gained a more interior connection to God through Margaret and that in this way she herself also benefited from their friendship.

> When I commend us and the friends which God gives us to you, then do not cease to open up your heart and take them to yourself, just as you would like God to accept you, and carry them with new loving sincerity from your heart into the merciful heart of Jesus Christ, so that they enter into his heart through your heart. Then they will hinder you no longer, indeed they will commend you to God so that to you just as many new mansions in God will be given, as you have ever gained in him.[116]

Because of Henry, Margaret became the focal point of many Friends of God. If Henry had been the advisor at the beginning, eventually it was he who sought advice from Margaret as from an oracle. With regard to eschatological questions, the supposed prophecies of St. Hildegard of Bingen were read and discussed. Also Henry wanted to know whether the plague, for instance, would really come about in the near future, and if so, how he should strengthen the people in their precautions or how he should otherwise advise them.[117]

Margaret's fame spread far beyond Medingen, as can be ascertained from Henry's letters. During Henry's stay in Alsace, Margaret became acquainted with Rulman Merswin, the famous Friend of God in Strasbourg, and also his wife. Through Henry she maintained contacts with the monasteries of Unterlinden in Colmar, Adelhausen near Freiburg, and the Dominican monastery of nuns of St. Agnes in Cologne, with whom she exchanged gifts. Through Henry's friend, the priest of the Abbey of St. Walburga, she was known in Eichstätt. Henry mediated her contacts with Queen Agnes of Hungary in Königsfelden in Aargau in Switzerland and asked her for a subsidy for the building plans of the monastery during the time when she held the office of "mistress of construction" and had performed this function successfully. This shows that even with her intensive mystical interior life she did not neglect the practical side of life. She understood how to develop a certain good business sense.[118]

The rich complex of human relationships that arose around Margaret as a result of her friendship with Henry shows how upright and intense the imitation of Christ as a way to God was when lived via common humanity with mutual personal responsibility. Despite her illness Margaret flourished due to rich interior graces and the guidance of Henry. The inner blessings of this highly graced woman made her "pain not painful," as Henry, full of wonder, appraised this transformation. Concerning her union with Christ, Henry claimed that Margaret was "elevated, united, and hidden in the hiddenness of his face." The phrase "hidden in the hiddenness" of Christ revealed the impenetrable darkness through which she was "formed" by Christ into "his most perfect likeness."[119] In this process Henry called Margaret "pearl of God," after the meaning of her name, making a connection between the formation of a pearl and the process of being formed into Christ. Henry veiled the finding of such an incomparably valuable and precious gem, whose origin and formation remain incomprehensible, with the biblical image of the abyss familiar to mystical vocabulary, when he wrote to Margaret, "there one abyss moves another, so that here in this time alone he calls out saying, *'abissus abissum invocat'* " (Ps 41:8).[120] Being confronted with the divine abyss opens the senses to turn toward fellow humans.

PART THREE

3.1 Elements of the Spirituality of the *Revelations*

We saw that the letters supplied a portion of the background of the *Revelations*, and they gave us a clue about the reason for writing them down. The goal was not to compile a literary work in the sense of an autobiography, since the *Revelations* offer only scant information about Margaret's external life. Following the wish of Henry to write down that which God had given her to say, Margaret, "reluctantly" and "in fear and dread" later recorded the course of her graced life according to the best of her knowledge.[121] Henry asked her to do this because during the time before his exile he had observed closely how her life had been held in tension in the struggle between "suffering" and "sweet grace." Thus he endeavored to acquire written testimony from an authentic source on the course of a rapturous spiritual life in its struggle with human nature in order to promote mysticism in the framework of his activity in the circle of the Friends of God.

3.1.1 The Question of Truth

Like Henry, Margaret also confronted the demands of truth. Her simple and occasionally dry reports of events showed a healthy skepticism with regard to mystical inspirations and visions. She recorded only those dreams she considered later on, after "long perceived great grace," to have been worked by God.[122] She doubted whether it was always God who was working in her or only the delight of her own soul. Contrary to her own will, she even began to doubt her faith, until she recognized God's activity in her "in the truth without any doubt."[123] In this time of continual change Margaret, deeply wounded interiorly, struggled with the mystical sword of grace deep in her heart, until she was thrust into "an indescribably wretched abandonment." She was regularly reassured in this terrible struggle with God by a sign "of a sweet grace," so that Henry recognized in her writings the same authentic worth as a "holy scripture."[124]

Her truth was Christ. He "really gave me everything He promised . . . when I began to write the little book."[125] She justified herself by this, since her goal was to live "a truthful life." She placed her writings under the protection of the Truth, frequently initiating a new passage with the words, "I present the following with appeal to nothing but the Truth, Jesus Christ." She perceived as the voice of God the words "You are a grasper of truth."[126] From the union with God she received "the light of understanding" as the "great gift from God." With such deep insight her facility with language and recognition of truth increased.[127] Above all, by this "new understanding" she recognized whenever anyone was lying. She had at her disposal a kind of intuitive knowledge of all things. She wished for herself, as the highest blessing, the complete comprehension of divine truth, which is in the Lord himself. "If I possessed this all the time, it would be like heaven on earth."[128]

Henry had also been tested by her according to the demands of truth. As she wrote, he won her trust because "I recognized in him an innocent truthful life." She did not want "the light of truth to weaken in him."[129] Everything that was directed contrary to love, peace, and truth, gave her pain. With regard to the worth and possession of truth, there can be no compromise.[130] Her whole life was directed to the possession of the living truth, namely, the possession of God.

3.1.2. Influence of the Dominican Order; Nature and Grace

One can infer from this that Margaret's pronounced feeling for truth and her great love for truth were strengthened by the motto of the Dominican Order—*veritas*. Above all, the memory of St. Dominic by word and in writing was carefully preserved in Medingen. The image of the Founder and the goal of the Order was forcefully promoted by the book *The Flowing Light of the Godhead*. Also available in Medingen were the writings of St. Thomas, who was referred to as "Thomas the Preacher." A high degree of familiarity with his person as with his works can be established in the monastery of Maria Medingen.[131] This was even more true because the prayer *Anima Christi*, frequently mentioned by Margaret (and mistakenly attributed to her), was also attributed to Thomas Aquinas. In recent centuries it has been mistakenly labeled the "sigh of love" of St. Ignatius of Loyola.

The thesis of St. Thomas that grace builds on nature and perfects it was attested to by Margaret in a clearly existential way. Margaret described being overcome by grace, whose force made her sick "from that day on." She "feared for her senses occasionally." God's interior presence assuaged her fear, and God answered her to her exceedingly great joy, "I am no robber of the senses, I am an enlightener of the senses!"[132] As with Mechthild of Magdeburg, Margaret reported that grace "flows through all the senses" yet does not destroy the body. The human being is grasped totally in all his or her powers, an occurrence that always leads to the development, not to the destruction of the senses. Thus the spirit of the Order and of its teachers is unmistakable.

Margaret's frequent mention of the "eternal wisdom of God" is all too clearly reminiscent of Suso's *Little Book of Eternal Wisdom*, whose Latin version, *Horologium sapientiae*, was loaned to Medingen by the abbey of Kaisheim for copying.[133] The striving for truth and wisdom fostered by the Order clarifies Margaret's subsequent reflection toward the beginning of the *Revelations* that she could report nothing about her first twenty years, "because I had not paid attention to myself," which meant that Margaret had not yet become aware of her potential to make the most of her talents and to cooperate with grace. Only later did she note that she began "to experience more visibly the grace of God inwardly and outwardly."[134] To the acquisition of truth and wisdom also belonged the need to seek advice, because judgment in one's own affairs may easily prove to be fallacious and thus cause general uncertainty. In just such a situation of helplessness Margaret complained, "I yearned for a human being, by whom I would be instructed, but at that time this was denied to me."[135] Only later, after hesitating, did she find "the true friend of God" as the invaluable advisor, for whom she waited, "because I want to direct all my desires according to your advice," as she wrote to Henry.[136]

3.1.3 Influence of the Liturgy: *Jesus Via Veritatis*

In addition to the spiritual imprint of the Dominican Order for the understanding of truth and wisdom, the daily liturgy with its times of meditation nourished an intensive spiritual life leading to the experience of God. Along with the frequently mentioned petitions of the *Pater Noster* Margaret had, according to her own statement, the custom of reciting the prayer *Jesus via veritatis*. At the recitation of these words "such a strong powerful grace" overcame her that with this "speaking" the "presence of God" was made known, bestowing upon her a "contemplative light" that permeated her with "immeasurable sweetness and flowed into all her members," so that she could not move for a long time. Since the faithfulness of the Lord had been shown to her in such an interior way, she no longer resisted and wanted herself "to become absorbed in his truth with joy, and with great yearning to give in to all his graces, the known and unknown," because, she continued explaining, "I recognized the truth in Him and perceived it from Him. I am sweetly consoled that He alone knows well my whole life and that He helps me in everything."[137] Liturgy and the life of prayer formed the fertile soil for her growth in the mystical life.

3.1.4 St. Francis, Model of the Radical Imitation of Christ

Next to St. Dominic, Margaret saw St. Francis as the model for imitating Christ in all ways. For this reason by the intercession of the Mother of God she longed to receive the stigmata of Christ, the "signs of love" of Christ. She asked for this, saying "a desire gradually increased in me to be given what had been granted to the praise-worthy lord, St. Francis, that I would be wounded with Christ's holy sufferings and have them impressed upon me as a true sign of love as it had been given to none other of His friends."[138] An intensive passion mysticism with the veneration of the Five Wounds was apparent also in *The Flowing Light of the Godhead;* however Mechthild of Magdeburg, unlike Margaret, never asked for the stigmata. Mechthild's passion mysticism of love included the intensity of being wounded by suffering with God in the sense of compassion at all levels for the passion of Christ.[139]

Since Bernard of Clairvaux, meditation on the humanity of Christ and also on his sufferings assumed an important place in the ascent to God, until with St. Francis it was manifested by a radical imitation of Christ called stigmatization. The imitation of Christ by way of the sufferings of the cross was emphasized by German mystics to varying degrees. In the case of Suso, imitation of the passion became frankly eccentric. By comparison, Margaret's veneration of the cross seems more moderate. The wounds or sufferings of Christ she called "signs of love," by which suffering lost its sting and was transformed by grace. In the sense of Bernard of Clairvaux, as with Margaret, the community of the suffering was founded upon unity in love from which the sweetness of the presence of God flows, thus forming an emotional state.

3.1.5. The Christocentrism of Bridal Mysticism in St. Bernard of Clairvaux

That Margaret derived inspiration from Bernard's writings is clear in the *Revelations,* in which he was mentioned three times. She wrote "of St. Bernard" as of "my lord," and yearned for the same graces that he had received: "the kiss" of God and "grasping of the heart."[140] "The kiss" was an allusion to Bernard's exposition of the Songs of Songs 1:1—"He kisses me with the kiss of his mouth." To this verse alone he dedicated seven of his eighty-six sermons on the Song of Songs. Apparently Margaret herself had read the works of St. Bernard. In conversation with the Child Jesus she asked about Bernard's statements concerning the vision of God, "since he writes about the soul's vision of God." The Child answered her, "What

Bernard has written, he has written in true love. He was enraptured with such great delight in me that he thought everyone should come to understand the truth, as he had, because I am the pure truth, who has written and spoken through him."[141] Bernard's writings served to clarify her own inner experiences for Margaret. Her language of bridal mysticism and the arrangement of individual spiritual experiences by type and time were nourished and supported by the spirit and by the language found in Bernard's exposition of the Song of Songs. Margaret reported that the Lord had said to her, "I am the spouse of your soul," and when she responded, "You are my spouse and I am your Beloved," she was using the traditional vocabulary of the mystical exposition of the Song of Songs, which had attained a high point with St. Bernard. The theme of Bernard's exposition on the Song of Songs, that in Christ, the Word, the Incarnate God was revealed and because of this incarnation the divine Son of God could be experienced, opened up for Margaret a broader horizon of understanding of her own inner experiences, since Bernard spoke not as a speculative thinker, but from experience, whether based on his own or that of others.[142] The certitude about inner experiences for Margaret as for Bernard rested not on externally acquired knowledge, but on the teachings of and union with the inner teacher, the friend and beloved, Christ. Therefore the question of the truth of her mysticism is christologically determined. How had Margaret come in contact with the teachings of St. Bernard? The Dominican monastery of Maria Medingen maintained close contact with the Cistercian abbey of Kaisheim. According to Henry's letters, books were exchanged between these two monasteries. It could be that the writings of Bernard came to Medingen via Kaisheim. In any case, the five extant letters of Abbot Ulrich III of Kaisheim show proof of mutual trust.[143] Bernard was also the authority for her lack of desire for food, when she wrote, "how long I went without eating, I do not know."[144]

3.1.6. The Motifs and Linguistic Influence of *The Flowing Light of the Godhead*

In his letters Henry borrows much from the thought and language of Mechthild of Magdeburg expressed in *The Flowing Light of the Godhead*, such as the image of the wine cellar and the mystical drink as expressions of inner union with God. He, like Mechthild, used the motif of the dance, and he also used her Marian titles of honor for Margaret, to some extent verbatim; for example, Margaret was like Mary, "a guardian against the devil," and so on.

Because Henry sent Mechthild's book to Margaret and especially recommended it for her reading, the *Revelations* were much influenced by this text. Only a few points regarding that influence can be mentioned here. The theme of burning desire to love God for himself is emphasized both by Mechthild and Margaret. Margaret called the relationship between God and the soul, "a sweet game," using Mechthild's vocabulary.[145] The theme of the vision "in the holy mirror of the Godhead," and the description "of delight of the holy Godhead," which was directed first to humans because they were always the first beloved in God, is stressed.[146] Also important is the image of the "desert of the Godhead," which described the process of stripping away and purifying in order to become totally free for greater union with God.

This brief sketch illustrates how Margaret, as a child of her time, was moved by various formative influences. But we must investigate the actual language and content of the *Revelations* in order to evaluate Margaret's significance in the history of medieval spirituality.

3.2. The Holy Name of Jesus

Margaret's understanding of truth, formed by her Christology, was the basis of her love for Christ, which progressed into Christ-mysticism. In a striking way this development was fostered by the veneration of the name of Jesus, so that from this attitude of piety a process of identification with Christ became clear.

"Your Name I have as the only refuge in my heart," was used as a prayer already known in the Egyptian desert.[147] The name here was thought to be almost identical with the person or to be an hypostasis of it, thus underscoring the importance of knowing someone by name. According to ancient and biblical thought, the name designated both the being and the task. "You should give him the name Jesus," said the angel to Joseph in a dream, "for he will save his people from their sins" (Mt 1:21, *RSV*). In the New Testament Jesus appeared and acted in the name of God as representative and as the one sent from God (Mt 21:9; Jn 5:43; 10:25). For that reason his own name was of such great importance. In his name there is hope, faith, salvation, sanctification and true life (Jn 21:31). According to Friedrich Heiler, for the first Christians the name of Jesus superseded the power of all ancient names of God and embraced them all, so to speak.[148] The significance of the prayer of Jesus from then on lay in the power that came forth from it. Already in the third century Origen (c. 185–c. 254) emphasized the actual power of the name of Jesus.[149] In the late sixth century the *Carmen de cognomentis salvatoris* was produced by Sylvius.[150] Since the Early Middle Ages veneration of the name of Jesus was promoted by Bede the Venerable, Bernard of Clairvaux, and Pope Innocent III, among others. This veneration found a home among the mendicant orders, beginning with St. Francis and his followers, and was also cultivated by Dominicans such as Thomas Aquinas and Henry Suso, who cried out, "that you might inscribe your holy name in me, so that you will never again depart from my heart."[151] The celebration of the feast of the Holy Name of Jesus (14 January), permitted to the Franciscan Order in 1530, was extended to the entire Latin Church in 1721.

Margaret possessed "the book of the sweet name, and of the rich love of Jesus," sent to her by Henry without stating the name of the author.[152] In her veneration for the name of Jesus, she belonged to a certain strain of formation and piety. What was the decisive meaning of the name of Jesus so frequently called out by her? The invocation of the name was no mere symbol for Margaret; it was rather an occasion of revelation with ever increasing transcendent power. In the revelation of the name of Jesus Christ, God appeared as Salvation, Power, and as Beloved. This was a direct placement of the self in relation to the name of Jesus. The living, true, holy and sweet name of Jesus revealed itself to her directly. The revelation of the name became a revelation of the Word and Being, which Margaret experienced existentially.

Her writings convey the increasingly great efficacy of the name of Jesus. The first time she experienced the effect of the name of Jesus occurred in the year 1332. After visiting some of the sisters' graves, she noticed a fragrance "of great sweetness" that came from outside and penetrated through her heart into all her limbs, whereby "the Name of Jesus was so powerfully impressed upon her heart" that she could pay attention to nothing else. In this irresistible grace it seemed to her that she "was really in His presence."[153] She perceived this fragrance for three days. In this condition she took no note of the circumstances in the monastery, so absorbed was she by the nearness of Christ.

In March 1334 she described the grace from the name of Jesus as the "greatest joy of all" and the "most excessive grace," so that she could neither eat nor pray in the usual way. This extraordinary condition of the nearness of God was brought about by an intensive veneration of the cross, which was accompanied by "very great grace and exceedingly sweet power" in her heart, so that she believed she could scarcely cease from doing this exercise and remain alive.[154]

In October 1334 and in the year 1335 she remarked that she went "to the common meal" when thinking about Jesus "with great joy and divine delight," because in thinking of him she perceived "the best taste of all and the greatest sweetness." She wished that the other sisters could also perceive it in just the same way. She could not understand their complaints about the food.[155] Margaret completed this statement about her inner experience with the conviction that interior insights should completely penetrate daily life in all its forms.

The great onetime mystical experience in the year 1335, which she called the "grasp in the heart of an inner divine power," and which could "not to be described in words," impressed the name of Jesus on Margaret's heart with such intensity that it could no longer be contained there, but broke forth into ecstatic "speaking." From then on this speaking held Margaret's life in tension with the "silence," which later suddenly took hold. The grasp of the heart was the exchange of her human heart with the heart of Christ whose "sweetest name" was now permanently within her. Margaret herself did not speak, rather it was "the powerful grace of the Lord" that spoke from her heart in sweet joy. "The speaking lasted until prime," and on such days she was so sick that she sometimes feared for her senses. Then she perceived from the interior presence of God within her "I am no robber of the senses, I am the enlightener of the senses."[156] Continuously, her heart repeated the name of the One whom it loved and desired, through whose sweetness and power the whole person would be transformed even in the senses. Here there was no discussion of an asceticism of the mortification of the senses,

INTRODUCTION

but rather a special value was placed on all the capabilities of the
senses and their transformation to a higher level of insight. This
required taking the limitations of the body seriously. The body could
at times be overcome by the extraordinary gracious power of the
Holy Name. Soon thereafter, on Saturday at matins in choir, the
interior "speaking" was intensified by the "sweetest grace" into
strong, loud, external speaking during which she repeated again and
again the name of her only Beloved, "God Jesus Christ" until she
was exhausted. However, "the grace, lightness, and sweetness and
divine joy" never left her. On the contrary, she perceived how "the
inner, sweet divine grace spread outward" through her body.[157] The
Holy Name had a uniform effect on body, soul, and spirit, alternately
penetrating, revitalizing, and strengthening them.

In the year 1335, the effects of the Holy Name were repeated
many times. According to the inspired words of the Lord, "Your
sorrow will be changed into joy" (Jn 16:20), the impression of the
name of Jesus occurred at this time so powerfully that her prayer life
nourished by the name alone was filled with pure joy.[158] In this joy
the nearness of God was intensified by perceptible divine power and
inner vision. When she heard the name of Jesus being sung or read
during prayer in choir, she no longer had the power to stop the
speaking that the Lord in sweet delight spoke from her. What others
said about her then left her unmoved and did not affect her at all,
because at that moment God was as present and as tangible in her soul
and heart and as perceptible in all the power God works in heaven
and on earth as if she had seen it with her own eyes.[159] At the same
time she was also aware that the speaking with the name of Jesus so
deeply moved her heart "that this could not remain a secret."[160] The
blessedness poured in through the "sweet Name" took away from
her any power over herself, but according to the witnesses standing
around she spoke "the Name of Jesus more than one thousand
times," powerless over herself, "unable to stop the speaking until it
was God's will." As an effect of this power of the name, Margaret
perceived "great lightness," as if she "had set aside her own body."
She interpreted this condition as a reference "to the lightness after
this life." Her body, at the same time racked by pain, seemed to show
signs of imminent death to those around her. She herself perceived

no pain. She seemed to have been anesthetized by "immeasurable inner sweetness" and "excessive joy." Out of ignorance she believed that God would take her from the world in this condition and confessed, "To me that would be the most joyous death I could have."[161]

Approximately twelve years later, in 1347, she described practically the same experience, only in much more intensified form and, as it were, justifying it by reference to 2 Corinthians 13:3 ("since you desire proof that Christ is speaking in me. He is not weak in dealing with you, but is powerful in you"). After the giving of the name and the accompanying painlessness, she sank down exhausted from her "speaking," with "eyes and mouth closed," despite "sickness" and her "great joy" in "word and voice." She could no longer speak out the name, but in her heart she continued to say it "without words of the mouth" until "for a thousand times without thinking of anything else" she was "firmly bound up" interiorly so that, as she stated, "I could not recite the name as forcefully as before," and she was compelled to be silent.[162] The name was the driving force of the outer and inner speaking, which continued uninterruptedly, even when the movement of her tongue and lips ceased. It continued to flow forth until the power of the divine name withdrew, just as when an electric circuit is cut off from its source.

In contrast to the hammering movement of power being released, a certain stiffness sometimes set in at hearing the name of Jesus. "Whenever I heard something about Our Lord, especially when I heard the name of Jesus Christ, I was inwardly grasped and so filled up by the grace of God and by divine sweetness, that I sat there a long time and did not move externally and could not speak a word."[163] Both conditions—movement and stiffness—expressed Margaret's peculiar inner relation to the Lord.

Margaret's characteristic veneration of the name of Jesus, and therefore of Jesus himself, was nothing less than the expression of her yearning for union with God and perception of truth. In 1347 she summarized the workings of the gifts of grace through the name of Jesus in the following way: "The Name of Jesus has a special place in my heart."[164] God himself had accomplished it when God had impressed the name four times "in the innermost part of the heart." The grace-giving sweetness, which flowed out from this place in the heart, extended to all parts of her body, so that her breath stopped and a sweet taste arose from within her heart through her throat and into her mouth.

The fourfold impression of the name of Jesus described stages of her experience of God in operation. The first two impressions emphasized the wonderfully penetrating sweetness throughout the body and the melting power and force of God in total divine possession, as was described also by Mechthild of Magdeburg in her writings. Concerning the third impression of the name of Jesus, Margaret spoke of a "new movement," which opened up a "new understanding of truth" in the sense of discernment of spirits. She recognized whether external speech corresponded to the interior intention. When something said was true, she felt "a sweet power of truth" in her heart. The fourth and strongest impression of the name of Jesus occurred during the exchange of hearts in the "grasp of love" (*minnegriff*). For Margaret, this was of "such strong, new grace" that she was filled with an "oversweet perception of the presence of Christ," which was revealed in his name and continued for a longer time than anything that had previously happened.

The name of Jesus was not a mere pious devotional platitude for Margaret. It penetrated body, soul, and spirit with healing power. It was filled with God's presence, power, and sweetness. Therefore, it was powerful in deeds and promoted "being reformed into Christ," even to the level of mystical experience. This recasting process increasingly developed into a strong personal relationship with God, as when God spoke to her soul, "You are a grasper of truth, a perceiver of my sweet grace, a seeker of my divine delight, and a lover of my love."[165]

The veneration of the name of Jesus reached its highest level in Margaret's longing to be permitted to rest upon the heart of Jesus and to drink from it as the apostle and visionary St. John had done.[166] This topos, beginning with Origen and continuing into the High Middle Ages, was widely used by both male and female authors such as Hildegard of Bingen, Mechthild of Magdeburg, and Gertrude the Great. It represented a high degree of vision and mystical union. For Margaret, this longing led to ecstasy, so that she "can scarcely utter the word anymore" and she "would like to die of love." She reached a "very deep grasp of truth," for which she "had never asked and indeed could never have asked." Connected with this topos is the idea of an unutterable mystical grace, accompanied by "the most sweet thrusts" and "all-sweetest movement" inducing even the bursting of the heart. This is similar to Mechthild of Magdeburg's change from "violent" love into the right measure of an ordered love so that her "limited human nature" could better bear this overwhelming grace. In this same situation, as earlier, Margaret heard the words of the Lord, "I am no robber of the senses; I am the enlightener of the senses."[167] Margaret summarized the effects of the veneration of the name of Jesus in this profession, "The Name of Jesus is the delight of our souls and the strength of our hearts and the help of our entire lives."[168] She reiterated her belief even more strongly at the end of her *Revelations* with the words:

> The Name of Jesus Christ . . . blossoms within me during the season of Advent with especially sweet grace and I can do nothing aside from what is given me with Jesus and from Jesus and in Jesus.[169]

3.3 The Childhood of Jesus

Since Margaret wanted to be "a true follower of the humanity of Christ," she asked about the course of events of the earthly life of Jesus. She wanted to know about it more precisely than the evangelists had recorded it. Her love for Jesus also increased by meditation upon and veneration of the sacred childhood and passion. The veneration of the Divine Child in whose littleness was hidden the almighty power of God was used as a theme in Suso's writings, where the motif of the child occupied an important place in *The Little Book of Eternal Wisdom*. Even earlier, Mechthild of Magdeburg's *The Flowing Light of the Godhead*, sent to Margaret by Henry of Nördlingen, had the same theme. It spoke about the childhood of Jesus in much more detail and therefore posed similar questions.[170] That the veneration of the Divine Child was a firmly established form of meditation and piety is shown by a letter written by Henry to Margaret at Christmas 1341. She received it prior to beginning to write down her *Revelations* in 1344. Using stark antitheses and paradoxes he placed before her eyes the unusual miracle of the Divinity incarnated in a little child.

> By the loving favor flowing from the mercy of the tiny newborn child, I wish you to be great and small in him, to be rich and poor, suffering and yet to be at home, to be lowly and yet exalted, hidden yet to be known in him, to be sick and strong, lost and found, pale and yet beautiful, dark and still illuminating, in him both blind and seeing, hungry and satisfied, sorrowing yet joyful, to die each day and yet have a foretaste of eternal life. Since He is so much greater this wondrous inequality raises you up interiorly for this young old child and plays with your senses.[171]

This strange paradox had but one goal—that the person be transformed into the Divine Child. "Oh, how well can he care for such an unequal thing, until he makes it into his likeness! Then he plays with it in a new way until they know that they are known, and love because they are loved . . . and must give you possession of the high nobility of God."[172]

The paradoxical turn, "this young old child," is reminiscent of the phrase in Daniel 7:9—"the Ancient of Days" as an expression for the eternity of God. It implies the christological belief that the Eternal Divine Word spoken at creation took the form of the "young old child" in the Incarnation. The basis for venerating the Child Jesus is the mystery of the Word of God becoming flesh, which, according to Meister Eckhart, should continue as the birth of God in the heart of the believer to begin the process of restoring the divine image in the human person.

In the same letter Henry recommended to Margaret a prayer to the Divine Child, demanding from her five things in allegorical form: "Give me your soul as a cradle, your heart for a pillow, your blood for my bath, your skin for a blanket, and all your limbs as a living offering for all my suffering."[173]

With such interior preparation, it was not surprising when Margaret, while reflecting on her process of writing to Henry in the year 1344, spoke directly for the first time of her veneration of the "childhood of our Lord." This does not mean, however, that she did not practice this devotion previously. For a long time she had pushed aside her writings because she either could not or would not write. When, under compulsion, she did begin to write, she reported that "the greatest happiness in the childhood of our Lord overcame me with the sweetest grace." She became "so very overpowered by his presence, that she had to speak about it." However, she felt "anxious and fearful in this grace," as if it had to do with objectionable things. Just as Mechthild of Magdeburg needed to let the truth of her book be confirmed by the triune God and Christ, Margaret gained interior certitude to continue writing by the inner exhortation of the Divine Child as Word of God from the scripture verse, "Whoever does the will of my Father, is my father and my mother" (Mt 12:50).[174] The miraculous nature of the Divine Child is the basis for the communication of her inner experiences. With this quotation from scripture the discord between the wish of the Lord and her inner uncertainty about the sense of writing her *Revelations* was removed.

The ever-increasing interior dialogue with the Divine Child and the graces bound up with that "more and more in all ways" demonstrated the stages of Margaret's spiritual ascent through meditating upon the Incarnation of the Divine Child.[175] Margaret developed a game of question and answer with the "childhood of the Lord" that basically concentrated on a deeper understanding of the Divine Incarnation. In conformity with the symbolic use of language of her time, the often concretely physical wording of a question was nothing more than an image for a supernatural aim and answer. The miracle of the Incarnation was explained in the following way: "How with great love he descended from heaven to earth and in what littleness he entered the womb of our Lady." The Divine Child said, "If you placed me on a needle you would not have been able to see me and yet I truly possessed all my limbs."[176] Mary's conception of Christ was understood as taking possession of the entire human by divine love precisely through the original action of union in love so that her heart and all her limbs were penetrated by the overflow of sanctifying grace, Margaret posed almost the same question about Mary as Mechthild had asked: How in her human body was she able to endure this great grace? Like Mechthild, Margaret saw in Mary the prototype of the lover of God, who could be sustained in the glowing fire of divine love only by the shadow of the Holy Spirit, "because the fiery power of divine love goes beyond all human power."[177] In this way Mechthild had already prayed to the Mother of God when she turned to her for help because Mary's human nature "was not destroyed in the sun of the fiery Godhead" during the time when she was most interiorly united with her Son.[178] Like Mechthild, Margaret sought help from the Mother of God to be able to master the bursting power of divine love. She compared herself in this experience of being filled with grace to the privileged status of Mary as Beloved and Bearer of God in order to gain power and strength from her.

The Divine Child revealed to her the secret of the Virgin birth. "I desired to hear something about his birth. Then he responded and said to me, 'I was born in total purity without any pain. And my birth was as wondrous as the Holy Scriptures relate and also as the mother of Holy Christendom believes.' "[179] Further strands of conversation reemphasized the divinity of the Child in order to bring out his human nature once again.

> My Salvation, Jesus also said that our Lady never suffered anything unclean from him, only that he was like other children in his natural weakness in love and sorrow. I asked further whether he had spoken with his mother using human words before he had begun to speak in a natural way. He said, "No, I spoke to her only in a perception of the sweet grace which flowed out from me into her."[180]

This response clarified that divine communication refrained from using natural hearing and speaking in favor of communicating by a gracious voice from within.

Further conversation gave evidence of formation through the sacramental life:

> I asked whether our Lady was able to fulfill all her desire for him with kisses and caressing him. Then my sweet Jesus said, "Along with her love, she had great awe and reverence all the time in virtue of the great power that she felt coming from me and recognized in me." He said this to show me that neither I nor any loving heart could have such a great yearning for the body of the Lord in holy communion that we would not also experience fear and awe at the same time.[181]

Although Margaret manifested great familiarity in relations with God, her attitude toward the presence of Christ in his divinity is characterized by profound veneration of this *mysterium tremendum*.

In the childhood of Jesus she recognized Christ as the power of the Father, from whom all other powers sprang. This power was imparted under the forms of bread and wine in holy communion. Just as the Mother of Jesus even with her great love showed deepest reverence before the divine humanity of her Child, so Margaret asked for this same attitude in view of the presence of Christ in the sacrament of the Eucharist.

The Child further revealed to her that he was really as poor as the Bible related. A critical question followed immediately. If the three holy kings offered such rich treasures, how can one say that the Child Jesus was poor? The Child answered, "The lowest good does not belong to the highest good. I did not descend from heaven in order to enjoy earthly riches. My mother gave them to the poor."[182] With this question and answer Margaret once again imitated Mechthild of Magdeburg, even if with her this theme was emphasized more. First, the poverty of the holy family and the Child Jesus was brought up, then the question about what Mary had done with the gifts of the three kings, since she had not bought a sacrificial lamb. Mechthild made Mary an image of poverty: "The holy flowing goodness and compassion for the needy and love for freely chosen poverty took the treasure away from me. My sacrificial lamb was Jesus Christ, God's almighty Son, who was born from my heart. . . . That is my true lamb of sacrifice."[183]

The veneration of the Child Jesus was also promoted by the actual image of the Child. An "image of the childhood of our Lord" transformed Margaret into a state of such great sweetness and joy that she perceived this exhortation from the Lord. "If you do not suckle me, I will draw away from you, and you will take no delight in me."[184] She explained this starkly physical image immediately by raising it up from its realistic level to a spiritual plane. The interior maternal intimacy with the Divine Child was the physical demonstration for the spiritual consequence of a progressive purification on the way to union with the Divine Essence according to the example of a truly great lover.

> But my desire and my delight are in the sucking, through which I am purified by his pure humanity. I am set afire by his ardent love coming from him and I am filled up with his presence and with his sweet grace, so that I am drawn into the true enjoyment of

his divine essence with all loving souls, who have ever lived in the truth.[185]

The motif of the mystical way and of union brought about by the image of the Child Jesus came to the fore once again when Margaret reported about a present of a Christmas cradle in 1344.

> On St Stephen's day my Lord sent me a loving gift for my delight. I was sent a lovely statue from Vienna—Jesus in a cradle attended by four golden angels. One night I had a revelation in which I saw Him with lively animation joyfully playing in the crib. I asked him, "Why don't you behave and be quiet and let me sleep? I tucked you in nicely." Then the child said, "I do not want to let you sleep; you must pick me up and hold me." So, with desire and joy I took him out of the crib and placed him on my lap. He was a dear child. I said, "Kiss me, then I will forget that you have awakened me." Then he fell upon me with his little arms and kissed me.[186]

The event portrayed here—the advance into mystical union using the image of the most intimate maternal love that could be sought —also appeared in Mechthild of Magdeburg, but in the form of lyric and erotic language used to express bridal love. "Whenever I bed down, I must hope, when I break flowers, I must love. When my Lord comes, I am beside myself, because he brings me such sweet string music."[187]

By imitating Mary in bearing Christ, Margaret was strengthened on her spiritual journey by intimacy with the Child Jesus and was completely transformed by him. Henry of Nördlingen supported her maternal yearning for Jesus when he wrote to his soul friend that "in your soul may the heavenly birth of the eternal Son of God be brought to completion," as with Mary "when she was pregnant with the Eternal Word."[188] He encouraged her with the words, "Prepare the earthly realm of your heart and bear for yourself and for us the Savior."[189] By this imitation of the Mother of God he called Margaret "bearer of God." Margaret's great veneration for the Mother of God was based on veneration of the Divine Child, who revealed to her that "nobody recognized my divinity and my true humanity, except my Mother and John the Baptist."[190] This response made clear that the concern with the childhood of Jesus made the mystery of the God-Man Christ the central and yet inexplicable question of faith.

3.4   The Passion and Imitation of Christ

Margaret's christocentric spirituality included devotion to Christ's passion and the appropriation of this in her own life. Central to this form of piety was the characterization of Christian life as imitation of Christ along the lines expressed by St. Paul: "We were buried therefore with him by baptism into death, so that as Christ was raised from the dead by the glory of the Father, we too might walk in newness of life" (Rom 6:5, *RSV*). Indeed Margaret could not comprehend any other form of spirituality. In January 1346 she stated, "When I heard about someone who led a great and perfect life, but did not follow the way of the sufferings of our Lord, I could not understand it."[191] This belief was very common in medieval spirituality, especially with St. Bernard, St. Bonaventure, and the German Dominican mystics. In a sermon once attributed to Meister Eckhart the incomparable value given to suffering expresses a common view of the German mystics. "If there were anything nobler than suffering, then God would have redeemed man by means of that."[192] Not only the nobility of suffering was stressed, but also the view of suffering as a personal means to union with God was commonly held. Henry Suso wrote of this in his *Little Book of Eternal Wisdom:* "If you wish to contemplate me in my uncreated divinity, then you must learn to know and love me in my suffering humanity for this is the sweet way to eternal happiness."[193] John Tauler, Margaret's contemporary and friend, preached of the benefit of suffering: "God's true friends take refuge in Him and accept all sorrow freely for His sake, thus suffering with Him and in Him. Or they lose themselves in Him in such a loving union that suffering ceases to be felt as such and turns into joy."[194] Margaret agreed with such an analysis of the Christian's response to suffering, since she believed that suffering in imitation of Jesus yielded joy. The imitation of Christ in his passion was the core of Margaret's devotional life, around which various other devotions were gathered. For example, she had a special devotion to St. Francis, who had received the stigmata; to the doubting Thomas, who had placed his hand into the wounded side of Christ; to

St. John the Beloved, who had rested his head upon the breast of Christ at the Last Supper. Not only her special devotions, but her prayers and practices reflected her attachment to the sufferings of Christ. She wished to treat every day as "Good Friday."[195] In addition, the image of the Crucified One was especially dear to her. She always wore a crucifix on her person; she pressed the cross against her breast; she kissed any cross she saw; and she even dreamt of kissing the great crucifix in the chapel.[196] She desired to receive the "kiss of love" as described by St. Bernard, "in no other way than through all your (Christ's) sufferings."[197] Margaret wanted to drink from the wounds of Christ as St. John had "sucked" wisdom from Christ's breast.[198]

She meditated upon all aspects of the passion of Christ, even upon Christ's loneliness in captivity, and imagined herself alone in the same room.[199] In order to meditate she often read the passion accounts from scripture or had them read to her, but as her compassion and commiseration for Jesus Christ in his suffering increased she was no longer able to read or listen to the passion accounts.[200] Eventually she could not even bear to hear the singing of office antiphons having to do with the passion, nor could she tolerate any mention of the names of Christ's persecutors.[201] In fact, as her personal participation in the sufferings of Christ intensified, she began to respond in various mystical ways to the experience of the passion. She was eventually forbidden to participate in the liturgical celebrations of the Paschal Triduum because of the disturbance this caused.[202]

Throughout the *Revelations* Margaret described various mystical responses to the passion, among which were binding silence (*gebundene swigen*), uncontrollable speaking (*reden*), loud outcries (*lute ruefen*), and the experience of the *sagitta acuta*.[203] She experienced the passion of Christ in "inner vision," as if she were truly present at the crucifixion.[204] These mystical responses grew more intense as Margaret progressed in her compassion for Christ. The "binding silence" came upon her, making it impossible for her to speak at all. This experience deepened into more profound silence and lengthened in duration over the years. The "uncontrollable speaking" most frequently entailed the constant repetition of the name *Jesus Christus* until she was exhausted. This likewise increased in duration and power. It also developed into what she termed "inner speaking," which seemed to indicate the same phenomenon at a more profound level. With this sort of speaking, no words were uttered aloud, but the sacred name or some other word would be recited thousands of times. The "loud outcries" also increased in intensity and duration of time. For Margaret, this was not simply screaming, for it also began with words such as, "Oh, no! Oh, no! My beloved Lord, Jesus Christ!"[205] Margaret constantly asserted that she had no power to induce or to end these experiences—their duration was due only to God's will.

Margaret experienced great physical and emotional suffering through the meditation upon and appropriation of Christ's passion in her own life. As early as 1312 she testified that the pain around her heart (with which her initial illness leading to deeper conversion had begun) was greatest during Lent and especially during Holy Week.[206] She interpreted her suffering as a means by which God was preparing her for union with God and thought of the entire process as a constant spiritual conversion into identification with Christ and eventual mystical union with God.[207] Early on she desired that her body be full of the "signs of love" or wounds inflicted on Christ. Her use of this term hints always at the motive of Christ's suffering—love. It was love for Christ that impelled Margaret to suffer with him. She included the passion of Christ among his "works of love," which she also used to describe any action of Christ in his earthly ministry, since all that he said and did were motivated by love for suffering humanity.[208]

In this regard Margaret was similar to both Mechthild of Magdeburg and Adelheid Langmann, among others. Both of these mystics, the first a spiritual mother of Margaret and the second a contemporary Dominican nun at the monastery of Engelthal in Nüremberg, had a devotion to the wounds of Christ. One wonders if Margaret's attitude toward the "five holy signs of love" may not have been directly influenced by Mechthild's *The Flowing Light of the Godhead*, for Margaret viewed the wounds of Christ in a way very similar to Mechthild, as interpreted by Margit Sinka. "Unlike her predecessors and contemporaries, Mechthild no longer associates woundedness primarily with the soul's sickness. . . . Mechthild reserves wounds mainly for her Christologically based journey of love. As she interprets wound imagery . . . she reveals all stages of Christ's and the soul's journeys to each other."[209] As set forth by Sinka, other similarities between Mechthild and Margaret are immediately evident. The imitation of Christ's passion is like Mechthild's golden coin—the crucifixion pictured on one side and a scene of heaven obverse.[210] "Earthly crucifixion and heavenly redemption; they fuse inextricably, the one necessarily implying the other."[211] Like her spiritual mother, Margaret experienced the depth of Christ's love by gazing upon the sufferings of the Crucified One, which necessarily called forth a response in love and an ardent desire to suffer for the sake of Christ. "The nature of true love, as understood by medieval man, necessarily involves reciprocity."[212] Since Mechthild spoke in greater depth of the devotion to the wounds, it seems her teachings served as fundamental background material.

Of the four ways that the soul may be wounded so that it resounds with the wounded love of Christ as expressed by Mechthild, three were prominent in the spiritual life of Margaret Ebner. Both mystics saw reception of the Eucharist (sacrificed Lamb of God), the kiss of the mouth, as union of human and divine, and the *sagitta acuta* as experienced response to the wounds of Christ. Even Mechthild's fourth response, being pierced with the sword of Longinus, may also be implied when Margaret described the painful thrusts against her heart.[213] There is also evidence of a relation to Adelheid Langmann's devotion to the five wounds. She recited the antiphon *Christus factus obediens* and prostrated herself five times to honor each of Christ's wounds. She recommended this devotion to Herman der Kramer, who had suffered from thoughts of suicide for years. She told him to recite five *Paters* and five *Aves* to honor the five wounds.[214]

Margaret's growth into spiritual suffering for the sake of Christ underwent a progression, beginning with a simple desire to be Christlike and culminating in the exchange of hearts in February 1335. This exchange or robbery of her heart symbolized total compassion with Christ and the acceptance of the same love motive for suffering. Her mystical development was signaled by increasingly difficult manifestations of those mystical phenomena already mentioned, which occurred during Lent, especially during the fourteen days before Easter. In this regard, the uncontrollable speaking lengthened, the binding silence intensified, and the loud outcries became incapable of giving her relief, and she became hoarse and unable to express her overwhelming emotion.

While suffering was an essential part of Margaret's existence, it was frequently tinged with joy. In 1338 she wrote of the pain that she had experienced while gazing upon a crucifix, but concluded that "sorrow for my Lord Jesus Christ came to an end in joy."[215]

She found it impossible to describe adequately her sympathy for Christ.[216] Yet she also claimed that for her nothing was more desirable than to die in the love and pain of her Lord's suffering.[217] Frequently she testified that along with the suffering she received great grace and sweetness.[218] A pattern of ever-intensified experience of suffering, grace, and sweetness continued Lent after Lent, and by 1343 she endured constant suffering during all of Lent.[219] Margaret identified herself with Christ Crucified. "So I am given suffering without consolation even as He suffered all His pain without consolation."[220] She wished to be drained of all human strength like Jesus.[221]

By 1344, in her ardent wish for this suffering and imitation, she prayed through the intercession of the Virgin Mary that she might receive the five signs of love (stigmata) like St. Francis. She prayed to learn Truth through the wounds of Christ and was glad of her suffering. "Then it was revealed to me with powerful loving delight that I was to share in every sort of suffering that God endured because I had given my life over to Him at that time."[222] It was also revealed to her that she must suffer greatly for the sake of his love during Lent.[223] Yet once again she maintained that she received great joy, because she had suffered during Lent and went on to claim that no good whatsoever could have been accomplished without the holy name of Jesus and his passion.[224]

Beyond all her other prayer practices, her *Pater Noster* was of greatest importance to her. In it was contained her theological vision, and as may be expected, her constant prayer in these petitions had to do with Christ's passion. Praying for all believers, Margaret asked Christ to "let us take delight in nothing but your holy passion and in your holy sacraments."[225] Further, she asked that all be "pierced through with the sorrow of your (Christ's) heart."[226] This clearly showed a desire to imitate Christ in his sufferings. More than simply suffering, she wished to "die of pure love," the kind of love that motivated Christ to die on the cross.[227]

Not only did Margaret suffer the wounds of Christ with an invisible stigmata, but she also had a devotion to the wounds of Christ very similar to the modern devotion to the Sacred Heart of

Jesus. As part of this devotion to the five wounds, she composed one of her most poignant prayers: "Jesus Christ, my heartfelt Love, have mercy on me! Jesus Christ, my pure Truth, teach me truth! Jesus Christ, sweet Love, teach me love! Jesus Christ, boundless Mercy, come to help me!"[228]

The climax of her suffering occurred on Laetare Sunday in 1347. She described the events of that day in the *Revelations*. "I was then given the greatest anguish I had ever suffered in all my life and I was drawn by strong love into the holy passion of my Lord Jesus Christ."[229] Soon after, she experienced the worst possible thing— doubt, which was overcome by an intense experience of the passion when "his suffering was as present to me as if it had happened before my very eyes."[230] All the usual phenomena associated with her passion occurred again, but to a maximum degree: the *sagitta acuta*, the outcries, the binding silence, and the speaking of the name of Jesus. This further intensified into an experience of bridal mysticism on 27 July 1347. The same cycle, yet again intensified, occurred in 1348, which was the last year recorded in the *Revelations*, even though Margaret lived on to 20 June 1351. Nothing is known of the inter- vening time, but if the example of other mystics may serve, Margaret had come as close to perfection as possible on earth and merely awaited the arrival of the Beloved.

3.5 The *Pater Noster*

Margaret's *Pater Noster* is the most concise expression of her prayer concerns, for in it are contained her constant intercessions and her theological outlook in a forthright and elevated style rarely found in her *Revelations*. The *Pater Noster* was her consolation in sickness: "I took up the *Pater Noster* and reflections on the works of love of our Lord and with these I got better and overcame my ill- ness.[231] At times this prayer form was "taken away" from her by God, with the result that she could not remember her petitions and had to resort to other prayers. She always rejoiced when God al- lowed her to recall these petitions, since they formed her favorite prayer.

Theologically, the prayers contained in the *Pater Noster* are significant for they express her understanding of salvation. Mercy and love flow forth from the Eternal Godhead, who is all Truth. The Father and Christ are both designated as Truth. Christ, the Word, flows out from the Father's heart, source of all joy. By Christ's Sacred Humanity salvation is brought about because Jesus is boundless mercy and goodness and his loving words and deeds help us to become purified and to be enlightened in the Truth. He pours himself into us to purify and cleanse us from sin by his sacred wounds, the "works of love" (*minnewerke*).[232] The grace of Christ helps us to be guided by his will and transforms us so that we have no mere human life within us, but rather that Christ lives in us and enables us to live in the truth. His grace surrounds us with eternal joy. Thereby the human being is graced by Divinity and is so formed by Christ that only the Trinity is seen in the soul, which is adorned with grace and love. Such are the chosen friends, the "elect" of God.

Her desires expressed in the *Pater Noster* portrayed just such a comprehensive understanding of the Christian life as lived in close connection with the providence of God and Christ's salvific actions. Margaret sought pure love and union with God, indeed God himself. She needed assistance for this to be accomplished and prayed for those things necessary to prepare for ecstatic union: to truly perceive what right love is; to have joy in nothing but Christ's passion and the sacraments; to renounce the world; to have a disregard of self; to recognize sin in order to repent; to have sorrow for past sins and omissions; to cultivate a sense of self-awareness in order to be victorious over evil by faith, hope and love; and to have assurance of salvation.

Her spiritual worldview was clearly christocentric. Christ was sent from the Father to save us out of a motive of love and desire for our salvation. This impelled him to live as he did and to make the ultimate sacrifice by the shedding of his blood unto death on the cross. Our appropriation of salvation continues in his church through the sacraments, especially baptism, which purifies, and the Eucharist, which empowers and strengthens us. We are transformed by his grace to experience the Divine Indwelling and union with God.

The *Pater Noster*, by its structure, by the use of titles for God/Christ, and by its content as set forth above clearly demonstrates a Thomistic perspective. The structure conforms to the *exitus-reditus* view of salvation history characteristic of St. Thomas Aquinas. The titles reveal that everything begins with God and ends with God. Christ is addressed as "Truth," "Goodness," "Eternal Wisdom," the "Way," "Mercy," and "Savior." The contents portray a real change in the believer brought about by the action of God's grace by means of the sacraments, especially the Eucharist. These characteristics mark Blessed Margaret as being thoroughly Dominican in her spiritual and theological outlook.

3.6 Mystical Phenomena

Mystical phenomena as spoken of here are distinct from the closely related devotional practices developed or used by Margaret Ebner. These mystical phenomena mark the growth in her relationship to God and the increased intensification of God's action working in and through her both for her own sanctification and for the good of others. Margaret, as a nun, observed the periods of silence required by monastic custom and thought to be necessary for a deepening in prayer. Silence was normally the rule, especially in certain places in the monastery and at certain times of the day. Beyond what was required, she chose to keep silence to foster a spirit of recollection and deep prayer. Her practice of silence was quite distinct from the "binding silence," over which she had no control to begin or to end, since this was brought about by the direct action of God. Whenever she heard any speech about God, whenever anyone mentioned the passion of Christ, or the holy works of love of the Lord, whenever she wished to speak unnecessarily, the silence overwhelmed her. This occurred also during certain times of the year, especially in Advent and Lent.

Likewise, her practice of oral prayer and the "speaking" that began and ended with the name *Jesus Christus* were distinct for the same reasons. The speaking was praying constantly aloud and later silently. This prayer was a gift from God, which Margaret could neither summon nor stop. The same was true of the phenomenon of the "outcry." She had no control over this either. She underwent this experience in sympathy and compassion for the sufferings of Christ, which she appropriated to herself. This mystical experience was perhaps an intensification of her compassion for the suffering Christ.

The *sagitta acuta* demonstrated her further growth in the spiritual life. It was a distinctly mystical experience as opposed to the pain in her heart, which had initiated her illness in 1312. In the experience of the *sagitta acuta*, Margaret spoke of the "thrusts" of love of God, which pierced her heart bringing both pain in association with the pierced heart of Christ and joy in the acceptance of his love. The *sagitta acuta* in turn progressed to the *minnegriff* (grasp of love), whereby the heart was captured and taken by the Lord, as had happened to St. Bernard and was indicative of the unity of hearts.

In addition to the above mentioned phenomena, there were other commonly accepted mystical experiences that were means of revelation for Margaret's own benefit or for the welfare of others in need of her intercessory prayer. She experienced rapture, ecstasy, and union in the manner of many other mystics, both male and female. She experienced inner visions of the crucifixion. She perceived lovely fragrances (internal and external). She enjoyed special perceptions of truth, and she also heard interior and exterior voices. All these phenomena clearly identify Margaret Ebner as an ecstatic mystic.

3.7. Conclusion

Gundolf M. Gieraths described Rhineland mysticism as being the harmonious blending of four elements: 1) scholastic origin, 2) neo-Platonic tinge, 3) use of the German language, and 4) emotional sensitivity.[233] While he applied these elements primarily to an analysis of Meister Eckhart and his influence on John Tauler and Henry Suso, these four elements could also be used to describe the mysticism of German women.

Fourteenth-century German mystics were rooted in the scholasticism of St. Thomas Aquinas and the High Middle Ages. For the Dominican nuns this assimilation of Thomistic teachings was accomplished through the careful spiritual guidance of some of the greatest minds in the Order of Preachers. While the friars had initially resisted any claim on their time and efforts by the innumerable monasteries of Dominican nuns, once that obligation had been accepted, the provincial of Germany was careful to send the masters and lectors to visit the various convents under his supervision. As with Maria Medingen, most monasteries had a secular priest as chaplain, but depended upon Dominican preachers for retreats and conferences. Such contacts account for some of the best sermons delivered by Tauler and Suso on the spiritual life. However, the nuns were not only influenced by such contact in which scholastic principles and thought were delivered, they also read the texts of St. Thomas Aquinas, available to them both in Latin and in Middle High German. Margaret Ebner and her entire community received many books as gifts from Henry of Nördlingen or in exchange with the Cistercian Monastery of Kaisheim or by purchasing them. Especially in the petitions of Margaret's *Pater Noster* the influence of St. Thomas and scholastic thought is evident. It can be seen in her use of titles for Christ (the pure Truth) and in the very structure of the petitions, which imitate a Thomistic schema of salvation history.

In this study a consideration of any neo-Platonic tinge in the writings of Margaret Ebner has not been considered. However, its presence is intimated by the use of titles applied to God or Christ (the Highest Good, Mercy, Eternal Wisdom, Love) and by Margaret's views on friendship. Her writings indicate a hierarchy of friendship with regard to God. Most people live at the level of an unrecollected life, as Margaret had prior to 1312. All are invited to a higher level of relationship with Christ. Some become his "special friends" or "elect." Margaret became one of the brides of Christ—a symbol of the highest level of relationship in this life. Margaret prayed for special wisdom in her *Pater Noster*. Such wisdom from on high derived from Wisdom itself. Acquisition of wisdom was a free gift to "special friends," by which they were elevated to a higher level. The sacraments, especially the Eucharist, provided the context for growth in wisdom by the grace of God. Also indicative of a neo-Platonic tinge would be Margaret's preference for texts from the Gospel of John, the Letters of Paul, and the Book of Wisdom.

While Meister Eckhart, Henry Suso, and John Tauler used both Latin and German in their works, generally the nuns, such as Margaret Ebner, Christina Ebner, and Adelheid Langmann, wrote in the vernacular. Their writings were sprinkled with Echkartian terms— *ingossenheit, ein, gotheit, luterkeit,* and so on. Their use of Latin was usually restricted to the sign of the cross, antiphons or hymns sung in choir, or scripture quotations. The nuns wrote about the spiritual life and mystical experiences in their respective German dialects with all the naturalness of the native tongue. They used the freshness of that tongue to express not only complex Latin concepts, but also to struggle with the attempt to express unutterable mystical experiences.

The fourth element of German mysticism was called emotional sensitivity by Gundolf Gieraths. This designates a process in which the individual turns from personal sinfulness to goodness, from the allure of the things of the world to enjoyment of the things of heaven, from the devil to God. This process entails a life of asceticism, in which the body is tamed by the spirit and the human heart is set on Christ and the things above. Margaret's *Revelations*, as a spiritual autobiography, demonstrates such a process of conversion in her life. Her withdrawal from the world and other people, the asceticism of her lengthy illness, her disdain of food and bodily comfort, her growth in compassion, and her dedication to prayer all demonstrate a nun in the process of deeper conversion at every level of her being. Her asceticism included real physical and profound emotional suffering, yet she rejoiced in it because she understood that it was necessary as part of the process. She desired to imitate Christ in his suffering, and by that imitation Margaret understood that she would be useful to others—the Emperor Louis, Henry of Nördlingen, and especially the souls in purgatory. Margaret frequently mentioned her joy in suffering, a joy that was neither masochistic nor perverse, since she understood the suffering to be a sign of spiritual growth. She believed firmly that if she died with Christ she would also rise with him.

Even though Margaret's spirituality and writings are evidently part of the great German movement as described by Gieraths, her spiritual formation and exemplary legacy go beyond his four elements. While not restricted to women mystics, bridal mysticism, mystical ecstasy, and elements of spiritual or mystical maternity must certainly be associated with women, and especially with Margaret. Her formation in these aspects of spirituality was influenced by the bridal imagery in the Song of Songs used to speak of the most intimate union between the soul and Christ. This was understood to be the ideal form of relationship, which would ameliorate sufferings endured by imitation of Christ. The mystical betrothal and marriage, the taking the heart (*minnegriff*), and even the painful thrusts of love (*sagitta acuta*) indicate Margaret's special status and her spiritual perfection. Bridal union represented the firm assurance of unalterable faith, love, and divine favor. It was the greatest and most personal gift of Christ. In becoming the bride, Margaret, as Henry saw her, could also be the mother, not of Christ himself, but of Henry and the Friends of God, the souls in purgatory, and all the living. Through her influence and intercessory prayer she would bring her children (especially Henry) to the fundamental insight of God's love for them and their need to return that love by imitating Christ in his suffering and by loving him with an undivided heart. The motivating force behind Margaret's spirituality was the love of Christ for every human being and God's wise providential care of the world.

1. Strauch based his critical edition of the medieval text upon the manuscript contained in the archives of Kloster Maria Medingen in Mödingen, Germany. This he designated manuscript *M*, which dates from 1353. The archives of Maria Medingen possesses seven copies of this manuscript dated 1676, 1687, 1728, and 1735, the rest being undated. Strauch judged *M* to be the best and most accurate version. Also, *M* includes the *Pater Noster*. Manuscript *l* is found in the British Museum and dates from the sixteenth century. It is noteworthy in that it contains drawings of the choir of Maria Medingen and the tomb of Margaret Ebner as they were prior to the total renovation of the monastery in 1717 under Magdalena vom Stein zum Rechtenstein. Manuscript *m*, "Papierhandschrift der fürstlichen Wallersteinischen Bibliothek zu Mayhingen," was copied by Sister Johanna von Mylen in 1735. Manuscript *n* dates from the fifteenth century and belonged to Sister Barbara Warrüsin of St. Katharine's Monastery. Manuscript *o*, the "Einsiedler Handschrift," dates from the fourteenth century and also contains the treatise *Von sieben Graden der rechten Demut*. Strauch also mentions a manuscript of the eighteenth century belonging to the Monastery of Melk.

2. Margaret Ebner was beatified by Pope John Paul II by reason of the antiquity of her cult, which perdured from her death to the present. The decree from the Congregation for the Cause of the Saints, which recognized and confirmed her cult, is dated 24 February 1979. Her feast is kept on 20 June.

3. Philipp Strauch, *Margareta Ebner und Heinrich von Nördlingen. Ein Beitrag zur Geschichte der deutschen Mystik* (Freiburg & Tübingen: Akademische Verlagsbuchhandlung von J.C.B. Mohr, 1882; reprint, Amsterdam: P. Schippers, 1966), pp. xiv–xxv. *Revelations*, pp. 1–161, "Der Ebnerin Pater Noster," pp. 161–66, Letters, pp. 270–83. German translations: M. David-Windstosser, *Deutsche Mystiker V: Frauenmystik im Mittelalter* (Kempten-Munich: 1919), excerpts from the *Revelations* and fourteen letters. H. Wilms, *Der selige Margareta Ebner Offenbarungen und Briefe*. vol. 5 of *Dominkanisches Geistesleben* (Vechta in Oldenburg: Albertus Magnus Verlag, 1928), excerpts from the *Revelations*, the *Pater Noster*, seventeen letters. Wilhelm Oehl, *Deutsche Mystikerbriefe des Mittelalters 1100–1550* (Munich: George Müller, 1931), pp. 333–43, excerpts from the letters.

4. Description of this manuscript in Werner Höver, *Theologia Mystica in altbairischer Übertragung. Studien zum Übersetzungswerk eines Tegernseer Anonymus aus der Mitte des 15. Jahrhunderts* (Munich: C.H. Beck, 1971), pp. 47–51.

5. Description of this manuscript in Philipp Strauch, fn 1, pp. xvii–xxiii.

6. R. Ringler, "Ebner, Margareta," in *Die deutsche Literatur des Mittelalters,* Verfasserlexikon, vol. 2 (²1980), col. 304.

7. Hieronymus Wilms, O.P., trans. *Der Seligen Margareta Ebner Offenbarungen und Briefe,* Dominikanisches Geistesleben, vol. 5, (Vechta in Oldenburg: Albertus Magnus Verlag, 1928), p. 25.

8. Ludwig Zoepf. *Die Mystikerin Margaretha Ebner* (Leipzig and Berlin: Verlag B. G. Teubner, 1914), p. 29. "Von wenigen Ausnahmen abgesehen muten die 'Offenbarungen' den Leser an wie eine ehrliche, gewissenshaft peinliche, oft trockene Aufzählung der von Gott erwiesenen Gnaden und ihrer Folgen."

9. Zoepf, p. 29.

10. Strauch, p. xxxiv.

11. Karl Bihlmeyer, "Die Selbstbiographie in der deutschen Mystik des Mittelalter," *Theologische Quartalschrift* 114 (1933): p. 522; Zoepf, p. 29.

12. Wilms, pp. 30–31.

13. This work was taken up by Fredericus Steill in *Ephemerides Dominicano-sacrae* (Dillingen, 1692; reprint with a preface by Dominikus Widmann, Dillingen, 1717).

14. Anton Michael Seitz, "Verwandschaft, Stammbaum und Wappen der Mystikerin Margaretha Ebner von Kloster Maria Medingen," *Jahrbuch des historischen Vereins Dillingen an der Donau* 72 (1970): p. 108.

15. Ibid., p. 91–108, esp. 93f.

16. Ibid., p. 17–41. A.M. Seitz, ibid., p. 92.

17. Strauch, p. 23,5: "Es kom min bruoder."—p. 40,14; "In dem zit [1335], do wolt min bruoder ein kind zu mir in daz closter tuon." —p. 110, 23: "Item do kom ze der selben zit min bruoder, den ich han in iener welt."—p. 186 (Letter XI, 56–57): "dein bruder und alle die dinen."—A.M. Seitz, ibid., p. 102ff.

18. Strauch., 7,4f.

19. Johannes Traber, *Die Herkunft der selig genannten Dominikanerin Margareta Ebner* (Historischer Verein Donauwörth: Don-

auwörth, 1910), p. 12. Jedelhauser (cf. fn. 20), p. 84ff. A.M. Seitz, ibid., p. 104.

20. Strauch, p. 13,10–11.

21. All supporting facts here are taken from M. Canisia Jedelhauser, O.P., *Geschichte des Klosters und der Hofmark Maria Medingen von den Anfängen im 13. Jhr. bis 1606,* Quellen und Forschungen zur Geschichte des Dominikanerordens in Deutschland (Vechta in O.: Albertus Magnus Verlag, 1936), p. 88. A hide was a tract of land used for agricultural purposes to support one family.

22. Traber (cf. fn. 19), p. 37,40f.

23. Seitz, p. 105ff.

24. The references here depend upon "Beurkundete Geschichte des ehemaligen Nonnenklosters Medingen, auch Maria Mödingen genannt bei Dillingen, und Monographien der ehemaligen Hofmarksorte Medingen, Bergheim, Schabringen und Stetten," *Jahresbericht des historischen Vereins für den Regierungsbezirk von Schwaben und Neuburg* (Augsburg, 1841), pp. 1–13, esp. p. 5, fn 19. M. Canisia Jedelhauser, O.P., *Geschichte des Klosters und der Hofmark Maria Medingen* . . . (cf. fn. 21), pp. 9–17.

25. *Jahresbericht* . . . 1841, p. 6, Jedelhauser, p. 95.

26. Jedelhauser, p. 14.

27. Ibid., p. 15.

28. Ibid., p. 108. A list of the prioresses from 1239 to 1606 is found on p. 109f.

29. Strauch, Letter XL, p. 238,74–78.

30. Friedrich Zoepfl, *Maria Medingen: Die Geschichte einer Kulturstätte im schwäbischen Donautal,* special volume of *Jahrbuch des Historischen Vereins Dillingen* LIX/LX (Dillingen, 1960), p. 72.

31. *Lexikon für Theologie und Kirche* 5 (²1960), col. 1245–50. s.v. "Kaisertum."

32. Zoepf, p. 141.

33. Strauch, p. 35,24: ". . . von der grossen entrichtunge der cristenheit."

34. Ibid., p. 102,25: "irsalin der cristenheit."

35. Ibid., p. 35,26–36,13.

36. Ibid., p. 36,6–7.

37. Ibid., p. 36,9–11.

38. Ibid., p. 36,11–13.

39. Ibid., p. 103,7ff.

40. Ibid., p. 103,1f.
41. Ibid., p. 220,26–29.
42. Ibid., p. 220,35–52.
43. Jedelhauser, p. 19ff.
44. Zoepf, p. 141.
45. Strauch, p. 6,15–17.
46. Ibid., p. 6,15f; Zoepf, p. 142; In the *Revelations* the psalm verse was quoted in Latin: "*Adorabunt eum omnes reges, omnes gentes servient ei.*"
47. Ibid., p. 6,5–10.
48. Ibid., p. 6,5–13.
49. Ibid., p. 103,9–12.
50. Ibid., p. 148,2–8.
51. Ibid., p. 148,8–12.
52. Ibid., p. 148,13–16.
53. Ibid., p. 148,13–21, 315 fn.
54. Ibid., p. 149,2f.
55. Ibid., p. 150,21–24.
56. *Lexikon für Theologie und Kirche* 6 (1961²) 1188, s.v. "Ludwig IV."
57. Strauch, p. 151,1–4.
58. Ibid., p. 158,16–20. Compare L. Zoepf, pp. 141–143. M. Roswitha Schneider, *Die selige Margaretha Ebner* (St. Ottilien: EOS Verlag Erzabtei St. Ottilien, 1985), p. 25 and p. 38f.
59. Schneider, p. 39.
60. Strauch, Letter LI, p. 263,70–81. Angela Rozumek, "Margaretha Ebner und Heinrich von Nördlingen," *Die christliche Frau* 36 (1938): p. 113.
61. Strauch, p. 8,6–12; Jedelhauser, p. 87; Schneider p. 25.
62. Schneider, p. 39.
63. Heinrich Gürsching, "Neue urkundliche Nachrichten über den Mystiker Heinrich von Nördlingen," in *Festgabe Karl Schornbaum* (Neustadt a.d. Aisch: P.C.W. Schmidt, 1950): pp. 42–57.
64. Strauch, p. 175,82f.
65. The reference to Psalm 138:17 is taken from the Vulgate. "*Mihi autem nimis honorificasti facti sunt amici tui, Deus.*" In all ancient versions of the text (LXX) the primary meaning of the Hebrew original was translated as "friend." However, in modern versions this verse is rendered, "How precious to me are thy *thoughts*, O

God" (*RSV*). This is the only place in the Hebrew scriptures where the root word is translated as "thoughts."

66. *Lexikon des Mittelalters,* IV (1989), col. 1586f by M. Gerwing. s.v. "Gottesfreund/Gottesfreundschaft."

67. Quoted according to Zoepf, p. 17.

68. See Wilhelm Oehl, *Deutsche Mystikerbriefe des Mittelalters 1100–1550* (Munich-Vienna: George Müller 1931; reprint Darmstadt 1972), pp. 387–410.

69. Strauch, p. 83,27–84,1.

70. Strauch, Letter XXII, p. 219,69–73.

71. Ibid., p. 16,3f., 24,4.

72. Ibid., p. 16,3f.

73. Ibid., Letter LXVII, p. 281,10–13.

74. Ibid., p. 282,31–34.

75. Ibid., p. 173,19–22.

76. Ibid., Letter XIII, p. 188,9–15.

77. Ibid., p. 188,19f.

78. Ibid., Letter XXXIV, p. 224,1; p. 194,9–18.

79. Ibid., Letter XXX, p. 215,1–4.

80. Ibid., p. 26,20–24.

81. Ibid., p. xxxiii with proof and fn. p. 290; 30,3; Letter XLVII, p. 254,24.

82. Ibid., p. 26,16ff.

83. Ibid., p. 24,3ff.

84. Ibid., Letter XXXVI, p. 230,20–29.

85. Ibid., Letter VII, p. 180,37–43.

86. Ibid., Letter XV, p. 192,5–8, (Jn 16:7).

87. Ibid., Letter XLVI, p. 251,36–252,60. Compare Margot Schmidt, "Das Reis als eines der Mystik-Zentren im Mittelalter," *Rieser Kulturtage,* vol. VI/I (Nördlingen, 1986), pp. 473–93, esp. p. 477ff.

88. Strauch, Letter XIII, p. 189,54.

89. Ibid., Letter IX, p. 182,30f.; 213,22f.

90. Ibid., Letter LXVII, p. 283,1f.

91. Ibid., Letter I, p. 170,25–32.

92. Ibid., Letter XL, 236,24–237,3.

93. Ibid., Letter LXVII, p. 282,55f.

94. Ibid., Letter XVII, p. 201,116f.; Letter XXVIII, p. 213,34–39.

95. Ibid., Letter XXXVII, p. 232,9–15.
96. Ibid., Letter XLI, p. 240,5–22.
97. Ibid., Letter IV, p. 173,15–22.
98. Ibid., Letter XVII, p. 197,4ff.
99. Ibid., Letter XLVII, p. 257,37–41.
100. Ibid., Letter LXVII, p. 281,16–24.
101. Ibid., Letter XXXV, p. 228,72–74.
102. Ibid., Letter VII, p. 179,10–13.
103. Ibid., Letter IV., p. 175,59–64.
104. Ibid., Letter XXXIX, p. 235,12.
105. Ibid., Letter XLVI, p. 251,29–36.
106. Ibid., Letter XVI, p. 195,43ff.
107. Ibid., Letter IX, p. 181,8ff; Letter XXXVII, p. 282,27; compare Letter IV, p. 175,56, and Margot Schmidt, "Heinrich von Nördlingen," in *Marienlexikon* vol. 3 (St. Ottilien, 1990).
108. Ibid., Letter IV, p. 173,10.
109. Ibid., Letter XL, p. 237,30.
110. Ibid., Letter XLVIII, p. 257,2f; Letter XLIII, p. 243,21ff.
111. Ibid., Letter XXI, p. 204,1ff; Letter IX, p. 182,26.
112. Ibid., Letter XXI, p. 204,27ff; Letter IV, p. 174,35ff.
113. Ibid., Letter XXXI, p. 215,1; Letter IV, p. 175,63ff.
114. Ibid., Letter VII, p. 180,34f; Letter XIV, p. 191,1f; Letter VII, p. 198,24.
115. Ibid., Letter XLVII, p. 255,71ff.
116. Ibid., Letter XLV, p. 250,11f.
117. Ibid., Letter LIII, p. 267,9ff.
118. Ibid., Letter XXIV, p. 207,32; Letter XLIX, p. 258,30.
119. Ibid., Letter X, p. 183,7ff.
120. Ibid., Letter XIII, p. 190,63; Letter XVII, p. 201,112–115. From Psalm 41:8, "Deep is calling unto deep."
121. Ibid., Letter LII, p. 266,55–58; Letter XLI, p. 240,10–13; p. 84,1–5.
122. Ibid., p. 30,9f.
123. Ibid., p. 90,1ff; 125,15; 126,16ff.
124. Ibid., Letter XLII, p. 242,39.
125. Ibid., p. 91,13–15; 79,15–17.
126. Ibid., p. 69,16f, compare p. 33,10; 109,14f; p. 69,16ff.
127. Ibid., p. 28,8–10; 129,15f; 98,3ff.
128. Ibid., p. 140,9f.

129. Ibid., p. 26,24; Letter LXVII, p. 282,40f.

130. Ibid., p. 17,19–23; 45,7f.

131. Ibid., Letter XL, p. 238,75ff; Letter XLIII, p. 244,59–61.

132. Ibid., p. 28,5–6.

133. Ibid., Letter XXXV, p. 229,83–87.

134. Ibid., p. 17,12.

135. Ibid., p. 22,20–23.

136. Ibid., Letter LXVII, p. 283,60–61.

137. Ibid., Strauch, p. 85,10–86,1.

138. Ibid., p. 46,1–4.

139. Compare Margot Schmidt, " 'Frau Pein, Ihr seid mein nächstes Kleid.' Zur Leidensmystik im 'Fliessenden Licht der Gottheit' der Mechthild von Magdeburg," in *Die Nacht der dunklen Sinne. Leiderfahrung und christliche Mystik,* ed. Gotthard Fuchs (Düsseldorf: Patmos Verlag, 1989), pp. 63–107; Alois M. Haas, "Die Arbeit der Nacht. Mystische Leiderfahrung nach Johannes Tauler," Fuchs, pp. 9–40; Otto Langer, "Passio und compassio. Zur Bedeutung der Passionsmystik bei Bernhard von Clairvaux," pp. 41–62.

140. Strauch, p. 21,26–22,2; compare p. 134,16ff.

141. Ibid., p. 104,11–18. Compare Roswitha Schneider, p. 19f.

142. Compare Ulrich Köpf, *Religiöse Erfahrung in der Theologie Bernhards von Clairvaux* (Tübingen: Mohr, 1980).

143. Strauch, Letters LVII-LXII, pp. 271,1–275,27.

144. Ibid., p. 134,13–16.

145. Ibid., p. 69,21.

146. Ibid., p. 76,8f. and 76,20f.

147. Compare *RAC* vol. XI (Stuttgart, 1981), s.v. "Gottesnamen," col. 1240ff.

148. Friedrich Heiler, *Erscheinungsform und Wesen der Religion* (Stuttgart: Kohlmann, 1961), p. 276f.

149. Compare *RAC,* loc. cit. col. 1262f.

150. *PL* 13, 378; Compare M. Manitius, *Geschichte der lateinischen Literatur des Mittelalters,* vol. 1 (Munich: Beck, 1911), p. 540.

151. Quoted from Strauch, p. 325. There is also a corresponding quote from Mechthild of Hackeborn, *Revelations* II,226.

152. Strauch, Letter XXXV, p. 229,91.

153. Ibid., p. 15,11–16,2.

154. Ibid., p. 20,14–25.

155. Ibid., p. 24,26–25,6–35,1–17. In the "Vitae" of the sisters

the monastic fare does not always fare so well. Compare L. Zoepf, p. 27, fn 6.

156. Ibid., 27,13–28,6; p. 28,5f.

157. Ibid., p. 30,19–23.

158. Ibid., p. 31,11–13.

159. Ibid., p. 32,1–13.

160. Ibid., p. 29,6.

161. Ibid., p. 34,9–26.

162. Ibid., p. 120,24–121,16.

163. Ibid., p. 35,19–23.

164. Ibid., p. 128,12–130,15.

165. Ibid., p. 69,16–19. Compare Zoepf, p. 77.

166. Ibid., p. 33,15ff; 74,15ff. On this topos according to John 13:25, see Hugo Rahner in *Zeitschrift für Katholische Theologie* 55 (1931), pp. 103–8. He traces the tradition from Origen to the Middle Ages. See also Hildegard of Bingen, *Vita* II, c. 16 (PL 197, sp. 116B); also Christel Meier, "Nostris temporibus Necessaria, Wege und Stationen mittelalterlicher Hildegard-Rezeption," *Architectura Poetica* (Fs.f. Johannes Rathofer) ed. Ulrich and Bernhard Sowinski (Cologne/Vienna, 1990), p. 314f. For further evidence see Zoepf, p. 76, fn 2.

167. Strauch, p. 76,4f.

168. Ibid., p. 100,13–15.

169. Ibid., p. 161,3–6. Compare Schneider, p. 49f.

170. Mechthild of Magdeburg. *'Das fliessende Licht der Gottheit,' Nach der Einsiedler Handschrift in kritischem Vergleich mit der gesamten Überlieferung*, ed. Hans Neumann, vol I, Text besorgt von Gisela Vollmann-Profe (Munich: Artemis Verlag, 1990), V, 23 (pp. 174–80).

171. Strauch, Letter XXXVIII, p. 233,4–15.

172. Ibid., p. 233,15–19.

173. Ibid., p. 234,47–50.

174. Ibid., p. 86,10–87,2. Mechthild of Magdeburg II.26, (Neumann, pp. 68,70). Margaret misquoted Matthew 12:50, "For whoever does the will of my Father in heaven is my brother, and sister, and mother" (*RSV*).

175. Strauch, p. 99,10–16. See also p. 87,22ff.

176. Ibid., p. 99,16–20.

177. Mechthild of Magdeburg V, 31 (Neumann, p. 191,26–31).

178. Ibid., p. 191,26–31.

179. Strauch, p. 99,26–100,3.

180. Ibid., p. 101,1–7.

181. Ibid., p. 101,18–26.

182. Ibid., p. 100,3–7; 101,13–17. Compare Zoepf, p. 127f.

183. Mechthild of Magdeburg, V, 23 (Neumann, p. 177,104–78, p. 127f). See also Margot Schmidt, "Maria, Spiegel der Schönheit: Zum Marienbild bei Hildegard von Bingen und Mechthild von Magdeburg," in *Maria für alle Frauen oder über allen Frauen,* ed. Elisabeth Gössmann and Dieter R. Bauer (Freiburg i.B.: Herder, 1989), pp. 86–115, especially p. 110.

184. Strauch, p. 87,3–9.

185. Ibid., p. 87,15–21.

186. Ibid., p. 90,22–91,9. Compare Josepf Dünninger, "Weihnachtliche Motive in der Mystik der Dominikanerkloster [sic] Maria Medingen und Engelthal," *Bayrische Literaturgeschichte in ausgewählten Beispielen* Band 1: Mittelalter (1965), ed. Eberhard Dünninger and Dorothee Kiesselbach, p. 338–48, especially 341f. Also Hans Wentzel, "Eine Wiener Christkindwiege in München und das Jesuskind der Margaretha Ebner," *Pantheon* 18 (1960), pp. 267–83, with nine illustrations. Wentzel concludes, "The statuette preserved up to the present in the Monastery of Maria Medingen is almost certainly the Christ Child that Margaret Ebner received as a gift from Vienna in 1344" (p. 282).

187. Mechthild of Magdeburg II, 2 (Neumann, p. 38,40ff).

188. Strauch, Letter XXXVI, p. 231,70–75.

189. Ibid., Letter XVI, p. 195,43. Letter XXI, p. 204,1.

190. Ibid., p. 102,1–3.

191. Ibid., p. 41,13–18.

192. Meister Eckhart quoted by Gundolph M. Gieraths, O.P., "Life in Abundance," *Spirituality Today* 38 Supplement (Autumn 1985), p. 20. He quoted Sermon CIV, which is now considered inauthentic. Nonetheless, it is a fourteenth-century document.

193. Ibid., p. 20; Henry Suso, *Büchlein der Ewigen Weisheit,* chap. 1; ed. K. Bihlmeyer, *Heinrich Seuse, Deutsche Schriften* (Stuttgart: Kohlhammer, 1907), p. 278ff.

194. Maria Shrady, trans., *Johannes Tauler: Sermons* (New York: Paulist Press, 1985), p. 53.

195. Strauch, p. 70,10–15.

196. Ibid., p. 20,18–25; 78,7–23.

197. Ibid., p. 22,4–6.

198. Ibid., p. 33,14–21.

199. Ibid., p. 17,1–3.

200. Ibid., p. 46,5–10.

201. Ibid., p. 55,4–8; 57,10–15; 69,9–13.

202. Ibid., p. 95,24–96,4.

203. Ibid., p. 54,8–14; 55,12–16. The *sagitta acuta* or "sharp arrow" was an image Margaret used for an experience she had of the love of Christ in Lent and on Palm Sunday in 1339.

204. Ibid., p. 55,19–25.

205. Strauch, p. 51,2–3.

206. Ibid., p. 2,10–12.

207. Ibid., p. 8,3–4; 13,21–22.

208. Ibid., p. 33,6–7.

209. Margit M. Sinka, "Christological Mysticism in Mechthild von Magdeburg's *Das Fliessende Licht der Gottheit:* A Journey of Wounds," *The Germanic Review* (Fall 1985), p. 124.

210. Ibid., p. 124.

211. Ibid., p. 124.

212. Ibid., p. 124.

213. The schema of Mechthild's progression of the four wounds is expounded by Margit M. Sinka, p. 124.

214. Philipp Strauch, ed., *Die Offenbarungen der Adelheid Langmann: Klosterfrau zu Engelthal* (Strassburg: Karl J. Trübner, 1878) p. 43,24–25; 44,7–17. "*Christus factus obediens . . .*" was an antiphon and response used in the liturgy of Good Friday. "Christ became obedient unto death, even death on a cross!"

215. Philipp Strauch, *Margaretha Ebner . . .*, p. 48,11.

216. Ibid., p. 51,5–7; 52,8–17.

217. Ibid., p. 52,22–24; 54,21–25.

218. Ibid., p. 53,17–18.

219. Ibid., p. 66,9.

220. Ibid., p. 29,17–18.

221. Ibid., p. 63,6–13.

222. Ibid., p. 88,15–18.

223. Ibid., p. 91,16f.

224. Ibid., p. 96,13–18; 100,15–18.

225. Ibid., p. 162,10–12.

226. Ibid., p. 163,17–21.
227. Ibid., p. 164,18–22.
228. Ibid., p. 109,11–17.
229. Ibid., p. 118,25–119,5.
230. Ibid., p. 126,3f.
231. Ibid., p. 4,18–20.
232. The *minnewerke* refer primarily to the wounds of Christ. Margaret also used the term to speak of any deed done by Jesus while he lived on earth.
233. Gundolf M. Gieraths, "Life in Abundance: Meister Eckhart and the German Dominican Mystics of the 14th Century," *Spirituality Today* 38 Supplement (Autumn 1986), pp. 13–20.

THE *REVELATIONS*
OF MARGARET EBNER

In the sweet Name of our Lord Jesus Christ and by His truth-filled life, by His loving works accomplished on earth for our salvation, by His holy works of love which He performed so mercifully for us and completed by His strong love for our salvation: may these complete the work already begun through the interior goodness of perfecting grace.[1]

In the year 1312 after the birth of Christ, God showed me His great paternal faithfulness on the feast of SS. Vedastus and Amandus before Shrove Tuesday.[2] God afflicted me with a grave and mysterious illness. Already during the previous year I had received continual inner exhortations to direct my whole life according to His will. How I had lived during the previous twenty years I cannot describe because I had not been attentive to myself.[3] This much I do know: God upheld me in His paternal faithfulness and protected me the whole time.

My illness began strangely with a great, unbearable pain which gripped my heart so that I could not easily breathe. My breathing could be heard even from far away. The pain then went to my eyes so that I could not see, and this continued throughout the illness. Then it went to my hands, and I could not move them. It affected my whole body except for my hearing, which I never lost. I endured this pain for three years and, during that time, had no control over myself. Whenever it went to my head I laughed or cried continuously for four days at a time or even longer.

During the first year I sought a cure through human means, but only got worse, especially during Lent and Holy Week when the pain was greatest. It was also during these first seasons of Lent that I could not speak because my tongue was bound. In this first year I endured the greatest internal and external suffering because I had not yet given myself over to God completely, for I still wanted to be healthy. A holy woman who lived in our monastery was especially dear to me and trusted by me. She told me I should give myself over to God completely and that I should pray when I could, because to suffer great illness for God would be the longest life anyone could have on earth.[4]

Gradually I learned by experience of the world's ways: those who had once been close to me now kept their distance saying they could not bear to see me suffer so. Then I understood that God alone remains faithful. He would never abandon me. So I gave myself over to the will of God and desired that He not let me recover my health; but then He restored me to health both in body and soul. So I devoted myself to praying, and as far as I could recall how sinful I myself was, I offered up prayers for the Poor Souls. Every day I prayed with great desire for all intentions, especially for health.

As the second year began, my interior suffering (I did not like being sick) was removed from me, and thereafter I was able to suffer all pain for God, and I devoted myself to prayer.[5] No matter how painful it had been for me, whenever I prayed I felt better.

Then when the third year came around I was unable to take a step alone and everyone said I was crippled.[6] Then a new sickness took hold of me, which lasted thirteen weeks. Every day from sunrise to nightfall I had no control over myself and I lay as if I were dead, neither eating nor drinking. Then my limbs felt as if they had been broken and the sickness left me.

After that, I was overcome by sweating, which I endured for twenty weeks; once each night and once during the day. The sweating was incredibly profuse. I was cleansed of this sweat by the palms of their hands—great pitchers full of sweat.[7] Soon after that my condition improved so much that I could walk, but only with difficulty.

After that, although I could get around somewhat once again, I remained so weak for thirteen years that I lay in bed more than half each year in great suffering. Often I was in danger of death, and often I myself presumed that I was dying. The sisters who were with me often thought my eyes would burst and I would die. But I improved so much that I could speak, and I devoted myself to prayer. It was only simple prayer: vigils and the psalter. Also my desires were simple at this time.

I withdrew from all people. I did not want to endure conversation or visits from anyone, except my sisters. I did not like to hear any speech, except about God. It was so totally unbearable to me when gossip or even harsh words were uttered in my presence that I often began to cry. This brought on a bad mood, which made me very ill. Perhaps it was due to my illness that I could not bear such disturbance. It happened often that I experienced such a bad mood for half a year. The whole time I lay in bed I longed for even greater suffering because I was not able to live according to the observances of my Order. I took up the *Pater Noster* and reflections on the works of love of our Lord and with these I got better and overcame my illness.[8] When my condition improved so much that I could walk, I always went with firm purpose and desire from the infirmary to Mass. I grieved much because I had not held the Lord's works of love so dear and I had not turned to them with as much concern all the days of my life, as I should have done, and I had not had such great desire for them.[9]

I was greatly concerned that I myself was not so well disposed to God with interior desire as I should have been, and also did not yet live truly according to His will. This bothered me especially because I did not have the necessary love and desire for the Eucharist and because I was not adequately prepared whenever I should receive Him in communion. I blamed myself and thought this was so because I had not withdrawn myself definitively from all earthly things. I was always distressed and concerned about this, and I refrained from talking and from visiting with others inside and from outside the monastery. I was reserved toward everybody. I did not go to the Friends of Our Lord because I thought no one could help me except God alone.[10] I have never performed great exercises in discipline or other great things except the severe illness, which God gave me in His goodness.

During these years I was not able to fast on Fridays or on other fast days, and this caused me bitter sorrow. As Lent drew near I was especially sad because I had been compelled to eat by my superiors. Frequently I annoyed my sister because I feared she was to blame for it. As much as I was able, I withdrew myself from all thoughts that disturbed me or hindered my prayer and devotions. I took careful note of all that I did, in eating and drinking and sleeping. Especially when I began the *Pater Noster* to the Lord's works of love, I never slept at night without worrying. I had a great yearning to pray for the Poor Souls.[11] In turn, they were very comforting to me in all my affairs and revealed to me the things that I wanted to know about myself and also about the Souls. I had great pity especially for one man who was in great sorrow and I prayed much for him.[12] It was made known to me by God and by the Holy Souls how it would turn out with him in his difficulties. In a dream I saw how our Lord grasped this same man beneath his arms and spoke to him saying He would never forsake him, neither here nor in the life to come. At the same time I was told by my dear Souls that this man would not have lived so long without my prayers. The Souls also told me that he would return safe and sound from Lombardy. When he was besieging Burgau, this verse was revealed to me in light during a dream: *Adorabunt eum omnes reges, omnes gentes servient ei.*[13] I considered him to have been given me by God. Then I received special grace and the inclination to pray for all his affairs and desires.

I always rejoiced on All Souls' Day, because I had received special consolation from the Poor Souls.[14] Sometimes they sent a Soul to me, who had been a sister of our monastery, and she thanked me for what I had done for them. Then I wished to learn from them whether I had ever helped a Soul reach God by my prayer, and I was told that I had helped many Souls. They revealed to me, to my great consolation, that my life was pleasing to the goodness of God and they showed me what pleased Him most about me—my deep humility. They told me much about the works of God's goodness toward them, especially in their final agony. Many Souls whom I did not know also visited me. They revealed their lives to me and asked me to keep them in mind.

At the same time the entire country, and especially our monastery, was in distress because of the strife, and we prayed a great deal because of this. It seemed to me as if our monastery were full of poor people, saying to me, "You should pray for them, whom God in His justice holds captive and whom He would gladly set free out of love; these are all believing Souls." I promised them a thousand vigils, because they helped me recover my health in soul and body. I began the vigils, but then I had to leave the monastery and return to my mother's home because of the war and the poverty of the monastery.[15] I read vigils there. I had a lay sister with me who was disturbed because I read them so diligently, and she complained much about it and said it would do me no good. One time she saw that the house was full of Poor Souls and they said to her, "Since you will not pray for us, at least do not begrudge us the prayers of others." Then she let me read and continue to pray. There in the world I was even more withdrawn than in the monastery so that my mother and my brothers and sisters were angry with me.[16] I did not like to see or to speak with anyone. The whole time I was in the world I do not think that I ever spoke before the meal, neither with my religious sister nor with anyone else.[17] At that time I was so weak that I could not walk. In the world I began to walk again. And when I returned to the monastery I was determined, as far as possible, always to live according to the will of God from then on. In His mercy He helped me to do that by frequent severe illness since He was preparing me then for Himself.[18]

It happened that the sacred regalia of the Empire were brought into our monastery.[19] I had a strong desire to go see them. Then I perceived that God was saying to me: "They are nothing to you. Go, instead, to the tabernacle in the choir! There and nowhere else will you find my Holy Body as truly as in heaven." I perceived this so strongly that from then on I went to the tabernacle more frequently and with greater desire; and I was prompted by God to pray at length during which I received great delight and grace. My burdens were lightened or completely lifted whenever I came to the tabernacle. I was often so sick that I had to be helped into choir for Mass. Then I kissed the tabernacle with great faith and yearning and desired that God give me strength from it. I received noticeable strength from it so that I could attend Mass without any problem. Often I perceived the grace of our Lord within me, yet I could not act upon it, due to the simplicity and limitedness of my life. I took great delight and joy in my prayer as well, especially in my *Pater Noster*. Often I could not sleep at night because of the anticipation of the delight I would have from praying it in the morning. I desired nothing more from God than a simple, plain life. Even when I heard from the Friends of God that God was doing great things with them I had no desire for anyone to know about the grace given to me and the deeds God had done for me.

One time I was standing before the tabernacle and all the sisters wanted to receive our Lord. Then my heart was so full that I could not comprehend it. I thought it was as wide as the whole world. This happened often when I received our Lord. But sometimes I felt hardness from the thought that there was no sister who did not have more grace than I, and I was burdened heavily by that thought. Yet often God let me perceive grace later in the day or on the next day. Once, while sleeping, it seemed to me that I was in choir with the sisters. Then I perceived grace and lightness so that it seemed to me that I beheld heaven on earth. Since then I have often experienced the same thing while awake. Whenever my life was shown to me while sleeping I took it as being true and have so perceived it ever since. I noticed, too, that when our Lord was playful with me in sleep then something physically annoying would happen to me. I was disturbed about that, and the greatest sorrow came over me because I did not give my will over to God and did not live for Him in thought, word, and deed with total detachment. That gnawed away at me constantly and stripped me of all human defects. Whenever I understood that I could not direct myself, then I was set at peace with all that God had created.

When I heard that someone was angry with our serving girls and had said to them, "You are not worthy to serve us," heartfelt sorrow overcame me so that I cried and thought, "God has never said that I was unworthy to serve Him." I could not bear the slaughtering of the cattle and when I saw that they were being slaughtered I began to cry and thought that God had never slaughtered me because of my misdeeds. I had compassion for all things and true compassion for everyone whom I saw suffering, no matter what kind of suffering it was. With God's help I have avoided afflicting anyone or being harsh with anyone, and also I myself was never afflicted by anyone.

Once I lay ill and the sisters and I thought that I would die. Then a voice said to me, "You are not dying; indeed many of the nuns will die before you." The voice named many of them who have since died. It continued, "You must suffer here on earth." That was proven true, because my sister and I were abandoned by our outside friends and by the community, leaving us without help or consolation for many years. "But when you die, you will go to heaven without delay." Then I asked what his name was who said this to me. "I am Ananias, Azarias, Misael."[20]

I had a sister, whom God had given me for consolation in body and soul and who was very faithful to me. By divine design she served me joyfully throughout the years and protected me from all things that could disturb me. When, in my illness, I was sometimes unkind to her while she served me, she did not hold that against me. This sister became very ill by God's design. Then we were both sick and in suffering and patiently endured much pain. Because of that I was greatly distressed out of concern for my sister. I slept little every night due to sorrow, and still I desired to see her even in her suffering up to my own death. We were both weak and sick and suffering from the Assumption until St. Matthias Day of the next year.[21] Then she died. The previous Christmas God had given me grace and strengthened me both outwardly and inwardly; outwardly by restoring my health, which was a wonder to me, and inwardly by a profound recognition that all things were as nothing to me by comparison to God alone.

At the same time, while asleep, it was revealed to me how I should receive the Body of our Lord. When I drank from the chalice I perceived great sweetness, which I tasted for three days. I knelt before the altar after compline, and the grace was given me to realize that I must suffer, but also that God would help me in this suffering. I received that revelation from Him with much crying, and I fell down before Him and gave myself over to everything His grace was working in me. Soon after that, as the death of my sister approached, I saw and realized that she must die. I would gladly have died for her. She asked me to go away from her and to say my *Pater Noster,* because she knew well that whenever I said it, whatever burdened me would be made easier for me to bear. So I left her alone. I went away from her in great sorrow and recited my *Pater Noster,* and with the greatest yearning I commended us both to our dear Lord's works of love. Then I returned to her, but during the days that she still lingered I was in sorrow and misery although occasionally God would give me relief. I was with her all the time until she died. Then I went into choir with her body and read the psalter.[22] Afterward I lay down and wanted to rest. As I lay there my heart was flooded with a very strong, very great light, with many graces and with much joy. I felt great joy in the thought that I should be suffering for God. Then I got up and went into choir again with great joy and read the psalter once more. When I saw her lying on the bier I found it hard to bear, despite the delight that I had even in my suffering. This delight lasted until prime when my usual sorrow overcame me again. When my sister died, I made a resolution to live in greater suffering from then on. I resolved, in particular, never to claim anything I needed as mine by necessity; instead I would take whatever was given to me, as if it were ordained for me by God. I also intended not to bother anyone about the food that I would eat or about what I needed or anything else. And truthfully I have done so ever since. Whatever was placed before me I enjoyed as much as I was able. I was always careful to eat only what I needed so that I would have no gnawing pangs of conscience about breaking off too much bread for myself. Our Lord gave me a wondrous grief for my sister and profuse tears. For a long time no day went by without my intense weeping. I could not pay attention to anyone else, and those who were previously dear to me I did not want to see. There were times when I thought I could not be without my sister and could not live without her. This sorrow was often transformed into a joy, which God gave me both inwardly and outwardly, but I could not actually be conscious of it. He gave me the grace never to be impatient in all my pain—great though it was— indeed greater than I am able to describe. I never thought, "Lord, why did you do it?" I considered it to be no mere human suffering; rather I considered it to be a true gift from God with which He wanted to prepare me for Himself.

Whether living or dead my sister was always true to me, and I received great solace from her while I slept. One time she said to me: "How can you carry on about me in this way? If you could have me as I am now, you would prefer to have me so! You should cease to mourn for me as I once was." Another time I saw her again. I asked her, "What is our Lord like?" Then she answered: "Like a mighty Lord of heaven and earth." And I asked, "Can He really be like a Lord?" Then she said with great desire and joy, "Yes, indeed." She meant that I would not be able to grasp that now. I asked again, "What is our Lady as Mother of Mercy like?" She said to me again, "Look above you." Then I saw the heavens open, and she showed me a throne near God that was prepared for me and no one was sitting on it. She came again. I asked her about the humanity of our Lord. She said, "When the Holy Trinity discloses itself then one sees the transfigured humanity in it." At these words I felt such a strong force with such great grace that I said, "Another word and my soul will not be able to stay in my body." Soon after her death I had been told by her that she was in heaven. I saw her once in a clear vision. She said, "God Himself wants to be there at your end with His saints and I too will be with Him." Thus I received so much consolation from her that I cannot write it all down. Even so, my sorrow for my sister was not relieved, because in her I had had that peace, humility, love, and real truthfulness that I desired. We had always been together in peace and in unity, and we did not concern ourselves with things that caused a stir in the monastery. Because of this I was anxious now to know where I should turn in order to flee from the whole world.

Now it happened in the first year after this sister's death that an official came and wanted to install a new prioress. This business was altogether repugnant to me.

It was on a Friday night and I had been to visit the graves. As I went into choir a sweet fragrance surrounded me and penetrated through my heart and into all my limbs and the name *Jesus Christus* was given to me so powerfully that I could pay attention to nothing else.[23] And it seemed to me that I was really in His presence. I experienced such great grace that I could not pull myself away. Then a holy sister named Adelheid, whom God gave me after my sister had died, came in and wanted to pray. I went up to her and, since I kept silence during the day, I made a sign to her wanting to know whether she noticed the fragrance. She could not understand me and I was frightened by this and understood well that she did not perceive it. I left her and said nothing to her about it until the day when I began to speak again. I perceived the fragrance for three days in the choir. As to all events in the monastery I paid as little attention to them as if they were happening in another monastery.

I was still grieving for my sister, when God sent His true friend to the monastery around St. Narcissus Day.[24] They asked me to go to him, but I went unwillingly because I still visited with no one and did not want to change. But when I visited him I listened gladly to his true teaching. I said little to him, and nothing to anyone else. This aroused fear in me that I did not love God as much as I claimed. Also I thought others spoke more profoundly than I and showed more devotion and love. I speak the truth when I say that I recognized myself as unworthy of all graces and gifts from God. By God's grace this well-prepared servant of God said to me, "Give me your sister." And I asked him, "Do you want her soul as well?" He answered, "What good is a body to me without a soul?" Then I received grace from his words so that the death of my sister was never again as unbearable as it had been.

After that, on the feast of the Purification of our Lady, after the anniversary of my sister, I had the greatest pain in my head and teeth.[25] It was so great that I could not bow my head for six weeks and all seemed bitter to me and I thought that I would rather suffer death each day. At this time I was miserable and had no one who did anything to help me accept God's will. Especially at night I had no one. I did not like to disturb the other sisters, so I placed myself with my Lord Jesus Christ in the room to which He had first been led captive.[26]

In His goodness God preserved me from becoming depressed or impatient out of misery or sorrow. Whatever anyone did for me I considered it good and whatever was not done for me I tried to endure also for God's sake. I spent almost the whole of Lent in great pain. After Easter I regained my health so that I could follow the nuns into choir and everywhere else with delight and joy. The sorrow for my sister was so diminished that I was able to give her over to God gladly. I began to experience more vividly the grace of God inwardly and outwardly. Especially when I came to my Lord with a grievous concern standing before the altar in the choir, it was taken away from me by the grace of God. It seemed to me that I was like someone who carries a heavy burden and lays it down. I was troubled when our monastery was not doing well in spiritual and material matters or when I saw that someone acted contrary to truth or peace or love or when someone rejoiced over the bad fortune of another or other such things. I suffered the greatest sorrow from this, and it gave me so much pain that I often went away crying. I treated this pain as a gift sent to me by God so that I would recognize that I myself did not yet live according to peace, truth, and love as I should.

Around that time I had a vision while sleeping. I was standing beneath a window and the gentlest breeze arose with uncommonly strong power. From this same power three utterly clear streams of water began to flow. The earth was covered by mounds, representing the sins of men. And the streams were flowing against these mounds. The water was so powerful that it was amazing that these mounds were not broken up by the water. Indeed many remained undisturbed. When all those that lay in the valley were washed away completely, a beautiful green pasture appeared. I was given to understand: Those who lay in the valley were the humble. Then one of our holy women, who is now with God, stood there and said to me, "See now that your Lord can show Himself as Lord indeed."[27]

Once again in Advent I lay in bed at night. The greatest fear engulfed me so that I did not know what to do. Indeed, God helped me to fall asleep by the greatest grace. And I was in this grace when I awoke during the same night, but I can not speak about this state of mine. My Lord Jesus knows that well. Then I got up and felt grace for a long time afterward.

During the same time when I was asleep, it seemed to me as if most worthy ambassadors from a Most High Lord were sent to me bearing a large document on which hung four golden seals.[28] Power was to be granted to me, which I might give to anyone whom I wished on earth and also in purgatory. Then I desired that my sisters have this power too, but I was asked, "Do they want to do what is really humble, loving, peaceful, and truthful?" And I was asked other similar questions that I do not now recall. The whole community of sisters was also there and answered foolishly, "We cannot abide by this." When I awoke I received great grace, and I lived through Advent and all its feasts in this grace.

Ever since my sister died I had the habit of maintaining silence from Thursday night until Sunday, for all of Advent and from the day on which the alleluia is no longer sung until Easter.[29] This silence suited me so well that I was set at peace and overcame all things in silence. Once during Lent great desire and powerful grace were given me to serve God more perfectly. I felt how our Lord's works of love increased powerfully in me. And I desired that my whole body would be full of the signs of love of the holy cross, as many as were possible to be on me, and that each one would be given to me with all its suffering and pain over my entire body.[30] Still I desire that there be no member of my body not wounded with the pains of my Lord Jesus Christ. I also had great yearning to hear something about the signs of love and works of love because I felt an inner grace-filled attraction toward them. Eight days before Easter the Lord gave me a most severe and unceasing pain. In this agony I heard about the sufferings of our Lord as the four Passion narratives were being read. As a result, I experienced immeasurable sorrow often thinking, "I can never be happy again." Frequently I left choir for my cell to see if it would be better there, but it was the same everywhere. Then I thought it might be better if I received our Lord on Holy Thursday.[31] And so it happened. But on Easter Sunday I was deeply depressed.[32] I thought there was no one on earth less joyful that day than myself. It seemed to me I should abase myself before all others because there was no one who had not spent the holy season better than I. But when I received our Lord on that day and went before the altar, the burden was lifted from me with great grace and immeasurable sweetness. Grace was granted, which welled up within me through the Name *Jesus Christus* and through our Lord's works of love. After that I went to table. I was not able to eat and, indeed, I felt the greatest joy and grace so beyond all measure, that I was not able to pray. Every cross I came upon I kissed ardently and as frequently as possible. I pressed it forcefully against my heart constantly, so that I often thought I could not separate myself from it and remain alive. Such great desire and such sweet power so penetrated my heart and all my members that I could not withdraw myself from the cross. Wherever I went I had a cross with me. In addition, I possessed a little book in which there was a picture of the Lord on the cross. I shoved it secretly against my bosom, open to that place, and wherever I went I pressed it to my heart with great joy and with measureless grace. When I wanted to sleep, I took the picture of the Crucified Lord in the little book and laid it under my face. Also, around my neck I wore a cross that hung down to my heart. In addition, I took a large cross whenever possible and laid it over my heart. I clung to it while lying down until I fell asleep in great grace. We had a large crucifix in choir. I had the greatest desire to kiss it and to press it close to my heart like the others. But it was too high up for me and was too large in size. Only one sister knew about my desire; otherwise no one else. She did not want to help me because she feared it would be too much for my human frailty. Now our Lord is mild and good and cannot refuse our desires. What could not happen to me while awake he granted to me one night while asleep. It seemed as if I were standing before the cross filled with the desire that I usually had within me. As I stood before the image, my Lord Jesus Christ bent down from the cross and let me kiss His open heart and gave me to drink of the blood flowing from His heart. I received much great, powerful grace and sweetness, which continued in me for a long time. Whenever I said my *Pater Noster* this grace was present to me again as it had been before.

My *Pater Noster* increased in me gradually just as my desire increased. But the long prayers that I had previously said decreased. I longed for and greatly desired to receive the kiss just as my lord St. Bernard had received it, and to be embraced by the arms of His love and to have my heart be grasped by Him.[33] This was fulfilled one night when it was revealed to me that God wanted to bring this about. Then I said, "I would like it and wish it in no other way than through all your sufferings." I was grasped so powerfully that I felt it both while awake and asleep for a long time. In the same Easter season St. John became dearer to me than before. During the night before the day when the Gospel read is *Maria stabat ad monumentum,* I saw my all-loving Lord Jesus Christ with His Beloved Disciple, St. John, who wanted to receive the blessing for the Gospel from our Lord.[34] He came down—both were floating above us in choir—and stood in front of me. My heart was so anxious that I dared not speak.

Now with sweet grace, the desire and the penances I had taken up with the cross and with our Lord's works of love came to me so strongly one day more than the others, and I often thought, "I will not be able to endure this and continue to live in this way." I yearned for someone who would instruct me and from whom I would receive real consolation. But it was denied me at that time. All this time I recognized that I was unworthy of the grace of our Lord and also that I did not make proper use of His grace. And as I have already written, this continued until the solstice. At the same time I was shown a visible image of a loving soul. For this reason I hurried so as to catch a good look at the image. All the time I felt great happiness inwardly and outwardly.[35]

When I was told that my brother was coming to see me, I was like someone who had been told a great sorrow, because I was entirely filled by divine joy and happiness and great wonder about what happened to me, and I was so taken up by my condition that I could not pay attention to anything else. Previously I had had the habit of offering up long prayers. Especially I read many psalms. This too decreased now. No longer did I offer up such lengthy prayers. Also I was no longer able to read the psalter. May the abundantly gracious humanity of our Lord Jesus Christ bring His eternal honor to completion in me.[36]

After my first sister had died our Lord gave me another, named Adelheid, a virtuous woman and a consolation to me in all things. But even she was taken from me. I mourned as much for her as for my first sister, especially because I had no one to whom I could go and to whom I could confide my concerns. I grieved for her with many tears and fell ill. One night after her death, I was seized by a great fear and I did not know what to do. Then I said to our Lord, "Oh, dear Lord, why are you doing this to me, and leaving me all alone, yet still you do not take away my fear?" And at that moment the fear was taken away from me with great grace so that I could fear nothing then. But my mourning continued until the eve of All Saints' Day.[37]

Then the Friend of God came to me—I say in all truthfulness that it seemed to me as if God had sent His dear angel in the light of truth.[38] When I was told that he was coming I went into choir weeping. After that I went to him, but did not go gladly because of my sorrow and lamentation for Adelheid. When I came to him, immeasurable grace coming from him enlightened me and an inner delight of true sweetness proceeded from his words, so that the yearning arose in me to speak with him about all my concerns. Now God is so good that He cannot resist true desire. So God ordained that he ask me to remain with him during vespers. I was happy because it seemed to me nothing less than a gift from God in heaven. When I left him that evening the grace of God was so alive in me from speaking with him that I could scarcely wait for daybreak in order to visit him again. And a great gift from the gentle richness of God was given to me at the same time: inner, heart-felt joy for a long time so that I felt no sadness and I experienced such an indescribably mysterious lightness of body; I did not even notice my body and it seemed to me as if I were floating upward. Jesus Christ, my wholly acceptable truth, knows this well. From that moment I never felt any desire for bodily food, no matter how long I waited to eat. Since then I have noticed too that, after eating, I never received the grace to speak or to do other things which I had done previously no matter how little I had eaten. All food except plain cloister fare seemed evil to me. Whenever I saw something tempting before me it also occurred to me to go without it joyfully for the sake of my Beloved.

When All Saints' Day had come and gone and the most faithful friend of our Lord had left me and gone away, I continued to live all the time in noticeable joy.[39] I neither complained nor cried anymore because I thought that God had provided me with an excellent teacher. I asked one of the sisters what the nuns were saying about me now that I had so happily let my dear friend go. She told me, "The nuns interpret all things about you for the best." This joy and divine grace continued in me until Christmas, when these increased in me more and more. On the same feast day my sister came to me once in the night. She brought me a white cup and said, "Your favorite, St. John the Evangelist, has sent this to you." I received it with great joy and as I awoke it was revealed to me with great grace that it had been my lord St. John.

Once after matins I was praying when no one was in choir. As usual I began to be afraid and looked behind me and saw something in a white garment. I was happy then. Afterward, I wanted to look more closely at it, but it was gone. I felt the greatest joy so that all fear left me at that time and for a long time after that I received special grace at the sight of that place.

My noble Truth, Jesus Christ, knows well that from His goodness He gave me such great lightness of body that I did not perceive whether I myself even possessed a body. He surrounded me with His divine sweetness and aroused an intense desire in me to live for Him alone in truth. My desire to know what true love for God is, was especially powerful and often I asked our Lady to help me to pray that God would fulfill my yearning.[40] I had such great desire that I thought I would gladly have given up my life to receive such love from God. Once after matins while praying my *Pater Noster* I had this powerful desire. In His goodness God answered me inwardly that He willed to grant me this, indeed so that the whole region would come to know of it. I was alarmed because I was fully content with this secret grace from God about which only the true Friend of God knew anything.[41] Since God in His goodness wanted to let me know this, I saw him while I was asleep and he wanted me to cooperate with him in faith. I said, "I shall gladly cooperate provided that you intend the honor of God by it." He answered that he meant it in no other way. I have always found that to be true and I recognize that he leads a truly blameless life. Although I always recognized that he was given to everyone in true divine consolation, yet I desired a true interior infusion of grace from God for him so that his human life would not be filled with worry. Then my blessed sister, who is with God, came and said to me, "Have no worry about him. If there is anyone on earth who leads the life of the apostles, it is he."

At the time when the alleluia ceased to be sung I began to keep silence with the greatest joy. In particular I experienced great grace on Shrove Tuesday.[42] On that day the following occurred: I was alone in choir after matins kneeling before the altar. Then great fear came over me. Yet in this fear I was surrounded by immeasurable grace. I present the following with appeal to nothing but the Truth, Jesus Christ. It happened that I was seized by an interior divine power from God that took away my heart, and I declare this in the Truth who is my Lord Jesus Christ. Since then I have never felt such a thing.[43] Immeasurable sweetness was my lot so that I thought my soul could have been ripped from my body. The sweetest Name of Jesus Christ was given to me with such great love that by the interior divine power of God I could pray only with continuous "Speaking." I could not resist it. I do not know how to write about it except to say that the Name *Jesus Christus* was constantly on my lips. The Speaking lasted until prime and I could do nothing else. Then I was silent. I could avoid speaking with other people, but I had no power to cease from this Speaking.

The next day I was very sick and began to wonder about what was happening to me. I perceived well what it was. It came from my heart and I feared for my senses now and then whenever it was so intense. But I was answered by the presence of God with sweet delight, "I am no robber of the senses, I am the enlightener of the senses." I received a great grace from the inner goodness of God: the light of truth of divine understanding. Also my mind became more rational than before, so that I had the grace to be able to phrase all my speech better and also to understand better all speech according to the truth. Since then I am often talked about. Often I responded to others according to the truth rather than according to their words. About this gift and many other gifts which were given to me I cannot write now; later I shall write about them as they increase in me. All this happened on the Tuesday when the grasp of love took my heart, as I should have mentioned in the beginning.[44] The grace of our Lord was so very powerful in me and was so unknown to my weak senses that I fell down before our Lord and yielded myself to His divine grace. On Wednesday after matins I wanted to say my *Pater Noster*. Then the Speaking came upon me again with great grace. And I repeated the Name *Jesus Christus* over and over again. In the midst of this other words were mixed in too, so that I could not say my *Pater Noster* until Friday. Then I recited it with great grace.

Once during the time when I do not speak I would have liked to send for the Friend of God, who had been given to me by God's grace, because I realized that this could not remain a secret. When Saturday arrived, I stood in choir and wanted to read matins of our dear Lady, but just then the Speaking came back to me with great grace. I had to go out from matins and went behind the altar Speaking loudly. A sister, who looked after me and who is my special friend, led me out of choir and read matins with me. After that I went into choir once more, and I wanted to say my *Pater Noster,* but then the sweetest grace overcame my heart with powerful loud Speaking. With this Speaking I often repeated that God, Jesus Christ, is my only Beloved One. In this condition I was brought to bed. The outburst of the Speaking was so strong by day and night that I could be heard outside of the room in the cloister walk. Occasionally it let up so that I could converse with other people. But the grace, lightness, joy, sweetness, and the divine delight never left me. On Friday I had an inner intimation that I might die the next Wednesday. I wondered about this a great deal: how it should happen, because I felt no natural pain except weakness whenever the grace with the Speaking was so powerful in me. Then the Friend of our Lord whom God had given me arrived. He recognized the merciful works of God in me. I revealed all my cares to him as my trusted physician sent to me by God. That happened on Tuesday. The following night went well. I felt nothing in me but the grace of our merciful God with great joy. On Wednesday morning, everything remained the same. But as the morning progressed, the Speaking came to me very powerfully and —with the Speaking—the greatest pain, so that my groaning was heard far from the room. But divine grace and sweetness were never withdrawn from me. I was anointed with holy oil because I myself and all who were with me thought the holy oil would prove useful.[45] We assumed that I was in the last throes. It seemed to me as if I were dead externally in all my members, but interiorly I felt divine grace and sweetness.

I had strong faith and powerful trust in God; yet, even so, I had a human fear of death. I was no longer sure that I would live and I awaited only the mercy of God to receive my soul. As I lay there I felt inner sweet, divine grace spreading outward through my body. I could feel myself again and came to myself once more with divine grace. Meanwhile the faithful Friend of our Lord and my entire convent had been in great sorrow because of me. They now rejoiced all the more because they had taken great pains for me before God by singing and reading. That Friday I awoke again with great pain and suffering, which was taken away from me again by great divine joy. It was revealed to me forcefully that our Lord wanted to accomplish in all His friends the words that He spoke to His disciples, "Your sorrow will be changed into joy, etc."[46] The Speaking continued until shortly before Easter so that I could not say my *Pater Noster.* Whenever I wanted to say that or other prayers that contained intercessions and petitions, the Speaking arose by the powerful grace of God, which I could not withstand. At the same time the Name *Jesus Christus* was so forcefully impressed upon me that since that time only prayers in which the Name of Jesus Christ came forth and those concerned with our Lord's works of love were consoling and appealing to me.

At that time I was also brought to a state where sleep no longer benefited nor suited me and bodily food no longer strengthened me. The little that I took of bodily food troubled and vexed me. I noticed that when I had eaten something that I found to be especially appetizing I became sick. Afterward I was depressed because I had eaten it. During all of Lent I never went to Mass because of the loud Speaking. Particularly, whenever I looked at the place where it had been given me by God and whenever I heard the name Jesus Christ sung or read, the Speaking began. But whenever it begins I am incapable of doing anything other than uttering what the powerful grace of our Lord speaks in me. Whatever anyone says or does to me in the meantime does not move my heart in the least. It is also beyond the grasp of my senses. I can only speak what has just been given to me. Neither can I break off from Speaking until it is God's will. My Lord Jesus Christ, the pure Truth, knows what this means. This was communicated to me powerfully by God: "I am He Himself and I want to accomplish it in you." And He promised to do me much good then. At the same time God was as present and as tangible in my soul and in my heart and as perceptible in all the power He works in heaven and on earth as if I had seen it with my own eyes insofar as this was possible for any human being. And I was also very joyful at the same time.

On our Lady's Day I went to Mass.[47] As the *Rorate Coeli* was begun I received most special graces.[48] The Speaking came again and continued throughout the Mass. Soon after that, I was able to say my *Pater Noster,* which began to lengthen and all my petitions increased. I was afraid of Holy Week because of the harshness which I had endured during the same week in the previous year, but God in His mercy let me live through the week with many graces and sweetness. Especially on Thursday and Friday I received great grace from my

Pater Noster and from all the things that I heard about our Lord's works of love.[49]

On the evening before Easter, the Friend of God arrived.[50] Through him, the grace of God always increased in me. Thus, I lived through that holy day with much grace and sweetness, especially on Easter Monday.[51] After Easter I began my *Pater Noster* again and the petitions were more forceful and extended and especially all my desires were drawn out. A powerful yearning overcame me to touch the open, wounded heart of Christ as St. Thomas had done and to press myself against it and to drink from it and to be wounded more powerfully with His pain than any other of His friends have ever felt.[52] And like my dear lord St. John, I desired to rest upon the beloved heart of Jesus Christ and to drink from it.

At the same time this was revealed to me powerfully in grace: I was told that God wanted to draw me up to the cherubim and seraphim, and ever since I have never heard them mentioned without special joy, sweet consolation, and delight. Throughout the year the Speaking continued and occurred often. Especially when I was alone in choir after matins, I grew anxious and with this fear the Speaking came, but with the Speaking the fear went away. When that happened I could never be afraid as long as it continued. At that time it often happened—and even now it still occurs frequently—that I am grasped by the powerful grace of God during the night, so that I have no external control and am scarcely conscious. Inwardly, however, I feel great sweetness and much grace and the true presence of God in my soul. I was then impressed with the sweet Name of Jesus Christ, which I repeated so often that I uttered "*Jesus Christus*" more than a thousand times according to those who were with me. I had no power to stop doing this until it was God's will. I felt the greatest lightness so that I thought I had laid aside my own body, and through this I attained a true idea of the lightness after life. Externally I appeared to be in great bodily pain. Those who were with me believed I would depart from this world, but I was not able to perceive it in that way because of the immeasurable sweetness, grace, and boundless joy that I had within me.

Sometimes I think God will perhaps take me home from this world. To me that would be the most joyous death that I could have. Lovingly, I was promised by the pure Truth, Jesus Christ, that He wanted to give me what no eye has yet seen, nor ear heard, and what has never yet come to the human heart.[53] It was revealed to me also at the time to go everywhere in great joy, no matter where I should have to go according to the will of God. I took special delight in the thought that I did it for the will of my Beloved Jesus Christ. I go to the common table especially with great joy and with divine delight because from the ordinary fare of my convent I often perceive the best taste and the greatest sweetness so that I think nothing better could be found on earth. I wish that the entire convent could perceive this. Whenever they complain that the food is not good and point out a certain failing, I have never found it so. I have a special craving for oil, because it suits me better and because I perceive more divine joy from it than from anything else.

This was revealed to me in that year: whenever I heard something about our Lord, especially when I heard the Name of Jesus Christ, I was inwardly grasped and so filled up by the grace of God and by divine sweetness that I sat there a long time and did not move externally and could not speak a word.

My conscience was not burdened by the sorrowful condition of Christianity, but often I had to go without the Eucharist. Our Order has never submitted to the commands, as others have done. Although our monastery was still bound by the law, we were permitted to act according to our consciences here.[54] All the while this conviction stood firm in my heart: if I knew that by receiving holy communion or by going to Mass I acted against God, I would rather die than act in such a way. I placed this before the faithfulness of our Lord and said, "Lord, if you let me do something wrong here, then you must do penance for me." God answered me, "You should come to me, because I will never leave you, neither here nor hereafter. Whoever desires me in true love, I will never renounce out of true love." I speak in the Truth, who is my Lord Jesus Christ, that the grace of God has never decreased in me because of this. At that time great grace was given to me by God when I received our Lord on such great feast days as Pentecost and the feast of our Lady, All Saints, St. John's Day, and also for all of Advent and on Christmas Day. On all these feasts I have great grace and immeasurable sweetness and divine consolation. Sometimes it comes to me with the usual Speaking, as I wrote earlier, sometimes in silence.

My Lord, who is pure Truth, knows well that since that time I have withdrawn myself as much as is humanly possible in thought, word, and deed from all things that are opposed to God. However, the thought that I did not live as I should, corresponding to the pure truth that is between me and God, disturbed me all the time. There were also longer periods of time when nothing worried me, and if anyone said something disagreeable to me I could receive it with joy. Sometimes a spirit of sadness is also given to me, which unsettles me greatly and causes me to cry. When that occurs, it ends with great joy. This happens sometimes six times during my *Pater Noster*. When it comes it is accompanied by the divine consolation that my Lord Jesus Christ gives to me out of true love to increase my reward. Often this happens to me without praying.

My Lord Jesus Christ in His goodness has also given me this: when midnight approaches keeping vigil is no burden for me and never causes me to become ill. During the vigil God gives me the most joyful, human peace, which strengthens me both inwardly and outwardly. It comes upon me with a feeling of lightness and ends in joy. The whole day I feel an increase of divine grace and bodily strength. Sometimes I look up and see little white lights before me, so that I think day is dawning. But indeed it is not yet day and the shutters are still closed. Then I see the altar and the walls in the cell and myself. This is given to me as an image of the peace which God has with loving delight in the loving soul, and that same delight the loving soul has for Him.

This was also revealed to me in prayer: when I wish to pray for anything that weighs heavily upon my heart or upon the hearts of others, and it seems to me that it is necessary, but then I cannot put it into words except to say, "Lord accomplish your most loving will." He fulfills many of my dearest wishes; yes, I say truthfully that He never denies me one. He brings it about in truly divine joy. But when I wish to pray for the Poor Souls, I can pray with greater desire for one than for others. Sometimes I cannot pray for a soul at first, but later I can begin to pray for it. I understood this in the following way: those for whom I could pray easily had led innocent lives; those for whom I could not pray at first, I believe this was due to the depths into which they had sunk. I could not help them with my petitions until the mercy of God and common prayer had purified them. I had to give up trying for some souls because I could not pray for them. Whenever I wanted to take them to join the other souls, I could not do it, no matter how much I desired to bring them along. When, for example, I wanted to pray for three souls, the one especially for whom I could not pray I had to let go. Also, I was constantly concerned for some souls and pleaded yearningly for them. Soon thereafter, to my greatest joy, I was told by God, that they had been delivered into eternal joy. And ever since I have been unable to pray for them. I say, "Lord, I know that they are in heaven; they told me themselves that they are with God." I am also asked to pray for many of the living with inner grace and sweet joy so that I may be a help to them in eternity after this life.

There was a lay sister in our monastery, who was given to me by the same special grace. She trusted me completely. It happened that she became sick and miserable. I never looked at her without experiencing true joy; this my Lord Jesus Christ knows well. Whenever I left the table, I had the custom of bringing her whatever I saw that would please her. I always went to her as if she were God Himself. In addition to all that I gave her, I had the desire that God grant her eternal life after this life and permit that she never go to purgatory. She lay there a long time suffering greatly. As I prayed my *Pater Noster* on the day that she died, it was revealed to me with great joy that she had been taken up into eternal joy in fulfillment of my desires.

Then another sister of our monastery died and I begged for eternal joy for her, but I was told, "Let me complete my justice in her." After that she came to me one time during the night. I asked her what the mercy of God had worked in her. She said, "I am not able to perceive mercy in the face of justice." After that she came to me again and said it was going better with her then, but that she had been in great misery. I asked, "Why so much?" She answered, "For all that I did against God." She thanked me for all the good I had done for her. One night my sister came to me. She brought with her a powerful lord who should have great power over us. Immediately He won great desire and inner love from me. My sister asked me, "Would you welcome such a master?" I answered, "That is true." Then he spoke to me very kindly. "Can you always hold me as dear as you do now?" And it was revealed to me that He was my Lord Jesus Christ. With these words He referred to the fierce love that I cherished for His holy works of love.

At that time my brother wanted to bring me his child and place her in the monastery.[55] That annoyed me because I thought problems

106

would arise from this. I saw the child often during the night before she came to me in the monastery. Her face beamed. With that, the joyous assurance was given me that she would become a holy woman. When she came to me in the monastery, with my own eyes I saw a great light over her as she lay sleeping. Before Advent, my usual Silence began and my Lord Jesus Christ granted His usual grace so that I spent the holy season in great sweetness, especially the holy day of Christmas. On the feast of the Holy Innocents the Speaking came upon me with the present grace of our Lord.[56]

On the Epiphany I received a great grace from the presence of God while praying my *Pater Noster*.[57] I had no control over myself and I had to be carried out of choir and be placed in my usual room, which is near the choir. From there I could hear the singing and the reading. I lay there the whole day in great grace and the Name *Jesus Christus* was present in my soul and in my heart. The delightful works of love of my Beloved Lord Jesus Christ always occupied me constantly and forcefully throughout my entire life, in all my desires and in all that I did. I spoke about them with sweet delight and always liked to hear them spoken about. Whoever held dear the sufferings of my Lord Jesus Christ was, on that account, that much dearer to me. When I heard about someone who led a great and perfect life but did not follow the way of the sufferings of our Lord, I could not understand it.[58]

When I wanted to say my *Pater Noster* after matins on St. Agnes' Day, my Beloved Lord Jesus Christ came with His sweet presence.[59] It brought forth in me the most powerful and extended Speaking. That happened very often during the day. And in that grace I had the greatest desire to receive the Holy Body of our Lord. Then we waited for our confessors, who did not arrive until after noon. They gave me our Lord, because I had not yet eaten. I was compelled to do this by great grace. Then I lay there during the whole day and only at night by candlelight did they give me something to eat.

On Shrove Tuesday I was in choir late after Vespers and was praying in front of the altar.[60] Before my eyes I saw three lights, round like disks. Then I received great grace with immeasurable joy from the presence of God. And the Speaking came upon me again. The whole of Lent I spent in great, sweet grace and inner desire to serve God in choir and in all places. I often had the special desire to press and kiss and drink from the five wounds of my Beloved Jesus Christ whenever I made a profound inclination.[61] In the sweet Name of Jesus Christ I was also compelled sometimes to say *"Jesus Christus"* after each verse of the psalms. I yearned greatly to speak about the grace of our Lord, but I had no one to tell, because the Friend of our Lord, who had been given to me by His goodness for powerful consolation, remained in Avignon.

On our Lady's Day I was stricken by a sickness about which I cannot speak.[62] Though in the greatest joy I felt a great chill, after the chill a strong fever and during the fever the sweet Name *Jesus Christus* was poured into me with such powerful grace that I was compelled to Speak. The Speaking always began with the Name *Jesus Christus*. My Truth, Jesus Christ, knows well that nothing in this world is sweeter or more delightful to me than the Name *Jesus Christus*. With it I am lovingly compelled and pressed into the suffering of my dearly Beloved Jesus Christ; by it arises from within me the most wonderful fragrance; in it I feel the sweetest grace with great power. Especially during my *Pater Noster* it often becomes more forceful by strong, mysterious grace that is beyond my human senses. I thought that I could not finish my *Pater Noster* alive due to the overflow of grace. It is so well with me then that I think, "Can heaven be better than this?" My human understanding cannot grasp this. Such a powerful love and such a strong faith are given to me that I perceive God's presence as real, so that all things become delightful. Even at the thought of hell I have no fear because the presence of God could be as little taken from me there as in heaven. Then great delight in God overwhelms me. This sickness, about which I have already written, continued for ten days, and this same sickness often returns, especially after Easter.

One Wednesday night I saw a light illuminating our entire choir with its radiance. I greeted it with great divine joy as a sign of the great grace which my monastery should receive that day from the Holy Sacrament. After matins I said my *Pater Noster*. Then I saw a snow-white luminous ring, which I received with great joy as the presence of God.

On the following Good Friday I said my *Pater Noster* again with great and sweet grace.[63] That lasted a good while. And then I prayed again and was silent. In this I perceived the presence of God more delightfully than I had ever before perceived it in the works of divine

108

mercy. As I read the psalter after prime, I was compelled by sweet joy in the Name of Jesus Christ to say at every verse: *Jesus Christus*. Later I went with the sisters to table for bread and water, which we usually have on that day. I understood the refectory reading completely. That I was not learned enough for this, I realized only after the reading was over.

On the following Easter Sunday I had special great grace when I came to table where I perceived such great sweetness and such a delightful taste from the food that the sister who was eating with me noticed it.[64]

Silence suits me so well and I have such great grace and peace from it that I practice it in Lent and throughout the year and am greatly annoyed with others when I have to speak. I am so content with this inner peace that I cannot suffer external speech, especially after Easter. My Truth, Jesus Christ, knows well that my soul heartily loves and holds dear this silence and solitude because I have perceived great grace from them.

I say this in the Truth from whom all truth flows: I recognize and know myself to be unworthy of the grace of our Lord, indeed more unworthy than I would ever be able to tell. I am in very great fear of our Lord all the time, because I do not live corresponding to the grace of God and do not receive it in true love, nor do I use it as I should in truth. I enclose myself in the loving, powerful works of love of my Lord Jesus Christ, so that they will complete what is lacking in me. The grace of the Silence and of the Speaking continued with me for two years. In all the mysterious ways that I had to go, I had no one, except the truly faithful one whom God had given me in His dear Friend. I received powerful consolation from his words and life all the time, so that I often wondered about it myself. But it happened according to the will of God that he was taken away from me because of the state of Christianity.[65] Then I had no more human consolation. I faced the greatest misery of my life. Moreover I heard nothing from him for a long time and was very distressed about this. Once in the night I was told by those who are with God that he was with them. I was humanly distressed by that and thought that he was dead. Then it was powerfully revealed to me by the grace of God that this referred to the real help that those in purgatory had received from his Masses.

A desire gradually increased in me to be given what had been granted to the praiseworthy lord St. Francis: that I would be wounded with Christ's holy sufferings and have them impressed upon me as a true sign of love as it had been given to none other of His friends.

After that, during a third Lent I felt great grace and a strong desire to serve God. Then I was granted a special gift from God: when I wanted to read something in which the Passion of our Lord was mentioned, such intense pain came upon my heart that I had to go away and was unable to continue reading. But I did not notice this as being due to Lent until vespers was being sung fourteen days before Easter when, at the beginning of the hymn *Vexilla regis,* I could not sing.[66] Moreover, searing pain and suffering came upon my heart so that I had to leave the sisters and go to my choir stall. But I was able to read it and to listen to it being read and I was able to go anywhere else: to choir, to the preaching, and to reading in refectory without feeling anything special. Then after Easter when I had wanted to speak about the Passion of our Lord I had to keep silence and could not say a word about it. I thought that was due to Lent and to the powerful works of love which were accomplished by our love at that time. Then one of our sisters took sick and wanted to die. She cherished the Passion of our Lord greatly and was in misery every day. Often I went to her because she trusted me and I wanted to speak to her about our Lord. Then from our Lord's works of love I gained the greatest and sweetest grace to speak, as well as other wonderful words from God about which I cannot write. That took hold of me so powerfully that a light with clear beams streamed out of my eyes from the sweet inner grace and poured into all my members. This made me so ill that I could barely breathe. I became so sick after the death of this sister that I lay in bed for four weeks. They wanted to give me meat, but in my mouth it seemed like something impure, totally unappealing as if it were uncooked. Then it was revealed to me by God that it was not His will that I eat it. Ever since then I have always done without meat.

The light about which I have written has appeared to me often since then. Sometimes a light was given to me that shoots out from my eyes like flames; at other times I am given small lights. But what all these lights mean, only the true Light, Jesus Christ, knows well. From them I received great sweetness and divine delight. Then when this sister passed away peacefully I could no longer speak about the

Passion of our Lord, but I was able to listen to it. This lasted the whole year. During that year I began to experience such pain at the sight of a crucifix that I could not bear to look at one. This happened especially at the sight of crucifixes I had never seen before. Once such a crucifix was given to me and because of it I was so sad and such pain came over my heart that I could neither work nor eat anything on that day. But as I prayed my *Pater Noster* in the morning I was moved to great joy in sweet grace. And I began lovingly to lament over the image, and to press it against myself, thus fulfilling all my desires with it. For this I would have gladly given up my life. And so sorrow for my dear Lord Jesus Christ came to an end in joy which He brought about in me, His unworthy handmaiden.

My tenderly beloved Jesus Christ gave me many delightful things in that same year . . . in which is sweet delight about which He alone knows.[67] Frequently when I began my *Pater Noster* my heart was captured by such a mysterious grace that I did not know what should come of it. Sometimes because of this I could not pray. Then I sat there in the delight of divine joy from matins until prime. Sometimes this was given to me so that within me arose the Speaking about which I have written before. Sometimes I was raised up so that I no longer touched the ground. Sometimes it was given to me to sit there in the wonderful joy of divine delight, unable to pray, but I could think about God and say whatever I wished. And with this it went well with me. Now He, from whom all grace flows, knows well what sort of graces there are, but to my human understanding these are incomprehensible. Also my Lord Jesus Christ knows well that I yearn for the dearest will of God all my life long. Whatever He gives me, I accept gladly. At all times, I desire to die in His love. Sometimes such great love for God takes hold of me that I cannot believe that God could ever have been so loved by another human being except by our tenderly beloved Lady and by His Beloved Disciple, St. John, whom I must rightly leave out of consideration. My Lord knows well that even more was given to me then: when I heard the Passion of our Lord taken in vain, I felt bitter sorrow and I thought that we were unworthy to mention it with true devotion. Once more this was also given to me, and it still happens that whenever I hear the Name of Jesus I feel the greatest joy wherever I go. And I wished eternal blessedness for them from whom I heard it. And then I thought, if I were not already happily in my monastery, I would gladly remain in it for this reason alone: I heard the Name of Jesus spoken so frequently there.

During Lent of the next year I was given this: when I heard the Holy Passion of my Lord during the preaching or reading, or when I heard it mentioned otherwise, my heart was shot through powerfully and this spread through my whole body. I was grasped and bound inwardly and outwardly, and could not move. This lasted sometimes half the day. I could not speak, nor could I suffer anyone to touch me, and I preferred to be alone.

One night I was given the sight of the five holy signs of love on me—on my hands and feet and heart. And I felt the greatest grace when I thought about it.[68]

After that I saw the most true, clear body of a man lying uncovered before me. I received the greatest grace and sweetness from the body because it shone brightly. Then it was revealed to me, all of us should eat of the body. It was inconceivable to me that the body should be divided and eaten. My sister said, "He is coming, the one who should distribute it." And after that it was revealed to me that it was the tender Eucharistic Body of our Lord, because we received communion soon thereafter.

During the same Lent, when the hymn *Vexilla regis* was sung, I could not bear to hear it, even less than previously.[69] I sat there silently for a long time, as I described before. This lasted the whole week, and I was so sick from it that I lay in bed. I was in the room where I could hear the singing and the reading and whatever else happened in choir. On Palm Sunday I heard the nuns singing the processional.[70] Then the usual Silence came upon me and lasted until the Passion was read during Mass. The greatest lamentation and pain from a present, perceptible suffering pierced my heart and spread to all my members. It overcame me so powerfully that I had to be held up. Then I broke out in a plaintive cry with the words, "Oh, no! Oh, no! My Lord Jesus Christ! Oh, no! Oh, no! My heartfelt beloved Jesus Christ!" And I could not break off from this Speaking until God wished it. I am unable to write about what love and desire and yearning I felt in sympathy for the Lord God present in me. The pitiable, hurtful plaint lasted until the canon of the Mass. Later I became sick and lay the rest of the day until vespers without anything to eat. I remained quite sick the whole week out of sorrow and also from the desire that I had for our Lord and from the delight that I had in the Holy Eucharistic Body of our Lord. I was not able to wait until Holy Thursday, so I received Him on Wednesday.[71] Even so, on Holy Thursday a lively sympathy for my Lord overcame me at matins in addition to the pain and sorrow that I have already mentioned. And it was the same when I read each of the hours of the day.[72] Already I was deeply concerned about Friday, thinking that perhaps I would be able to do nothing then, since I had lain in Silence the whole night until prime. This left me with a feeling of great lightness. I went into choir and read the psalter and was able to listen to the Mass too. Even though I suffered much during the day, still often I also experienced great grace. But on Easter Sunday I was so well that I said my *Pater Noster* and went into choir and could sing and read.[73] What had been given to me the year before, that is, not to speak of the works of love, was increased this year so that I was not able to listen to anything about them. From this the Silence bound and held me as I have already noted. That continued the whole year.

During the following Lent this Silence began to increase again two weeks before Easter. I grew very sick from this binding Silence and from the Speaking, which I experienced constantly until matins of Holy Thursday.[74] When I began matins the greatest pain came over my heart and also a sorrow, so bitter that it was as if I were really in the presence of my Beloved, my most heartily Beloved One, and as if I had seen His most painful sufferings with my own eyes and as if all were happening before me at that very moment. Until that time I had never yet perceived true suffering in my whole life. My pain and the bitterness of my sorrow were so great that I thought nothing more painful could ever have happened to another human being, and I do not wish to exclude St. Mary Magdalen. When I had read three lessons of matins I could not read anymore. This present suffering lasted until matins had been sung. They laid me down and it was so painful for me that I would have given myself up to death: indeed nothing in the world seemed more desirable and delightful to me than to die in the love and in the pain of my Lord's sufferings. I lay in bed in the dormitory—not in the room near the choir—since I could not bear to hear the singing. I was sick until after prime. I could neither read matins nor the other hours of the day. Indeed I could not utter a word due to my sickness. I could only make a sign that I wanted to receive the Holy Body of our Lord. Thereupon our confessor came to me. I was not able to speak at all, but even so I could still confess by

God's help without any mistakes, and so I received our Lord.[75] That happened both inwardly and outwardly by His goodness. Then I lay there that day and night. On Good Friday the binding and grasping Silence overcame me again while reading matins and I was grieved, believing I would not be able to do anything during the day.[76] Then I was given great lightness by the goodness and faithfulness of God, and I got up and went into choir. That amazed all the sisters. I read the psalter and heard Mass. During the Passion I had the same great sweetness and grace that I have during my *Pater Noster*. This continued in me until *Sanctus, agios* was sung.[77] Then I was grasped again by the Silence until the sisters returned from table, after which I went into the refectory and ate bread and drank water. Afterward the greatest desire came over me to hear the Passion read in German. I asked a sister to do it for me, but she did not want to do it. Then I told her how much good the Passion had done me during the Mass, and so she read it to me and as she began I was bound by the Silence once again. This intensified so much that I began to cry out loudly.[78] That had never happened to me before.

During the night of the Vigil I heard someone swearing by the holy suffering of my Lord. That happened to me again in the same way and lasted throughout the year.[79] But when I was given to loud exclamations and Outcries by the gentle goodness of God (these were given to me when I heard the holy sufferings spoken about), then I was pierced to the heart and this extended to all my members, and I was then bound and ever more strongly grasped by the Silence. In these cases I sit a long time—sometimes longer, sometimes shorter. After this my heart was as if shot by a mysterious force.[80] Its effect rose up to my head and passed on to all my members and broke them violently. Compelled by the same force I cried out loudly and exclaimed. I had no power over myself and was not able to stop the Outcry until God released me from it. Sometimes it grasped me so powerfully that red blood spurted from me. Then such sorrow came over me that I thought I could not endure life for long. It would be a great consolation for me to die of this love. My Lord Jesus Christ showed His ever present help to me: at its passing it left me truly happy in sweet grace and I remained so for two days. During this time I preferred to be alone and did not want to hear what was being said in my presence, because it was revealed to me interiorly that all would go well with me in this way. After this I usually had to lie down for three days or longer.

In the same year, after Christmas, I was made unable to listen any longer to reading or singing about the holy sufferings of my dear Lord as I had been able to do previously. As soon as I heard of them I became very sad, as I have already said. In Lent it was stronger still. Then it came time for vespers, which began with the hymn from Holy Week, and I wanted to have vespers read to me.[81] No one wanted to help me so I read it alone.

After that I remained still in the binding Silence from vespers until the sisters returned from table. Then I broke out with loud crying and exclamations, and I did that for a long time, and was very sad. I lay in this condition the entire week. On Palm Sunday I cried out again at such length during matins that the entire community despaired of my life.[82] They thought I would die, and I thought so too. On Monday the same thing happened again before matins. It arose because the holy Passion of my Lord Jesus Christ was shown to me in inner vision. I was so sad that I cried out loudly again. And that happened to me frequently at that time because of some inner vision especially during Lent, even when I did not hear or read the Passion. On that Wednesday when I had read vespers, the entire Passion came to me again with strong Outcries and exclamations.[83] On Thursday after that at matins I was again grasped by great sincere sympathy inwardly and outwardly. Then on Friday the Passion was so really present to me while reading the office that I cried out when I read one of the hours.

I had lain in bed the whole time and was so wounded externally from the interior suffering that I could not bear to have anyone touch me. At the close of the hymn at matins on Holy Saturday I was carried into the little room where I usually stayed.[84] At prime, I lay there still very sick, but since they wanted to go to Mass at daybreak and since I did not want anyone with me, I bade them all to go to choir. I was alone. Then during the *Gloria in excelsis* the greatest power flooded into me with the greatest grace, indeed an inner grace by which I was fully restored to health. This was revealed to me by the faithful help of Jesus Christ: I had suffered with Him; I should also happily rise with Him now. After that one of our nuns, who usually cared for me, came to see how I was. She found me in great joy and in good health and she was greatly overjoyed and amazed because she had left me in a condition of great sickness. When I showed her that I was well she said, "For two weeks I have seen you in such pain that I cannot believe that you have recovered until I see it with my own eyes." Then she asked me to walk around the room. When I offered her my hand, she said, "You must stand up without any help." So I stood up with great joy and without any difficulty and walked around the room three times. I could have gone anywhere I wished to go, but I did not care to create a sensation over myself. When I went into choir at matins on the holy feast of Easter, the whole community was overjoyed and everyone marveled at the merciful works of the Lord. I recited my *Pater Noster* with great grace and sweetness and received our Lord and went to choir during the whole week with great joy. Ever since then I have been brought to a state in which I can no longer listen to the hours which have anything to do with the Holy Cross. I cannot read about it with anyone else, nor about anything having to do with the Holy Sepulchre and the like without special sadness or strong inner feelings. Neither have I been able to speak about our Lord as well as I could before so that now I cannot speak about His holy works of love even though all my desire and delight is in them.

It also bothers me that, when I speak with other people, I fear that they are deceiving me. This fills my heart with sadness and hinders me from talking. And so I suffer interior anxiety from this. Now my Truth, Jesus Christ, knows well that neither love nor sorrow remain longer in my heart than God allows. I am always occupied with the mysteries communicated to me by God and the matters already known.

During Easter week the Silence—about which I have already written—came upon me at compline on Thursday.[85] I remained in this state until after prime. It increased in me from week to week, each week beginning progressively earlier. By Pentecost it had lengthened so much that I began to keep silence from Thursday at noon and I remained silent on Friday.[86] Thursday I ate at nine in the morning, but not at night. During the day I remained without any food.

After that on St. Lawrence Eve—it was Thursday—I had it again.[87] And from then on it increased until St. Michael's Day.[88] After that the Silence was given to me on Wednesday and in such a way that I remained silent from Tuesday night until Friday at mid-day. Meanwhile I had no control over myself, took neither food nor drink, and could not get a single drop of water down my throat. I did not suffer from this lack of food and drink and did not desire them. I preferred to be alone. It annoyed me to listen to other things, and I could not bear to have anyone touch my head, hands, or feet. My greatest joy was in the strong bonds, in which none other than my Lord and my God Jesus Christ had caught me and bound me. With this I was assured by Him that He delights in me with true love and that He wants to fulfill several of my wishes. When the Silence begins in me sometimes it comes with joy and ends in weeping. Sometimes it begins with sadness and ceases with joy. The time does not seem long to me because I have the sweet grace of the presence of God. Sometimes I have no consolation, indeed sometimes I am inwardly closed and bound just as I am outwardly.[89] But I can give God my willing obedience and these words come forcefully to mind, "If I live, I live for the Lord; if I die, I die for the Lord."[90] So I am given suffering without consolation even as He had suffered all His pain without consolation. I gain sweet joy then from the thought that I should suffer in and with the sufferings of my Lord. In this way the merciful sweet bonds tighten around me from Tuesday to Friday noon.

Also, often I suffered a great deal during the same days—both night and day. Such a strong pain seized me that sometimes I thought I would die from it, if the Lord had wished it. Now my Lord Jesus Christ is merciful, faithful, and good and is full of all graces, which He distributes generously. He sent me powerful grace in His dear Friend, a faithful servant of truth.[91] He came to me and saw me lying thus bound.[92] And it seemed remarkable to him that I lay there without any sort of human nourishment. He would gladly have arranged things differently for me, but it was given me by God. As a faithful Friend, he thought to give me the Lord when I was able to receive Him. Then I was terrified because my mouth and my teeth were closed shut so that I had no power to open up either my mouth or teeth. However, I received the news with great joy and with divine trust. I meant, I wanted to try it. This was on All Saints' Day.[93] He said the Mass. Through God's goodness and the Holy Mass I was freed and in the sweet grace of God I was prepared for the Holy Sacrament. Truth Himself knows well that I recognized His divine power working wonderfully in this. After Mass, he gave me the Lord, whom I received more easily than I had ever done before. But I was not equally able to drink from the chalice.

After that, on All Souls' Day—it was Friday—I came to myself with great joy and went into choir.[94] He said the Mass and gave me our Lord once more.[95] Then that faithful Friend of God took leave of me on Sunday.[96] From Monday at noon until Friday at midday the strong bonds of our Lord and the pain bound me fast so that I lay caught in these bonds as I had described before. This continued until St. Nicholas' Day, which was on a Thursday.[97] Then, after matins toward morning, I felt a powerful release from all the bonds that had bound me in great mysterious pain, and the sweet grace of God was given to me inwardly with its true sweetness and the sweet Name *Jesus Christus* was given as well, and I recovered. So I went to prime in choir and received our Lord and my entire community sang the *Te Deum* out of great joy because God had given me back to them.[98] Since then, I have received our Lord once each week.[99] My Truth, Jesus Christ, knows well that, out of His goodness, He gives Himself to me, the least worthy one, to receive Him with inner delight in my soul by true, sweet grace because I receive Him so frequently. Sometimes great fear overcomes me because of my unworthiness, and because of His greatness, and because I receive Him so often. Then I desire certain knowledge from Him that it is His will that more grace be given to me on that day. And, in His goodness, He has not denied that to me. Sometimes, when I had received His Eucharistic Body, He revealed that He had accepted me, for He was nothing but sweetness in my mouth. I cannot describe it. I had no perception of the substance of the host. Whenever I receive our Lord I have neither special prayers nor petitions in mind. Most often I pray as it comes to me at the time. Wonderfully by His grace, He gives Himself to me to have desire and to make petitions. My Lord Jesus Christ knows well that I always take inner delight in the reception of the Holy Sacrament along with all those whom I see receiving Him. And all of this delights me with the result that I am able to accomplish much in Christian love through this delight. It is my custom to receive Him every Sunday. That was taken away from me once. Then the greatest pain in my heart came upon me with much weeping, which lasted the whole day. And when I should lay down at night the pain was so great that I thought I could never survive through the night without our

Lord. So I went to choir for matins on Monday and when I heard that the priest was coming I was filled with joy so great that I cannot describe it. I was also given this by our Lord: when I wish to receive Him, interiorly I receive grace with the same delight and with the same desire as when I actually receive Him, even before the priest comes. On such days any bodily food is especially repulsive to me. I pay no attention to it either. I prefer to be alone on such days and would rather not work with others. When I heard about the sad condition of Christianity and learned that those who had received our Lord should be punished, I desired to honor Him by having to eat bread and water until my death. That would be an inner joy for me.

When I lay there held in the binding Silence and then came to myself again on Friday, I was drained entirely of all my human strength. Then I thought, all others, even if they led perfect lives, would not be able to gain for me my desire to suffer for the Lord to such a degree that I would be totally satisfied in having all my strength consumed by the sufferings of my Lord, just as He had suffered from Thursday until Saturday. Yet this was often promised to me in true joy by our Lord, that He longs to accomplish this in me out of love.

Every Saturday throughout the year I felt sweetness and grace and lightness as it had been given me previously on the holy Vigil of Easter.

The following Lent I was sick again from the same illness already described, which I have during every Lent. Fourteen days before Easter I was bedridden as usual. During those fourteen days I lay there without being able to utter a word. Even if I wished to speak I could not. My mouth was so tightly closed that I could not pray. I could read only the hours and nothing else. Sometimes such a great pain overcame me that the Speaking, about which I have written previously, returned with great grace. Thus I could speak using powerful words while feeling no sickness. When it ended it left me in great sweetness, but then I was made silent so that I could not utter any word at all. At the same time great suffering plagued me continuously, which God, in His goodness, had given me as a true sign of love of His suffering: these were the loud Outcries and the exclamations that I have whenever I hear the holy suffering of my beloved Lord mentioned. At the same time I am also unable to read the hours as they are read in choir. Antiphons other than those read in choir had to be read to me, and some things had to be changed in the reading so that I could bear to listen to it. I also thought it would be impossible for me to confess, but on Wednesday God surrounded me with such great grace that I could confess and pray.[100] For three days I could not read the proper matins and had to read others because I could not bear to read or to hear the proper office. On Friday I remained alone in the little room during Mass.[101] Then God gave me great grace and inner delight to desire to make intercession through His holy works of love. He gave me the special desire to pray for a soul who had died a year ago and who had received great consolation from me as she lay dying. Then God revealed to me that she would enter into paradise on that day and there she would await the resurrection until Easter Day and then pass on into eternal joy. When I wanted to pray for her then, I was only able to say, "Lord, I know that she is in eternal joy!"

At Easter it was revealed to me that I would not be able to listen to the *Credo*.[102] I had to leave Mass whenever it was sung and the same thing happened when the holy sufferings were mentioned in the Gospel. Also, I could not bear it when someone mentioned by name those who were guilty of the sufferings of our Lord. Hearing these evil names was more painful to me than all else except hearing about the intense sufferings of my Lord Jesus Christ. And from this feast day on I experienced the binding Silence throughout the year. It began each week on Tuesday at vespers and stayed with me until morning after prime and then on Thursday at vespers until after prime on Friday.

Then, when St. Nicholas' Day came around again, the binding Silence was taken away from me with great grace.[103] The next Lent I was given the greatest joy on the Tuesday after *Laetare* Sunday.[104] And with that a fit of laughter came over me, which I was unable to stop. I had to leave choir because of the laughing and could do nothing else. And by this it was revealed to me that it meant suffering for me. And so it happened. In the night the grasping and binding Silence began with severe illness and bitter suffering both inwardly and outwardly. And it began every day after noon and lasted until morning after prime. Only then did I read matins. Also I could go neither to Mass nor anywhere else during Lent. With great effort I was brought to bed in a place where a window overlooked the altar. From there I saw our Lord every day. All through Lent I was in great pain. In particular I was bound by the Silence, about which I have already written, so that I was inwardly closed up and was preoccupied with my own concerns. I found that very puzzling, for afterward whenever I was to eat I could take food only with great effort. I was constricted inwardly by something that I find mysterious and about which I am not able to write. But my Lord knows well that however much my body is still in pain, I have joy in my heart all the time because of the wonderful works of our Lord. No one can believe or understand that except someone who has experienced it.

In His mercy, God has given me this: I have never broken the fast a single day in six years whenever our Order or Christendom ordered a fast, no matter how little food I had taken or how much pain and sickness I had to bear. I was often so sick that they thought I would die. This is how I spent the whole of Lent. In the last fourteen days it was stronger. I spent them as I have already written last year concerning the fourteen days before Easter, only it was stronger. Then I passed the time with mysterious things.

When Easter Day came I rejoiced greatly in the resurrection of our Lord.[105] I went to matins in choir and wanted to recite my *Pater Noster,* but when I wished to begin it I had forgotten all the petitions and could remember nothing. When I wanted to begin, I could not say a word. I sat there and kept silent. I had hoped it would go better when I received our Lord. For that reason I received communion before prime. After that, I sat there silently because it was good for me to be in the presence of our Lord. During the Mass God allowed me to pray whatever I wanted with great, sweet grace, except for my *Pater Noster.* I had the greatest sorrow due to the loss of the *Pater Noster.* To me, death would have been preferable because I did not know how I should spend my time day and night. I broke out in a flood of tears weeping uncontrollably. During the night, especially when I remembered that I was not able to recite my *Pater Noster,* the greatest sorrow and grief came over me and I wept incessantly. But the Truth, Jesus Christ, knows that I submit myself in willing obedience to all that He works in me according to His dearest will. When I saw that I could not say my *Pater Noster,* I turned to other prayers. I said fifty Our Fathers after matins for all His suffering and pressed and wrapped myself in it. I then said fifty Our Fathers again for His truly holy life and commended all my mysterious ways to it. Now my living Truth, Jesus Christ, knows well that my greatest desire is to devote all my time and my whole span of life to Christian works and to live for God alone in truth. But the all-sweetest Master, from whose loving heart all knowledge flows, must teach me how to do this.

Praying and in suffering, I came to the Sunday after Easter.[106] Then I was given the presence of the Lord in the night with the greatest sweetness and the mysterious grace of God. The Speaking —about which I have already written—returned. And when I came into choir after matins, my *Pater Noster* was restored to me, but the petitions seemed obscure and strange. I did not remember all my petitions and did not feel the same desire as before. It remained so until the Ascension of our Lord, and did not fully return until Pentecost.[107] At that time I was so weak physically that I often thought I would die. But on Ascension Day this feeling diminished. After that, on Pentecost, my *Pater Noster* was restored to me completely with the petitions and the desire and the sweet grace. Then I went into choir with the sisters. When I stood in choir on Monday after Pentecost, and we sang the *Veni Creator,* I heard the sweetest voices in accompaniment but cannot write about it. And I was flooded through by the grace of the divine presence and was inspired with the revelation that these were angels of the Lord. The whole feast day I lived in great grace.

After the feast day, the great Silence—about which I have already written—was given to me. Just as I had it the previous year on Tuesday and Thursday, so now I had it Thursdays and Fridays until the third day after the feast of St. Martin.[108] At that time this was revealed to me by God with powerful grace:

> You are a knower of truth, a perceiver of my sweet grace, a seeker of my divine delight and a lover of my love. I am the only husband of your soul. This delights me and honors me. I have a lovely work in you that is a sweet game to me. Your love compels me to let myself be found so that your soul is satisfied and yet your body will be unharmed. Your sweet delight finds me, your inner desire compels me, your burning love binds me, your pure truth holds me, your fiery love keeps me near. I want to receive you happily and embrace you lovingly in the only One who I am. That is not too much of my goodness. Then I want to give you the kiss of love which is the delight of your soul, a sweet inner movement, a loving attachment.[109]

And, from the High Godhead flows down mercy, from the

tender humanity of Jesus Christ flows goodness, from the loving works of the Holy Spirit flows love. And love gives peace and from peace comes grace and from grace comes delight, from delight comes desire, from desire—deeds, from deeds—fruit, from fruit—eternal life.[110]

After that, I began Lent with the intention of making all days "Good Friday" with desire and with the presence of His entire Holy Passion. I delighted in this and felt the presence of divine grace every day, as if it really were Good Friday. I did this because I could never celebrate Good Friday, yet my Lord knows well that I love to honor the laws of Christianity.

One Sunday several of the sisters wanted to receive our Lord with me, but I was forcibly bound by the Silence. As the time approached when I thought they had received Him, I had the most painful yearning to receive the Body of the Lord. Then my help, Jesus Christ, came and gave me joyous, lightning relief, so that I perceived nothing but His grace. I got up joyfully and went into choir. When I arrived they had already received Him, but the chaplain was still in the choir and he gave me our Lord. When I had received Him the Silence came upon me as powerfully as before. During Lent I was continuously bound and caught by the faithful goodness of God. As the fourteen days before Easter approached I was bedridden again and lived through those days as I had done the two other Lents about which I have already written—with the Speaking, the binding Silence, and the Outcries. I could not pray or read the hours for three days. But on Tuesday of Holy Week the power to pray was granted me again, so that I could pray whatever I wanted.[111] After Easter I was very sick and on the next Friday the binding Silence set in once more, increasing in me so, that it continued on Saturday.[112] By the sweet grace of our Lord I was well for the entire week of Pentecost.[113] After that the Silence lengthened further so that I had it often the entire week, except for Sunday. But usually I had it only Fridays and Saturdays. During the entire Octave of the Assumption of our Lady I was well and experienced great grace and sweetness.[114]

At the same time I wanted to receive our Lord on a Sunday. When I wanted to begin my *Pater Noster* I could not recite it, and the Speaking came upon me with the most powerful grace. The sisters would have liked to come to me, but I had locked myself in as I usually do. So they broke the lock and came into the room. When the Speaking ceased, the chaplain came. He brought our Lord to me in choir and I received Him with great grace. In that year I was also granted this: whenever I wished to say or read something in which the Lord's works of love happened to be mentioned—even when I uttered no word whatsoever—then my heart was grasped by such a great pain that I had to bend over clutching my heart and could utter no word for a long time. This happened to me frequently. Similarly I was sometimes so moved inwardly by the grace of God whenever I said something about our Lord that I had to keep silent again and was unable to speak. My Lord knows well that to hear or to engage in any speaking, except *the* Speaking, is annoying to me, and I suffer great pain and sadness when I must carry on even necessary conversation.

In that year our Lord sent me His beloved Friend with great and powerful consolation and with especially great grace, which I received as soon as he gave me the Holy Body of our Lord. He gave me communion twice during the binding Silence. For this God prepared me inwardly so that I received it without any disruption of my spiritual delight. Especially, he gave me our Lord on St. Denis' Day.[115] Then he took leave of me. I felt special great grace on that day when I came to myself and realized that he had left me, but I wished that God never be parted from his soul or his heart. After that the Silence increased in me so that it always began on Tuesday at vespers, and I was silent all night until prime. That went on for the whole week until Sunday and continued indeed for fourteen days. Then it took hold of me so strongly that I thought it must let up or I would not be able to live yet another fourteen days. The most sweet and clever binder, Jesus Christ, bound me so powerfully at that time that my hands swelled and death spots appeared on them.[116] The Speaking began again during the same fourteen days. When I went to matins on St. Martin's Day, although I had lain in bed, all this was taken away and I was given the great joy that I always have with powerful grace during every Advent.[117]

In the years about which I have written, the petitions of my *Pater Noster* and all my desires increased from day to day, and the grace of our Lord and the presence of God increased powerfully in me. Whatever I desired to know about the fidelity of God was communicated to me by the Truth of God during my *Pater Noster*. Especially when I asked whether I should take a certain course or not, and whether He wished to show me His grace in it, then I was answered, "As little as my divinity can separate from my humanity, so little do I wish to separate myself from you in this matter or in any other." By that I am also given to know that I cannot ask for just anything that I would like. In the same way I am sometimes wonderfully brought to think about some intention I had never thought of before. I came to understand that this was the will of God because of the sweetness of the grace. I experienced the strongest, sweetest, and most mysterious grace during the *Pater Noster* and all my petitions. I cannot write about it, and any heart that itself has not felt the grace cannot understand it. Because of this the most powerful love came into my heart so that I felt sweet joy from one *Pater Noster* to the next. And the desires became so strong in me that I yearned with all my heart to give up my life for the sake of this love, which He had shown me in each petition of the *Pater Noster*.

In particular, very sweet grace was given me by God in my love for His beloved disciple, my lord St. John. Whenever I remembered how my lord, St. John, rested upon the dear heart of my Lord Jesus Christ, such sweet grace stirred in me that I could not speak a word. When I recalled the sweet drink he drank and sucked from the sweet breast of Christ, again I could not speak at all, and I sat there with delight and desire so that I would have gladly died out of love.[118] And when I desired that this be given to me too, just as he had received it, then I was so moved again that I had to sit a while. This was given to me last year in Advent and has intensified this year. Whenever I remembered this and the intense desire I was not able to say the words well, but I was moved inwardly and I sat there longer. It gave me a sweet inner joy in God and a powerful grasp of truth whenever very hidden things were given to me which I had neither desired nor could desire. Then I felt, in the fullness of grace, that no one can give this except God alone. It illumined in me the light of true Christian faith, so that for me all things were comprehensible which are with God or flow from God. But all my strength and all my power came to me through His most worthy humanity, His truthful life, His holy, and His powerful sufferings, and all my desire to live and to die comes from nothing else. Often, I felt such a strong, powerful grace from my desires that I thought I could not survive from one desire to the next. I felt the sweetest thrusts against my heart with the most powerful grace and the sweetest movements, so that I thought my heart would fly to pieces from His raging love and would like to dissolve from His grace. But then He acted like a clever, knowledgeable lover and withdrew the turbulence from me so that my frail humanity could better bear it. Sometimes the following happens to me: when, because of ignorance, I fear for my human senses, then I am answered as before, "I am not a robber of the senses, I am an enlightener of the senses." This is given to me for the faithful, true teacher of our Lord, for whom I long at all times, when I pray that God would keep him in His fatherly care: "He is a true joy to my holy Divinity and a sure follower of my holy humanity. He shall delight in me with the cherubim and look on me with the seraphim." And,

> I will give him my tender humanity against all natural weakness, my true pure life against all dark senses, that my divine grace has not yet moved, my ardent love by which all unconverted hearts will be moved through him, and as a firm foundation, the pure truth that teaches him the way that I desire for him out of love, by which he will accomplish my eternal honor. I will draw him into the Incomprehensible Essence of my Holy Godhead in which he shall lose himself out of love for me.[119] And I will lower him into the holy reflection of my Sacred Godhead where he will see my divine honor clearly in the image from which his pure soul has flowed. And I will complete in him what is written there: "The lowly shall be exalted."[120] I desire this for him because of his great humility. And, in pure truth I am found, with burning love I am bound, with fervent desire I am compelled, in true purity I am held.[121]

Ardently I desired to be any place where no one knew of me except God alone. If that were the will of God, I would gladly assent to it. After my death I want it known by someone, such as my confessor, that I remained in my monastery, because as my Lord knows well, I prefer to be in my monastery provided I am not disturbed. I desire nothing other than detachment from all things and the accomplishment of His most precious will in me to His eternal honor. I have great desire to be with Him in eternal joy. Oh, that the day still has not yet come! Were it the will of God and to His honor I would gladly die! Then I was also granted this: should I have to live a thousand years according to the will of God and for His honor I would gladly do so and do all that He had ordained for me as well.

One time I was standing before the crucifix in choir and desired with great earnestness that He draw me to Himself. Then I was answered: "Because of your continuous prayers I cannot cease to do the deeds which I had planned to work through you out of such great love."

Another time during the holy night at Christmas such a powerful, great, sweet grace was poured into me that it penetrated all my members. And it was revealed to me that this was the very moment in time when our Lord had been born.

One day I wanted our Lady to help me so that the five signs of love would be impressed upon me with the same feeling as they had been impressed upon St. Francis. On that same day I asked her to help me to perceive what divine joy there would be with her dear Child. Then I was answered lovingly by her, "You ask me for such dissimilar things that I do not know what I should do for you." I received that answer with great grace and joy. I have written much about grace and the good that God has done for me, but what I have omitted or done for the sake of His love and how I have lived according to His grace, that I credit to His inner goodness, because in truth I confess that I have never lived corresponding to His divine grace as I rightly should have. Whatever there is came from His great mercy. From His Goodness He has granted to me that I was able to renounce all things which were desirable and delightful for my body, whether food or drink or other such bodily comforts. I could give these up for His love. The thought that I could no longer endure this misery often roused me from sleep; so too did the very great delight that I had in serving God during the time that was still left to me.

Often from His goodness God gives me an invitation saying, "Get up, I want to give you special graces today," or sometimes, "Get up, I want to give you what no eye has seen nor ear has heard and what has never yet come to a human heart."[122] That was all granted to me lovingly with the sweet Name *Jesus Christus*. But what has drawn me away from delight in eating and drinking is the great delight and sweetness that I feel from God and which I await from Him in Christian love—to enjoy Him eternally in His divine clarity. That makes me grasp all the true Christian belief that is given to me with the vivid light which illumines the recognition of the truths of

God and which guides me into the love of God and then sustains me according to His dearest will. The power and my ability to relinquish all personal adornments and to see these as abhorrent for myself and for others came from the most worthy humanity of Jesus Christ and from his holy, loving sufferings. I thought that nothing could adorn us before God except a sincere, innocent life and the perfection of virtue. But uncleanliness in dress or in food or drink, my Lord knows well, I cannot endure. I have special delight and desire because I have forsworn all delights that come from the world for the sake of my Beloved Jesus Christ. Indeed I have lived thirty years without drinking wine and without taking a bath; indeed neither water nor soap have touched my head or body in these same thirty years. And I am so well accustomed to this by the help of God that I never had any trouble from it. I have also given up fish and meat. I took especially great delight in fruit. Then it was revealed to me with great joy, "I want you to give it up for the sake of my love." And I had the desire to give up all sweet things for the sake of the sweetness I received from God. I also had the desire to rest according to the custom of the Order.[123] Then it happened that they sometimes placed a pillow beneath me because of my illness. After that, when I said my *Pater Noster* great sorrow overcame me and from that I received these words from our Lord, "Should a spouse of Jesus Christ rest on pillows? And if she should die, she should not be found lying on a pillow." Then I promised by the loving heart of Jesus that I would never do it again, even if I would be compelled by the command of my superiors.

With my whole heart I desired that the pure Truth, my Lord Jesus Christ, be my agent, helper, and teacher my whole life long. It was read to me that our Lord was on earth for 12,412 days. Then an interior desire arose within me to honor each day of His truth-filled life by reciting an Our Father for myself and for others for whom I desired it as much as for myself that we would all be forgiven by His true life for not having lived truly according to our Christian vocation and our spiritual calling. And after every fifty Our Fathers I said the *Anima Christi, sanctifica me,* and desired then from His holy sufferings that we would be able to resist all evil in thought, word, and deed, and then I also desired powerful assistance by which we would live according to the pure truth and the Truth would live in us.[124] I also had an inner desire to write down all these desires, which are truly and vividly presented to me by the faithfulness of God. They begin in this way: "I ask you, the all-good, most worthy humanity of Jesus Christ, by the power of your holy sufferings and in the love of your holy death and by the power of your Holy Sacrament and by the holy, sweet Name of Jesus Christ and by your pure and true life to give us a pure, truly humble life and a loving death, etc."

For a long time I have liked to ponder six points of meditation, and to hold in honor especially those in which God had given us particular gifts. The first is how He came down from heaven to earth into the womb of our Lady and lived there for forty weeks. The next, how He was born according to nature and how He thereby truly came among us and after that—out of love for us—he lived a genuine human life for thirty-three years. The third, how love for us moved Him to die on the cross and to perform all His works of love. The fourth, how He gave Himself to us and gives Himself to us and gives Himself every day in the Holy Sacrament. The fifth, how He has given Himself to all pure hearts and souls and gives Himself daily. The sixth, the love in which He has worked and continues to bring about His goodness, love, and mercy daily in everyone, and from which He excludes no one—as He has often shown and continues to show every day.

Before I go to table I also have the custom of saying these words before the Blessed Sacrament: "I ask you, my Lord, to feed me with your sweet grace, strengthen me with your pure love, surround me with your boundless mercy and embrace me with your pure truth, which encompasses for us all your graces so that they may increase in us and never be taken from us until we enter into eternal life."

I was also given very great power and help by three things with great grace in the faithful truth of God. First, I had great desire for and took delight in the Poor Souls. That made me predisposed toward God and eternal life. I have often wished that everyone would perceive this, so that the Poor Souls would have more help from everyone, because the Poor Souls were the beginning of all the good that God has worked in me. But my whole life long, my ability and all my strength have been given to me from the loving desire and the delightful works of my Lord Jesus Christ. These were given with such great powerful gifts and with such sweet grace that it cannot be put into words, neither in writing nor in speech because of the mysteriousness and greatness of the grace. This is beyond my human understanding. And I desire with all my heart that everyone should place all their delight and desire and all their abilities in the works of love and delve deeper into them. Third, the strong power of the noble suffering of my beloved Lord has drawn me lovingly into inner joy and sweet delight in the Holy Eucharist of our Lord, which is so perceptible to me with sweet grace and in Christian love by the power of His true presence.

One day I began to fret because of my daily carelessness. Then during my petitions it was revealed to me with great joy that I should recite five *Misereres* for the five signs of love and then say the *Anima Christi, sanctifica me* for every *Miserere.*[125]

And so I began: Lord, in your highest love and your greatest and sweetest mercy, how they have ever flowed from your eternal Godhead, from heaven to earth, I ask you to preserve our souls in uprightness, our hearts in purity, our lives in true innocence, and all our desires and all our thoughts for our whole life in pure truth. May your boundless mercy prepare us and may your perfect love draw us so that we live in the truth according to your dearest will. And I ask you, my Lord by your holy sufferings that you forgive all the evil we have done in thought, word and deed and all the carelessness of our lives. And may the power be given to us to overcome all human evil with ever increasing heartfelt love for you. I desire also that we be given the pure truth by the power of your five holy wounds. May Truth be impressed upon us and may we be led by it so that it may live in us and we in it.[126]

My Lord knows well that to me there is nothing more desirable and delightful to write than the admonitions and desires of my *Pater Noster* because of the great grace that I have received and felt from them.

I was asked by the true Friend of God whom He had given me for my entire life as a great consolation to write down for him what God had given me.[127] It was my opinion that he himself should be the author, but that could not be. He said that I should begin it and write whatever God gave me. It was difficult for me, and I began reluctantly. When I wanted to begin I feared and dreaded it. Then I called upon the merciful help of God and upon His beloved evangelist, my lord St. John, to help me write by the truth he had drunk from the sweet heart of Jesus Christ. I began to write it during Advent before the arrival of our dear Lord Jesus Christ, when the sweet grace of our Lord is given to me more sweetly than at any other time in the whole year. It was my will and desire that I act according to the dearest will of God and His honor and also that I obey him who asked me to do it for the honor of God. My faithful Jesus Christ was my powerful help in this, and He promised me thereby to accomplish much good. He said He would not excuse me from it, and He assured me that He would give me more grace in the holy season of His birth than He had previously given. The Truth, Jesus Christ, accomplished this in me and gave me grace in many ways especially from His holy works of love with sweet grace, and also at the moment of His birth and by such loving grace from the sweet Name *Jesus Christus.*

On my lord St. John's Day I had the grace to receive our Lord again.[128] So I did that and I had great grace then in the presence of our Lord. On the feast of the Holy Innocents before vespers I enjoyed the sweetest grace while reciting the *Pater Noster* to honor the true life of Jesus Christ, as I have previously written.[129] Now I have the custom to say after every *Pater Noster,*

> *Jesu via veritatis,*
> *Fons immensae pietatis,*
> *Per quem vivunt omnia,*
> *Tibi laus et gloria.*[130]

Then when I wanted to say *Jesu via* I was grasped so powerfully and with such great grace that the Speaking came upon me with God's presence, as I have written previously. And with this I was granted a visible light. It pierced me with its immeasurable sweetness and flowed into all my members and grasped me so strongly that I was not able to move for a long time. And if I had wanted to speak during the day, still I could not utter a single word. I had to lie down during the night without reciting vespers or compline. I did not read them until matins. Thus the true promises of our Lord were given to me so lovingly that from then on I wanted to devote myself to His truth with delight and with desire to all His gifts, known and unknown, because I recognized the truth in Him and perceived truth from Him. I am sweetly consoled that it is He alone who knows well my whole life and helps me in everything. I desire the living Truth, Jesus Christ, to help me too. He has given Himself to me here in the presence of His sweet grace and has granted me here true trust in Him and has supplied me with loving Christian faith and has promised that I shall later enjoy His very self from His divine clarity and that later my life will be praised by divine Truth, without whose praise no praise has any power until we receive true certainty from the Eternal Word of God.

I am compelled to write by the will and the command of God and by the faithful promises which God has made me. He will increase His grace in me here and hereafter with all of the graces in which He has given me Himself. I have actually delayed a long time because I could never write it down. Then, while I was writing this little book, the greatest delight and sweetest grace came upon me concerning the childhood of our Lord. Also, the delight in His holy works of love was made stronger in me. By His love and by His presence I was . . . had been lovingly compelled, that I told him.[131] I was anxious and fearful in this grace. Then I was answered by my Lord and God about my anxiety: "My mother was the most pure and chaste maiden, and because of that you should not forget that you have received your purity from all my sufferings." I thought to myself, there is no one more worthy than his tender mother. Then I was answered by my beloved Lord: "Whoever does the will of my Father is father and mother to me."[132]

I have a statue of our Lord as a child in the manger. I was powerfully attracted to it by my Lord with delight and desire and by His gracious request. This was spoken to me by my Lord: "If you do not suckle me, then I will draw away from you and you will take no delight in me." So I took the image out of the crib and placed it against my naked heart with great delight and sweetness, and perceived then the most powerful grace in the presence of God so that I began to wonder how our dear Lady could have ever endured the continuous presence of God. Then I was answered by the truthful words of the angel Gabriel, "*Spiritus sanctus superveniet te.*"[133] But my desire and my delight are in the suckling through which I am purified by His pure humanity. I am set afire by the ardent love coming from Him and am filled up by His presence and by His sweet grace so that I am drawn into the true enjoyment of His divine essence with all loving souls who have lived in the truth.

Since I have begun to write this little book I have taken great delight in the childhood of our Lord—especially when I am actually writing—and also in His circumcision, which I treasure because of the shedding of His all-powerful, holy blood, poured out in love. I have such desire and longing that I would gladly give my life for it. My desires take hold of me so powerfully by day and night that I am unable to sleep during the night because of the truly divine desire and delight that I have for the presence of God's grace that is granted me in choir.

Since then it became customary whenever I sat down to recite my *Pater Noster,* for me to be so powerfully compelled by such a strong love that I had to press Him against my heart. Then I was granted the greatest grace and sweetness, and could take note of nothing except that He is. I remained in this sweet delight, and the grace was transferred from the infancy to the holy sufferings of my beloved Lord. Then it was revealed to me with powerful, loving delight that I was to share in every sort of suffering that God endured because I had given my life over to Him at that time.

I have a large crucifix by which I was compelled in great love and through the presence of God to take that cross and press it against my naked heart as hard as I could using all my strength, and from the delight and the sweet grace that I had from that I could not feel it and pressed so hard that I received death spots on my heart and on my body.[134] I was often lovingly and sweetly admonished by my Lord: "Spare yourself and let us be together nonetheless. I take delight in your true love." Delight and desire are so strong and powerful in me that they strongly compel me, whether I wish it or not, and I cannot break off the whole time I suffer the divine presence with such powerful and sweet grace. On days when I received our Lord, the vivid presence of God was given to me inwardly and was received immediately in my soul with strong Christian love. It compelled my soul in love and I knew that I had the living power of God within me: His Holy Body and Blood. During the day I let him accomplish in me whatever He willed in love and mercy, and then the delight I had taken in the statue changed into delight in the Holy Sacrament.

One night I lay there as matins was being read, and I was grasped by the usual Silence and did not think that I could get up. Then I was exhorted by my most beloved Lord: "Stand up and come to me in the choir. I want to do something good for you as I have always done." So I got up with great joy and recited matins and went into choir.

Then great delight in the childhood of our Lord came over me, and I took the statue of the Child and pressed it against my naked heart as strongly as I could. At that I felt the movement of His mouth on my naked heart and I felt such a great holy fear that I sat a while and did nothing.[135] The fright was taken away from me with great joy and grace, and this fulfilled my prayer. Now my Lord, who is Truth, knows well that I have no great doubts concerning the gifts which God has given me, except for that one, whether it was truly Himself or whether it was only my desire for the Lord. Then I was answered by the true faithfulness of my Lord: "As truly as I have bound myself to you by my holy suffering and by my Holy Sacrament, just as truly is this my gift given out of love for you." Yet I had no courage to dare tell anyone except the Friend of our Lord who was given me by God. Soon after that the sister, who was close to me and who had written that for me came. She said to me, "I offered you your child this night in a dream, and it was a living child and you took it from me with great delight and placed it against your heart and wanted to suckle it, and it puzzled me that you were not embarrassed since you are so shy!" And I heard about her dream with true joy and thought that it was given to me by the will of God, and then I took courage joyfully and thought I should let it be known, and wrote it all down as I had experienced it powerfully.

On St. Stephen's Day my Lord sent me a loving gift to delight me.[136] I was sent a lovely statue from Vienna—Jesus in the crib, attended by four golden angels. One night I had a revelation in which I saw Him with lively animation joyfully playing in the crib. I asked Him, "Why don't you behave and be quiet and let me sleep? I tucked you in nicely." Then the Child said, "I do not want to let you sleep. You must pick me up and hold me." So with desire and joy I took Him out of the crib and placed Him on my lap. He was a dear Child. I said, "Kiss me, then I will forget that you have awakened me." Then He fell upon me with His little arms and embraced me and kissed me.[137] After that I desired to know something about His holy circumcision. Nothing was revealed to me by Him, but from His face I received great grace and sweetness.

My Truth, Jesus Christ, really gave me everything that He promised me when I began to write this little book. He promised to give me special grace that He had not given before. Then He said I must suffer greatly for the sake of His love during Lent. He sent this suffering powerfully to me on Wednesday, when I began to be silent. That was the Wednesday before the alleluia ceased to be sung.[138] On the same night the binding Silence began powerfully and commenced always at midday continuing with wondrous suffering until night-time. The sickness decreased when the Child Jesus was given me with sweet delight. This grace was so great that I usually lay in bed unable to sleep because of my sweet painful yearning for the Child. But the binding Silence was not lifted until matins. Then when matins was read I got up, physically very ill, so ill that I thought no one could believe it. But then such deep desire was granted me to serve God and to say my *Pater Noster* that I overcame my discomfort. I read compline all the way to matins. Then when I read matins I went into choir, still very sick, and began my *Pater Noster,* and said it with such help from our Lord's great grace that I felt no ill effects from my bodily sickness. Thus I was able to complete all the prayers up to none as usual. But then the illness began again and was never worse than when I was to receive food, not out of any distaste for food, but by the wondrous powerful thrusts against my heart whenever I should take food. Then I cried out loudly and could be heard every-where, crying until I seemed to be lanced through with the pain. I could not drink because of the same suffering. I suffered the same sickness from eating and drinking until the Easter Vigil.[139] I could not eat on Sundays from the time when the alleluia was no longer sung until Easter Sunday.[140] But I received much great consolation from the presence of God, granted me in such love that I received it with the delight of divine grace and for the most worthy grace which God had wanted to give me at that time. I received it in the same love with which He bore such powerful thrusts against His own loving heart for love of us, and by which He saved us through His death on the cross.

As I have written, when it began all this increased powerfully from day to day until *Judica* Sunday.[141] That day the whole monastery had prepared to receive our Lord in holy communion. During the night before matins our Lord's holy works of love came to me so powerfully in my heart that I thought I would begin to cry out loudly. After that as I read matins it became worse by God's will. While reading matins an Outcry came over me and continued powerfully for a long time.[142] Thereafter I was granted the vivid presence of God in my soul and heart. In His mercy, He told me that I was one of

His most beloved ones upon earth and that it was because of love that He would not end my sufferings. He also said He would accomplish in me, by His holy works of love, the greatest work that He had ever accomplished in anyone on earth and would give me intense suffering to endure this for fourteen days. I was told so much about the goodness of God that I cannot write it down. I had great hope every Lent that God would take me to Himself. Then I was answered that He still wanted to accomplish much with me, and that I should consent to it, because in His love, He did not want to shorten my life. Then many bodily things were taken away from me with grace so sweet that I desired it would always be so. Then my Beloved spoke, "If you were not human, you would be an angel!" With the same grace, I received our Lord at dawn and I had great grace the whole day through. But I was then so sick that I had to be carried out into the small room where I usually stay during the fourteen days before Easter. I could not speak from that day until Tuesday before Easter.[143] But whenever anyone read to me I received great grace. I could not utter a single word and could not pray, but I experienced great grace and desire, and His love sustained me in my suffering during that time. Every night before matins the holy sufferings of our Lord were presented so forcefully in my heart that I released loud Outcries. These continued so long and so powerfully that the sisters despaired of me. These recurred at prime. And this continued until the Monday before Palm Sunday.[144] And after that on Tuesday I wanted to try to read the Passion, but then I began to cry out aloud once more.[145] Thus every day until the Easter Vigil I could neither recite prayers (except for the Our Father or the Hail Mary) nor think about anything that had to do with the Holy Passion because it caused such very intense pain.[146]

But then on Maundy Thursday I received our Lord and felt great grace that day.[147] Then after the meal the usual Speaking about which I have already written came upon me with great grace and with the vivid presence of God. This persisted all day and long into the night. Then I was so sick that I thought I would never be able to pray on Good Friday.[148] But in the morning God, as He well knows, fulfilled my desire to honor Him on that day with all other Christians. And I read the psalter and prayed the Our Father and the Hail Mary. I could think of nothing else until midday. Then, according to the custom of my Order, I ate bread and drank water, as much as I thought appropriate. After the meal the Holy Passion presented itself in my heart with the greatest pain and affliction so that I thought I would die. After that the usual Speaking came upon me with grace, with pain and with tears continuing until compline. I also noticed that the Speaking had been granted me with sweet grace so that I might recover my health and be cured of all the sickness that I had endured throughout Lent. God's goodness and his mercy can be seen in me, though I am undeserving, since I came out of that agonizing Lent with some human strength remaining.

Then on Holy Saturday I was able to read the hours and to pray as usual, except for my *Pater Noster* and matins, which I must avoid each year on the same three days at the request of my monastery and the command of my confessor.[149] When I left the table the great pain that I usually had from eating, from the presence of other people, and from everything during Lent, was lifted. But I was later given great pain and suffering, because I had to surrender myself to another year of suffering. I also experienced great joy because I suffered most grievously during Lent by the will of my Lord Jesus Christ and in honor of His Holy Passion. And then on Easter Day I went to matins in choir and said my *Pater Noster* and received our Lord.[150] But nothing changed and I still could not speak or hear about the sufferings of our Lord. Also at Easter, when the *Regina Coeli* was being sung, God's goodness granted me to hear wonderful, sweet voices among the nuns. These I accepted with great joy and grace.[151]

Then on Friday of Easter week the usual Silence was given to me to its ordinary degree from Wednesday night until Sunday.[152] It lengthened further so as to last all week until Sunday when I received our Lord. It began again after vespers and continued until prime. When it came upon me I accepted it with great desire in order to suffer for the love of God by the wonderful gift that it gave me. I had to sit up the whole night and could not lie down, yet I was not sick and—as I have already said—this ceased when I invoked the Name of Jesus Christ. The Silence continued until the Assumption of our Lady.[153] Then it ceased for ten days and continued again until the feast of the Angels, which was on a Thursday.[154] Then I commended myself in trust to our Lord, especially to His Holy Passion and His innocent childhood. And I received our Lord and I did so with much grace. Then the Silence left me for ten days.

After that, on St. Martin Day my inability to say the *Pater Noster* was taken from me so that I could recite it.[155] I had not been able to recite it since Easter, except for the days when I did not have the Silence. But I was so sick that it was thought I would never again be able to go with the sisters into choir or refectory. Then, on Saturday, the eve of Advent, I received our Lord with the sisters and was greatly favored with the presence of God along with profound inner sweetness and a wonderful experience of His healing in my body.[156] Then I was granted by the presence of God to go to choir and there to praise God, and I received such wonderful health that I thought I could do all things well for the honor of God. I was also given great grace and sweetness in my *Pater Noster* and a vivid increase in awareness of the works of God. I could not pray for myself in all the mysterious gifts from God except when I was given power and a strong, sweet, compelling force, which brought forth my desires and petitions. This happened with a sweet inner delight in the sure power of God, by which God's pure Truth enlightens my heart and my soul, giving me knowledge and perception of all things. This occurred in every instance when, by God's will, I was moved to pray for both the living and the dead.

I had a noble friend who came to me desiring counsel and help. I recognized well that he required the mercy of God, because I knew him to be in a state of sin. I would gladly have prayed for him, but I was not able to offer up prayers for him, so I included him in my prayer for those in mortal sin. I would gladly have made the Sign of the Cross over him, but I could not move my hand in the slightest. By His goodness God revealed to me that He would not forsake this man. He wanted only to show me his evil condition. So I did not give up. When I received our Lord on the next Sunday a powerful impulse to pray for him was given to me. This meant that his welfare had been entrusted to my prayers. I received this from our dear Lord with great joy, as I have previously written in connection with other souls. Powerful grace increased in me through the gentle gifts of Jesus Christ by a true recognition of the greatness of God's mercy. Sometimes when I wish to pray for a soul, I cannot. Sometimes souls are burdensome for me and I am barely able to lift them up in prayer. Later they become light and then I pray for them happily. After that they become delightfully sweet and I notice this when they are brought to me for prayer. I experience this with such rejoicing that I am filled with profound awe and feel a heavenly joy. And then I can pray for them no longer, except to wish that those who have been delivered by God's mercy and power may enjoy His divine clarity in pure truth in heaven in company with His chosen friends.[157]

As I have written, the childhood of our dear Lord, Jesus Christ, is especially close to my heart. And my devotion to it increases more and more in every way. I am granted constant, sweet, powerful grace and true, loving responses by the Infant Jesus Christ. All my desires are answered by Him in this way: how with great love He descended from heaven to earth and in what littleness he entered the womb of our Lady. And He spoke, "If you placed me on a needle, you would not have been able to see me and yet I truly possessed all my members. With great delight and love I possessed her heart and with great, sweet, overflowing grace I penetrated her heart and all her members. She bore me in great joy and without difficulty." I asked, "My most beloved Child, how was she able to have these great graces the whole time and contain them in a human body?" Then He responded, "*Spiritus sanctus superveniet. . . .*"[158]

I desired to hear something about His birth. Then He responded and said to me, "I was born in total purity and without pain. And my birth was as wondrous as the Holy Scriptures relate and also as the mother of Holy Christendom believes."[159] He also said to me that He had suffered during the night because of the severe frost. I asked, "My Child, they say you were so poor. Is that true?" He answered, "It is true. This had to be fulfilled in me for the sake of the salvation of all." "My Child, is it also true that Joseph wrapped you up in his pants? I have never liked that detail." He said, "He wrapped me up in whatever was at hand. He had nothing more suitable for me."

Also, for a long time I had desire and took delight in His holy circumcision because of the great love and humility He showed toward us by it and because the sweet and saving Name of Jesus was given to us then. That Name is the delight of our souls and the strength of our hearts and the help for our entire lives. I say it in the Truth, who is my Lord Jesus Christ, that without the Name of Jesus and without His holy sufferings, no good whatsoever could have been accomplished. I also have complete trust and firm faith that whoever is drawn to it by the mild goodness of God, will grasp the pure truth in Him. I asked how the holy circumcision happened. He answered, "Joseph held me because my mother was not able to do it on account of the great pain she felt. She cried bitterly too and I cried and endured great pain and shed much blood. After that my mother took me to herself with great love and calmed me." My Salvation, Jesus, also said that our Lady never endured anything unclean from Him, only that He, when sick, had been like any other child in love and suffering. I asked whether He had spoken to His mother using human words, before He had begun to speak naturally. He answered, "No, I spoke to her only by the communion of the sweet grace that flowed from me to her."

He said, "With great love and with strong faith the three kings sought me. They found me with great joy and brought me worthy gifts both inwardly and outwardly. I said, "My Lord Jesus, did you grab one of them by the hair?" He responded, "Yes." After that I asked, "My Salvation, Jesus, what happened to the great gifts that had been given to you, since you remained so poor?" The Child said, "The lowest good does not belong to the Highest Good. I did not descend from heaven in order to enjoy earthly riches. My mother gave them to the poor."

I asked whether our Lady was able to fulfill all her desire for Him by kissing and caressing Him. Then my sweet Jesus said, "Along with her love, she had great awe and reverence all the time in virtue of the great power that she felt coming from me and recognized in me." And He gave me an example of this, that neither I nor any loving heart could have such great desire for His Eucharistic Body without likewise feeling awe and reverence for it. He said, "Nobody recognized my divinity and my true humanity according to the naked truth except my mother and John the Baptist."

Then I had desire for my lord St. John. My beloved Child Jesus said, "My mother and John were prepared for this in the womb, but my beloved John drank and sucked it from my heart with sweet grace.[160] He was given complete understanding on the holy day of Pentecost when he received the Holy Spirit. And the noble Simeon was enlightened with my divine grace as he took me into his arms and recognized that I was the light that had enlightened the whole world, and he also knew that his life would soon end even as he spoke to my mother." I cannot describe this or anything else in connection with His suffering. But I can ask Him about it in the great desire and strong love of receiving an answer from Him so that I might feel all His holy suffering with sweetness and such bitter pain that I often cried with the Child, when He related this to me as truthfully as it is contained in the Holy Scriptures. And it was more present to me than in any other way. Were it the will of God, I would rather write about this than about any other thing since I know more about it.

I had much great desire to know the will of God with regard to the present confusion in Christianity. No response was given me except that it was caused by the sins and weakness of men. It was also revealed to me that, because of this, it would be good for those who ceased to receive holy communion out of right love and fear of divine love during this time. Nevertheless, to those who received the Holy Eucharist in right love and total trust, Christ would also give Himself in true love for He alone would know the whole truth.[161] I also had the desire to learn something about the lord who is a cause of that confusion and who has been given to me by God before other men. Then my beloved Child Jesus Christ said, "I will never abandon him, neither here nor hereafter because he bears love for me, about which no one knows, but I myself." Often he says to me when I ask Him about someone or about something, "Whoever is dear to you, is dear to me too, and what you intend, I also intend."

I desired to learn something about the Friend of our Lord, who has been given to me by God. He was physically ill. Then the dear Child Jesus Christ said, "I want him, and have made him healthy again in body and soul. And I have still much in mind for him to accomplish for the sake of my honor, for I have chosen him for myself and I will bring to perfection my delight in him." Often I asked about the Friends of our Lord with whom I am acquainted. The He said, "They are dear to me for the sake of the love they have for me." Also I ask especially about those whom I bear in faith and desire. Then I am sometimes answered well and gently by Him, but also at times strongly and firmly—which makes me fearful. But indeed all His words are such that mercy must be recognized in them. Often I have great desire to learn something about the welfare of the nuns in our monastery. He says, "Oh, that they would give themselves over to me completely! Then I would gladly give myself to them."

Also I wanted to know something about the degrees of perfection and dignity of the saints. Then the loving Child Jesus Christ said, "John the Baptist and my beloved John are in the same order of perfection in my sight." After that I wanted to know if it were true that St. Mary Magdalene and St. Peter had received the crown of virgins. He answered, "Yes, because their great love brought them to it." And He told me about other saints too, and in what great grace and dignity they stood. In particular I asked about St. Bernard, who wrote about the soul's vision of God after this life of suffering. He said, "What Bernard has written, he has written in true love. He was so enraptured with such great delight in me that he thought everyone should come to understand the truth as he had, because I am the pure Truth who has written and spoken through him."

I desired to know something about the essence of God and about the workings of God *ad extra* in all creatures, and also about the hierarchy of heaven. But the gentle Child Jesus Christ revealed this to me saying with great grace, "How could your heart receive what no heart is able to grasp and what no tongue can utter?"

I had greatly desired that He speak to me using audible human speech. Then I was told, "Is that which is in your soul and in your heart not sweeter and more perceptible than what is heard by your ear?" Sometimes I asked Him, "My most beloved Child Jesus, do you want to do something gracious for me tomorrow?" Then He answered, "I want to give you special grace." And my Truth, Jesus Christ, never breaks His promise. That happened to me especially when I wanted to receive our Lord. The following has happened to me twice in this year when I wanted to receive our Lord. As I came into choir for matins and wanted to say my *Pater Noster*, the Speaking about which I have already written much set in with the most powerful grace and sweetness. It lasted a long time, and they had to bring me our Lord in the small room in which I usually pray. I sat there until prime unable to do anything. But I had great grace and sweetness as always happens to me by the goodness of God when the Speaking is granted me.

Great grace was given to me in a special way on St. Augustine's Day.[162] The Speaking returned and I received our Lord and the great grace and gift were given to me that ever since I have never perceived the matter of the bread in the Holy Sacrament; rather I perceive nothing but great sweetness and a wonderful taste whereby He flows into my heart and soul. The real truth, in which He has given us His Holy Blood and Flesh, was as present and perceptible to me as if I saw it physically and ate and drank in just the same way as the holy Christian faith teaches us. And that is more suitable to me and still more desirable than simply the matter of the bread, because this gives me such powerful strengthening in the true Christian faith. I felt myself drawn by grace to receive our Lord with my sisters, because I always feel special graces then. Also, I never see anyone else receive our Lord without having the desire to receive Him as well. Also, I never see anyone in sickness or in some distress without desiring that she receive the Lord, because then I think that she would be helped in every way. Also, whenever I perceive that anyone is in great sickness, pain, or dejection, I wish to suffer it too out of true love and for the sake of God's honor. Nothing seems so hard to me that I would not want to bear it for the sake of love. Also, I never see anyone depart from this world without desiring to go along into eternal joy. It also happened to me when I saw someone dying, that I could not pray for the individual no matter how much I tried, until confession had been made. I was admonished by one of our sisters to think about our founder, whose anniversary it was, and to pray for him to God.[163] I undertook that with the sweet consolation in which it was revealed to me that God wanted to grant my prayers for him. So I prayed to God for him the entire year with all the earnestness my unworthy life would allow. And on St. Andrew's Day he was taken from me filled with joy.[164] I cannot describe the joy I feel whenever a soul is taken from me. I can say only this: it gives me certain knowledge of the sweet delight of eternal happiness and a powerful way to the pure truth. They are usually taken from me on great feast days or on the feast day of a saint who had been especially dear to them. It was also granted to me sometimes, when I wished to obtain mercy for someone who lived lawlessly or sinfully, to be unable to pray except to say, "Lord have mercy on all sinners." Whatever that signifies, I commend to the pure Truth, Jesus Christ.

After that, on the holy feast of Christmas, I awoke with sweet grace and got up and for that day and for the whole season God was present to me all the time with the powerful works of His sweet grace and especially on that same day the Holy Name *Jesus Christus* came flowing with sweet power into my heart, so that I was compelled to say the Name *Jesus Christus* at every petition of my *Pater Noster*.[165] Then the usual Speaking came upon me, but on the feast of my lord St. John and during his octave I received special grace and merciful gifts.[166]

On the feast of the Purification of our Lady the nuns wanted to receive our Lord later than at other times, and I was annoyed because

I would have no grace in receiving our Lord so late.[167] Then our faithful Lord Jesus Christ came to my aid with His sweet grace that was my special delight and joy, and I had such great grace the whole day through that I had nothing to eat until nighttime. But as the day progressed the joy was mixed with sadness because the binding Silence came over me at compline and continued until matins. My lovely Child Jesus Christ had told me that I and all who were with me would despair of my life. Then I wanted to know whether I would die or recover. He answered, "Leave that to my goodness." And that was accomplished in me. When the alleluia ceased being sung, the binding Silence began every day at midday and I suffered great woe, which lasted until matins.[168] Then, on Wednesday after Shrove Tuesday, it happened again that I could take food only with great suffering—as I have previously written. Also, I said my *Pater Noster* every day after matins, but was robbed of all my strength between matins and midday so that I often thought my life was about to end. Despite this, I was able to offer up all my prayers with the help of God. I fasted every day, too. But throughout this time the binding Silence set in after noon with severe illness and suffering. This lasted the whole of Lent.

As I came into choir for matins on Wednesday after *Laetare* Sunday and heard the antiphon to the *Benedictus* being sung, the suffering of the Lord took hold of my heart so powerfully that a loud Outcry began, repeated sometimes six or seven times.[169] That lasted until the eve of Palm Sunday.[170] And from the Outcries I became so hoarse that I had no voice left and felt considerable pain though I accepted it with great delight. In what love God gave it to me, I will yet write. My hoarseness was taken away from me after three days and the usual Speaking always began with sweet power after an Outcry. At that time I could not pray nor could I read the minor hours, nor meditate, nor think about the sufferings of our Lord.[171] But the Name *Jesus Christus* was given to me so powerfully that in sweet delight of heart I earnestly invoked it. Because I was not now able to meditate or think about the sufferings of my God, I turned to these sufferings invoking the Name of Jesus Christ and said five times each in honor of the five wounds: "Jesus Christ, my heartfelt Love, have mercy on me! Jesus Christ, my pure Truth, teach me truth! Jesus Christ, sweet Love, teach me love! Jesus Christ, boundless Mercy, come to help me!" And I said many other words similar to these. By God's goodness I was shown a sure way to everlasting life so that I could go to death as if to bed, without fright or fear, so great and strong was the divine trust I had in the mercy of God and so sweet my desire to enter into eternal joy. On Monday after Palm Sunday I could read the minor hours and pray again, but could recite no prayers other than the Our Father and the Hail Mary.[172] I was able to do that before midday, but in the afternoon I lay again in the binding Silence until matins.

During the same time, this was revealed to me in sleep. I thought I came into choir to the place where I usually pray. There I saw a beautifully painted table with nothing on it but a loving soul lying sick. Then it was revealed to me by the mercy of God that this was my soul. Likewise, it was also revealed to me when I came to that same place, and I found my Child Jesus laughing and He said, "Has not all that I have told you come true?" And then He began to cry. I perceived from this that I must still endure much suffering. However, after that one night a very old man, shriveled from age and disfigured, came to me. He was scarcely as big as a child, but he thanked me for the good I had done for him. Then I realized that it was a soul, and it was then revealed to me that it was our founder, who had been taken away from me on St. Andrew's Day—as I have already written.

Again while sleeping, I saw that the choir stall in which I usually pray was illumined by the bright sun. And likewise my brother in the world came and brought me a whole human body that was wound in a white sheet. But when I opened it, there was a human body on a crucifix and I perceived it was the Holy Eucharist of our Lord.[173]

But on Wednesday before Holy Thursday the Outcrying came upon me more powerfully than before and the greatest thrusts that I had ever received came against my heart.[174] Then on Holy Thursday, at night during the first period of sleep, the greatest pain and the most bitter suffering came upon me inwardly and outwardly, so that all my strength and inner consolation vanished.[175] At first I thought it would get better as soon as I read the psalter, as had happened in earlier years. Then when I was reading the psalter a great sadness befell me out of a sorrow so bitter that I cannot describe it. No one can understand it except my Lord Jesus Christ or someone who has already experienced it. I went to Mass in this sorrow and then the loud Outcrying came upon me with such great pain that it was beyond my human senses and I thought that with every scream my life would end. And all who were with me despaired of my life as powerful thrusts came against my heart. Thus I lay there sick the whole day.

Then on Holy Saturday at prime great delight came upon me with the sweet Name *Jesus* in my heart. By it I was made strong inwardly and outwardly so that I could pray all day; I went to confession and took food as at other times, which I had not done during Lent, and I had great consolation because I had suffered so much from the pain at that time. But I had terrible misery and great lamentation because I remained here alive. And then on Holy Easter Day I went to matins in choir with great joy and said my *Pater Noster* and received our Lord.[176] For that week all my sickness was taken away, both internal and external. As my Truth, Jesus, knows, at that time I was given such sweet delight with the powerful consolation of divine grace that I cannot write or speak about it because no one can understand it except God alone or someone who has perceived it—as I have already written. Then on the Thursday after Easter week—in fact from Wednesday until Sunday—the binding Silence came upon me every day after the evening meal so that I could scarcely come away from the table.[177] This continued for two weeks always from Wednesday until Sunday and afterward every day except when I wished to receive our Lord. Then, during Mass, I set about asking our Lord to help me so that I could receive Him in the morning, and this He never denied me. And often I was told by Him, "Delight in me, then I shall delight in you." In His mercy, our Lord has given me great delight from His Eucharistic Body and always gives me this whenever I receive Him. My desire in receiving Him is to partake of the Eucharist with a clear soul, a pure heart, and a truly Christian life, as He grants me out of His goodness. And for that He Himself must be my recourse so that this will be perfected in me in truth. By custom I always prefer to receive our Lord on Sunday, but when I receive Him on Saturday for some special reason, then I have the binding Silence on Sunday as on other days. During Pentecost week it left me for three days and also for three days during the Octave of the Assumption of our Lady, and also for three days at the Exaltation of the Holy Cross.[178] My Lord, Jesus Christ knows well that I could have no thought, desire, or prayer contrary to it, no matter how gravely I suffered by it. Then it happened that I was in such suffering that I wanted to pray for God to come to my aid, and I had to say, "Lord, do all that you will and never forsake me." One night in the binding Silence I was told with great sweetness and grace: "No one knows what compels you except Him who loves your heart." And I had to ponder this message for a long time.[179] After that the usual Speaking came upon me. "I am the spouse of your soul and the strength of your heart and the faithful helper for your whole life and the generous giver of all my sweet grace to you," as I have previously written. This remained in me until Thursday night before the beginning of Advent.[180] Then all this ceased with very great consolation and the sweet graces that are usually given to me every Advent.

When I wished to write all this down, it was made present to me with the very same inner grace as when it had first happened, and with a richness and fullness of meaning that I could scarcely begin to put into words.

After that, in Advent, grace came to me as it usually did in earlier Advents so that I could serve God always and everywhere with great delight and joy. I received special grace from everything I did with great lightness of body, so that I lay down every night in true divine joy and arose in true joy with a sweet desire to serve God. I could complete my *Pater Noster* and the other services of our Lord in true, sweet grace. Every day I visited a particular sister who was sick and in suffering. It was as if I were visiting our dear Lord. I always have this thought and desire whenever I go to visit the sick and I feel great grace in my heart and want to speak with them. Whenever I see such sisters suffering greatly I rejoice deeply because I see in it a preparation for their eternal blessedness and a drawing near to eternal life. And I liked to send them whatever I had or whatever I could get to suit their tastes with the hope and purpose that they regain physical and spiritual health.

On the holy day of Christmas while praying before matins great grace came upon my heart, which revealed to me that this was the hour in which our Lord was born, just as it had been revealed to me before. When the matins bell was rung I got up with great grace and sweet delight and longed from my heart to be able to speak so that I could wish my sisters a happy year. And when I had read matins, I went into choir to my stall and the sweetest, most powerful grace came upon me with the Name of Jesus Christ and at that I recited my *Pater Noster* with strong desire. I was also filled with grace throughout matins and during the Mass of the Nativity and after the same Mass I received our Lord with great grace, and was given two hosts. At first I was alarmed for I could only receive one; the other remained under my tongue and I could not swallow it.[181] So I showed the priest. He took it out of my mouth and gave it to a sister, who wanted to receive with me. And when I returned to my stall the usual Speaking returned. After this Speaking I took up my *Pater Noster* again where I had left off before. That has happened to me only once since then. Usually I cannot pray after the Speaking. Also I passed the day and all the feast days of Christmastide, especially St. John's Day, with great grace and sweet delight.[182] And then after the New Year I felt sad toward nighttime and this has increased continually ever since, and it seemed as though I was entering into a mysterious suffering. And sometimes the sweet Name *Jesus Christus* is locked up in me so that I can neither ponder Him in my heart nor name Him with my tongue. And that ceased, when God wished it, at the Name of Jesus or with His true promises to me. But it was never taken away from my heart, so that I could always think, "If I live, I live for the Lord! If I die, I die for the Lord!"—as I have previously written.[183]

At this time one of our sisters lay dying. She had served God earnestly in suffering and poverty. And since she had already lain four days without eating I went to her and told her I noticed that she wanted to go to God before me. Then she clapped her hands together for joy and laughed so that it was heard everywhere in the room. One of the sisters said to her, "You are acting like someone who has just come from a wedding." Then I replied, "You act like someone who wants to go to a wedding." Then she laughed so loudly that I noticed that God had granted her special grace. She assured me that this was true. And at that I laughed like her and was so happy that I could not sleep much that night because of the joy in my heart over the eternal joy for which she longed.

In the summer before, a lamentable thing had happened. A woman from the village of Medingen, at the counsel of the evil enemy and with a perverted Christian heart, went into our church at Stettin, where our Lady shows herself to be especially gracious. The woman took two unconsecrated hosts from the pyx and carried them into the city of Lauingen near to our monastery. She offered them for sale or in pledge for money to the Jews. A Christian woman saw this, and since the Jew wanted to give that woman nothing for them, she informed the court of the theft. The woman was apprehended. When she was sentenced to death, a child was cut away from her. It was baptized and then they were burned.[184] Because of this, I was so filled with sadness at such dishonor to God that I was unable to look from my window toward the place where it had happened. Throughout the summer I could neither listen to anything about it nor speak about it. I could not endure it if anyone felt sorry for her, because I thought that anyone who had dishonored a dear friend could not expect mercy from the one who had been dishonored. Often I tried to pray for her diligently, but I have been unable even to desire to pray to God for her as yet.

The following things cause the Silence, by which speech is taken away from me with great power. First, when I want to speak about God or even when I hear talk about Him, it moves me with inward sweetness and grasps and binds me so powerfully that I cannot speak. Second, when I want to speak about the Lord, I fear that someone will respond and even mention before me or to me, what I would not be able to listen to: the holy suffering of our Lord. For a long time now I can neither speak about it myself nor hear others speak about it because such wondrous sorrow comes upon me that fear forces me into silence. Third, the holy works of love, especially the most painful and loving suffering of my dearly beloved Lord, which binds me and grasps me, sometimes with heartfelt pains, sometimes with the inexpressible love with which they had been accomplished for us, and I am once more unable to speak. Fourth, when I say or want to contradict anything that is neither useful nor necessary, I am compelled to inner silence, so that I am no longer able to speak about it, because my Lord Jesus Christ knows well that it is repugnant and totally annoying to speak or to hear anything that is not about Jesus Christ.

Then when the alleluia is no longer sung, the binding Silence came upon me with great pain every day at noon lasting until matins, so that I could not bear to place one hand upon the other, nor could I open my eyes.[185] My teeth were closed shut and I could not make a fist with my hand. They remained rigid and my back was bent so that I could not stand up straight. I could not move my feet and could not endure anyone to touch my head, hands, or feet. I had to make a signal with my head or with my hands, and even a slight gesture was very difficult. When Lent began my great sufferings with the thrusts during meals returned and lasted until the Easter Vigil.[186] The suffering continued in the same way as in previous Lents—as already described. But a singular exception occurred on *Laetare* Sunday, when I had received our Lord early in the morning.[187] I was then given the greatest anguish I had ever suffered in all my life and I was drawn by strong love into the Holy Passion of my Lord Jesus Christ. I was enwrapped in it with much mysterious suffering. It began with many tears and I was given perceptibly to understand how great were to be the sufferings that lay before me until Easter. I accepted this in true love and I wanted to suffer willingly for His love and desired by His mercy that He see me through it. It was like this for me in the morning during my *Pater Noster* and at Mass.

Then on Monday morning at matins I felt sick and could not come to choir and could not recite my *Pater Noster*.[188] Then pain so intense overcame my heart so that I could not pray and at that Jesus Christ came to me with sweet power in my heart. Thereupon the pain left me and the usual Speaking returned. And when that left me I was relieved of the pain and could pray with great delight, but not my *Pater Noster,* and I was sick. Tuesday was like the preceding Monday, except that I was just as sick after the Speaking, so that I could not pray as well as on the previous day and I perceived clearly that the great suffering would come to me, namely my strong Outcries.[189]

On Wednesday between the two signals rung for matins I went into my small room and began matins.[190] Then the loud Outcries commenced and lasted a long time. And I exclaimed in a loud voice, "Oh, no! Oh, no!" This screaming was so loud that it could be heard everywhere in the monastery and in the court. I could not have cried out so loudly by my own power, even if someone had wanted to kill me. This came upon me seven times before nightfall with the strong thrusts hitting against my heart so violently that three sisters had to hold me up using all their strength, one under my heart on the left side and another against her behind me and on the other side. They said they had to lean against one another with full strength and under their hands they felt something living, moving inside me and nowhere else. The third sister held up my head. Sometimes I could not endure it when the strong thrusts came against me for they harmed my insides so that I became greatly swollen like a woman great with child. The swelling arose under my face and on my hands so that I had no control over them. And the Outcries sometimes recurred 100,

140, 150, or 250 times or more, sometimes 200 times. And following the previous Outcry, on that same Wednesday, lengthy Speaking came upon me with such great delight in the sweet Name *Jesus Christus* that I could not feel whether or not I was still sick, and all my limbs became strong. I could sit up by myself without any help and could speak with great joy using my full voice. All this was granted me by God, my Lord, in the Truth, which He Himself is. Thus I could not speak one word by myself—as Paul said, "*Ad experimentum quaeritis eius qui loquitur in me Christus?*"[191] And after the Speaking I fell down and my eyes and mouth were closed so that I had to be silent as before, and I could not say "*Jesus Christus.*" But I could still experience Him in my heart. For fourteen days I noticed, both this year and last, that I could name Him in my heart without uttering words from my mouth, sometimes a thousand times before midday, without any other thought, but after midday I felt more strongly bound within so that I could not recite the Name as forcefully as before.

On Thursday before matins the loud Outcries came over me and six times until midday the Speaking was as long and happened in the same way as on Wednesdays—as I have written about previously.[192] Then at compline the loud Outcrying came once more and the Speaking twice and after that during the first period of sleep an Outcry occurred once and the Speaking four times. And after that at midnight a loud Outcry returned and the Speaking twice. And with this Outcry a wondrous hoarseness came upon me so that my voice sometimes sank into my heart and the full Outcry could not come forth. That was worse to me than all my other suffering; with it all inner consolation was taken away. Sometimes the hoarseness was taken away from me so that I could then cry out loudly, and at such times I thought I had never suffered so before. Then the pain, which was enclosed in my heart by the hoarseness, broke out with violent thrusts into loud Outcries. In the same way the interior of a house burns violently indeed and when the fire breaks through the roof and flames up it subsides within. So too, when the new wine is in the vat the wine fumes and froths violently, but when the tap is opened so that it may breathe, then the vat becomes quiet. The same thing happened to me when the Outcry was trapped in my heart and then blurted out. I speak truthfully when I say that this was not under my control.

At the same time I came to realize that whenever an Outcry was about to occur I would perceive a sweet taste in my mouth before. And after that, in the following week, I came to understand that when the Outcry strove to rise up from within my heart into my mouth, this would be preceded by a sweet taste in my mouth. The sweetness lasted as long as the Outcry continued and then, after that, the same sweetness increased during the Speaking. Note: *"De ore prudentis procedit mel . . . ,"* and also *"Favus distillans, etc."*[193]

What the cause of these Outcries and this hoarseness and the loss of all inner consolation is, I understood and knew well, but cannot speak about it because of the strong power, the full grace, the great love, and the abundant delight with which my Lord has possessed, bound, grasped, and compelled them by such great force that my mouth, in the Truth who is my Lord Jesus Christ, may not speak about it. He, who closed the mouth of Zacharias, has closed it up. I would like to speak about it, but I cannot. It becomes painful for me so that I feel very sick and have a pain in my heart, which often prevents me from sleeping. After that, I can speak well, since it is given to me in that love wherein the Eternal Father gave it to His only-begotten Son, and in the same love that the Son received it and suffered for all. By God's grace my greatest desires have been fulfilled now. I declare by the Truth, who is my Lord Jesus Christ, what I have has been given to me out of His goodness, so that in these ways and in this wonderful manner He accomplishes His greatest, most powerful work in me and with me, equal to any that He is now achieving in this world. Note: *"Heli, heli, lamah, etc."* and *"Laboravi clamans, rauce facte, etc."*[194] And note also, *"experientiam horum in Christo pro modulo suo experta est sicut aliquis hominum nunc viventium et tunc gemens et flens hec verba ex profunda humilitate scribi."*[195] Now my Lord Jesus Christ must preserve this in me out of His mercy for His eternal honor and His highest praise because I am unworthy to receive His divine grace. May His holy beneficent wisdom preserve me in His merciful work.

After that, on Friday, a loud Outcry came over me ten times between matins and compline.[196] And I was so sick after the first time that I could not speak as after previous Outcries. For after the other spells of Outcrying, the Speaking had begun and during it I returned to myself, but this time I was so sick from each episode that I and all about me despaired of my life. But then, after compline, a loud

Outcry came upon me with deep lamentation, with profuse tears and with bitter suffering because of the great misery and suffering of my Lord, that had come powerfully into my heart. This remained there, but I could not break out into my usual Speaking and this caused me immeasurable woe. It lasted so long that my sisters who stood around me had despaired, abandoning all hope for my life, as they later told me. And during this loud Outcry that hoarseness came upon me in a very painful way—as I have already written.

The same night, before matins, my Lord Jesus Christ placed me into such indescribable misery and a feeling of abandonment that it seemed as if I had never experienced the grace of our Lord in my whole life. I had lost complete trust in His mercy. Whatever I had received was taken from me totally. The true Christian faith—which is in me at all times—became darkened. And what was more painful to me than any previous suffering—worse too than any martyr's death—was doubt. I began to doubt against my will and wondered whether He and His works were acting in me or not. Indeed, it remained for me only to want to suffer willingly, patiently for His sake. And that seemed right to me because of my sense of guilt. And then I felt an inner, deeper humility and out of these depths I cried out to the Lord and desired that He show me His mercy, which He had shown me so lovingly before, and to show me truly by some authentic sign whether it was He and His work acting in me. Since His Spirit gives witness to our spirits that we are children of God, so my Lord is good and merciful and cannot ignore the desires of the poor and the humble. He came like a friend after matins—note, it was a Saturday—and gave me His true help.[197] This is the natural virtue of the Lord: to whomever He gives sorrow and pain, He then comforts. Whomever He afflicts, He then makes glad. And in His holy suffering He gave me the sweetest delight and the greatest pain and the most incomparably severe sorrow. And His suffering was as present to me as if it had happened that day before my very eyes. And then, compelled by the power of God working in me, I broke out crying in lamentation, moaning and saying with many tears, "Oh, dear, my Lord Jesus Christ! Oh, dear, my Lord Jesus Christ!" I said that frequently over a long period of time. I could do only that and nothing else, because of a heartfelt sorrow so great that I would have certainly died had God wished it of me, for this would have been enough to cause death. When that finally left me I was granted sweet grace and with this I recognized in truth without any doubt that it was He alone who worked His merciful deeds in me. What I had wished to know earlier in my suffering He now revealed. I was now as full of divine grace and joy as earlier I had been full of misery and a feeling of abandonment. In this sweet grace great delight was given to me and desire for the Holy Eucharist. And when I received it the usual Speaking came with great grace, through which I experienced sweet strength. And after that loud Outcrying came upon me on Saturday, so frequently that those who were with me, by God's virtue, could not count the cries because they came so quickly.[198] Sometimes I spoke afterward, sometimes not. And since I was so sick I merely bore my desire for God, for I could only lie there during the holy season and thus I could not serve my Lord according to Christian practice. So may He give me great suffering as satisfaction for my service to Him.

At the same time I desired earnestly to depart from this misery and to go to my Lord. And my Lord Jesus Christ heard my desire and gave me such great pain in my sufferings after compline by pressing against my heart so powerfully that the loud Outcries continued uninterruptedly throughout the night until matins. Sometimes I was quiet approximately the length of the *De Profundis*, but then the loud Outcries returned again with the hoarseness as I have already described.[199] In great longing and joy I thought that my life would come to an end.

And this immeasurably great misery in bitter pain lasted until *Judica* Sunday and then the whole week until Friday, so that this suffering with the strong Outcrying was sometimes greater and louder than was humanly possible. Sometimes—usually with the hoarseness—it continued day and night at least seven times in the same way as I have described before. This means that it will be shorter for me now.[200] The Speaking came upon me often, sometimes not at all as I have already described it. Then, from Friday until *Domine ne longe* Sunday, this Outcry and the other kind ceased and I lay there powerless, externally silent and unable to pray.[201] But internally, in great joy and with sweet delight, I possessed the sweet Name *Jesus Christus* in my heart and was so powerfully grasped and afflicted that I could not bear to have anyone near me, and I took fright whenever anyone came near me because of the powerful works of my Lord Jesus Christ in my soul. When I can utter the Name of Jesus nothing is lacking, but when it remains locked up I am poor and miserable and am robbed of all consolation. I perceive in truth that the sweet Name *Jesus Christus* has a special place in my heart, one which He Himself has prepared in me through His grace by impressing Himself so mercifully in a special way—four times as I recall—into the innermost core of my heart and with a new grace of an inner movement. And when I lie down on that spot or touch it with my hand or lay something on it or press against it, I feel such great grace that it flows into all my members and powerfully grasps my heart so that I can barely breathe and a sweet taste arises from my throat into my mouth. The first time this happened was on Easter Sunday as I received His Holy Body and went away from the altar, since He had been so very hard on me before.[202] It happened to me a second time on a Friday as I went away from the graves into the choir after vespers. As I came in through the choir doors, I perceived a sweet fragrance, which seemed to me to fill the choir. With that the sweet Name *Jesus Christus* was impressed into my heart so that it filled my heart with great power and possessed it with might. And from the rich fullness of this overflowing grace I felt a wonderful, penetrating, sweet, and melting power in all my members.

The third time it was granted me after matins before receiving the Eucharist—again with great sweetness and with a new movement of interior grace in which many new gifts were given me. I could understand, read, and write what I could not before, as I have already written. In particular, a new understanding of truth was granted me, and with it I can often detect when someone speaks untruthfully in my presence. When that happens I can answer nothing except that I often have to say, "I believe that is not true." Sometimes I notice that someone intends these things in the heart differently from what comes out of the mouth. Then I respond according to the intention and not to the words. I feel the sweet power of truth in my heart whenever I hear someone speak the truth, just as if I had seen some pious deed performed. The fourth time it was granted me according to the great desires which I had for it, so that God grasped my heart with love. Once while sleeping God granted this to me, as I have previously written. His grasp was so perceptible it seemed to me as if my heart were taken away from me, as once before. Then the Name *Jesus Christus* was powerfully impressed into my heart with new grace and with an excess of sweet feeling for his presence revealed in the Name. I felt that for a long time afterward, so that I could pay attention to nothing that I had seen or heard before. I do not write about dreams except when I feel great grace from them for a long time afterward. Along with these four gifts, I was given at the same time both the Name *Jesus Christus*, as I have described, and the desires that I have with my *Pater Noster*. And the four impressions of the Name *Jesus Christus* were given to me one after another in little more than a year.

Before the meal on Palm Sunday the Outcrying and the Speaking had already set in three times with particular intensity, when, during the Passion, I experienced deep sorrow even though I did not know that it was being read at that same hour.[203] On Wednesday the Outcrying and the Speaking resumed with great pain and even greater intensity than during the reading of the Passion.[204] On Holy Thursday as I received our Lord, I saw so many hosts in the ciborium —for the other sisters had not yet received the Lord—that I felt the greatest grace, and prolonged Speaking came upon me with sweet delight.[205] And after that, whenever I thought about the sight of the hosts, I felt a renewed sweetness and a new inner sort of Speaking began—my mouth remaining closed, with inner words which no one understood or noticed except for myself. These same words formed a sweet unvoiced sound in my mouth. Note: "*Ego vox clamantis in deserto, etc.*"[206] Note also: "*Fac me audire vocem tuam, vox tua dulcis, etc.*"[207] This happened often during the year. Then my mouth was forcibly shut so that I could speak no word, even if I were to die of it. This same inner Speaking—about which I have written much— happened to me with a joyful lightening of heart, and it began just as a sweet composition for strings is begun, with notes arranged masterfully with a sweet introduction and ending with a sweet echo. At such times I taste supernatural sweetness. Were there no other heavenly kingdom, I thought, I would still be fully satisfied, and no creature would be able to turn me away from God by one hair's breadth. When I fell asleep after that, the loving arrows of my Lord awoke me with a swift shot (*sagitta acuta*) from His spear of love, meeting my heart with great pain.[208] And then by His grace I understood intellectually and perceptibly that this was the hour when my most beloved Lord began His Passion in prayer on the mountain with His sweating of blood. That had been granted me the previous year also around the same time and in the same way. Already, I had felt it in my heart the fourteen days before with great pain at the same time without knowing the hour. Indeed, I thought it was the same hour. But to know this for certain had been given me at this hour for the second time—as I have just now written—just as it had been granted to me to know and to perceive the hour of His human birth at Christmas with exceedingly great joy, about which I have already written. Also at this hour, I often had this feeling before I clearly perceived or recognized what it was. I am also still awakened from sleep and when this occurs I am alarmed at first because of the great grace and the inexpressible joy felt in my heart.

After matins on Good Friday the Outcrying and the Speaking came upon me three time before Mass.[209] And during Mass the loud Outcry came upon me, but with painful lamentation afterward, so that in bitter sorrow and with the shedding of many tears I often repeated, "Oh, no, my Lord Jesus Christ!" Indeed this occurred very often, and I was then full of heartfelt sorrow and painful misery so that nothing could console me because of my clear perception of all those painful sufferings that He bore for us on that day. It was as present to me as if I had seen it at that very moment with my own eyes. And because this vision of the Martyr overwhelmed me, I could not be aware of His eternal honor, His beauty, or the glory He has in heaven, nor could I be consoled by these thoughts even though the sisters, who were with me, wanted to console me by calling them to mind.[210] I felt an inner pain in my hands as if they were stretched out, torn, and broken through, and I supposed that they would always be useless to me thereafter. In my head I felt a wondrous pain as if I were pierced and broken through. That seemed so excruciating to me that I began to tremble and shook so violently that the sisters had to hold me fast. I trembled while in their grasp and I felt this trembling for a long time after Easter whenever I prayed earnestly or read or talked, and I perceived the same painful brokenness in all my members especially on both sides and on my back, arms, and legs, so that it seemed to me I was in the last throes and that all this suffering would continue until death, if it were the will of God. I hoped for this, *"cupio dissolvi."*[211] And beyond anything that could give me pleasure now, I experienced a great yearning for death, *"mihi vivere Cristus et mori lucrum."*[212]

I fainted from the bitter suffering that was upon me then. The Speaking, which usually eases my suffering, did not come upon me.

And then the same sorrow and suffering came upon me in the same ways as before during the Mass, except that it broke and wrenched all my members more painfully. Both times I felt the most painful thrusts against my heart, any one of which was strong enough to kill me. After that, the Speaking came upon me with the usual sweetness, which strengthened me and eased my pain. Indeed, I lay the whole day through in great sickness. With all this great pain I could eat nothing even when conscience forbade me from fasting, for I perceived with utmost certainty that I needed nothing, and that for the work my Lord Jesus Christ performed in me, no bodily food or medicine was needed. How long I went without eating I do not know. Whatever I ate and whatever I was given I took no delight in. For me no hour is more unpleasant than mealtime. "*Augustinus ad alimentum sicut ad tormentum ivit et Bernardus similiter.*"[213]

On Shrove Tuesday I became ravenously hungry and this continued throughout Lent until Holy Saturday, when I was to eat at midday.[214] This has happened to me in other Lents—as I have already written—though I cannot really explain it, for it can only be understood from experience. I will say just this: food and drink pass unhindered down my throat, but when they reach the place between the ribs near to my heart where I perceive the first movements of grace from which all divine sweetness is sent to me (the fragrance too), then I have a reaction to the food. My internal organs are jolted, so that I must groan loudly and I am often full of pain. With that I am often given to wailing and weeping, and suffer much human grief. This continues every day throughout the mealtime and a little afterward until the food has passed on. Then the loud moaning ceases and after that I can say nothing until matins. No matter how much suffering I feel on account of the food I submit to it for the sake of His love. I eat only as much as I need for nourishment each day, and I perceived indeed that food does not really serve to give me nourishment. All through Lent my faithful Lord did not give me His strength and help in this. So that I should suffer this for His love, He gave me great delight, and I would gladly have borne it until my death, if He had wished it. Of all bodily food and drink I take the greatest delight in water. It seems so sweet to me that I wonder why everyone does not prefer water to other drinks. And yet I do not trust myself to drink enough of it out of fear that it would make me sick, and that would be contrary to the will of God. And as often as I receive the

Holy Body of our Lord I suffer no discomfort. When I wish to receive Him I perceive an inner readiness, given to me by God's goodness—just as if He were to say, "Give me all your will, then I can prepare a place for you." And often His holy human body, as when He walked upon earth, is so present to me that I see Him before me and think about that with great delight and joy that I should truly receive His flesh and blood. Often I ask my little Child, "My little, beloved Jesus, shall I receive you?" Then He answers, "Yes, because I cannot do without you and you cannot do without me. Your delight is in me and mine is in you." Then He adds, "Come, I want to do something good for you." Then I grow so expectant that I do not sleep well through the night and can scarcely wait until dawn. And sometimes the usual Speaking comes upon me with great sweetness because of His truthful sweet promises. Once He astonished me completely, when I asked Him about a sick sister. He answered and said, "She is dying." After that, she got up and walked back and forth as she wished. And soon after that, she died on the third day.

Again during the night before matins a sweet lightness came upon me giving me inner strength. I rejoiced greatly because of the resurrection, since I had spent the holy season with such great suffering and because I could praise God again in my prayer, which was usually taken away from me for these fourteen days. Yet I felt misery and sadness because I was still left here on earth. But I was often reminded that God still wanted to accomplish much with me before I die, "*Heu mihi! quia incolatus meus prolongatus etc.*"[215] And great joy was granted to me when my human strength decreased, yet divine power increased in me and continued in accord with the words: "If I live, it is not I who live, Jesus Christ lives in me."[216] "*Etsi is, qui foris est, noster vetus homo corrumpiter.*"[217]

Then on Holy Saturday I prayed the psalter, which I had not prayed previously on Friday, and I managed it in the usual way without any pain or mistakes.[218] And then on Easter Sunday I awoke before matins in great joy and grace eager to serve my Lord since I had been unable to do so before. I was joyful and filled with delight the whole of Easter week and had to get up every day before matins. I thought this was the hour of His resurrection, but I am not as certain about this as I am about the hour of His birth and of His suffering. After Easter—usually for a day or two or three—a great chill came over me with great heat in which I felt the greatest warmth, joy, and grace. And sometimes the Speaking came upon me; at other times it did not. After the eighth day I was caught, bound in a prison of Silence—about which I have already written—and this happened to me every day after noon and lasted until sunrise. However, when I intended to receive the Holy Body of our Lord early the next day, the binding Silence would cease the evening before. This continued more and more every day until the Monday before St. Alexius' Day, which fell on a Tuesday.[219]

On St. John's Day—at the summer solstice—the chill and heat about which I have written came upon me again and with that a great flow as well.[220] And I did not drink from Wednesday until Sunday, and during these five days I felt all the time as if there were sweet sugar in my mouth accompanied by pleasurable sweetness in my heart. And when I took liquid on Sunday the sweetness decreased.

On St. Alexius' evening, out of His goodness God sent me His worthy Friend with whom and from whom much has been given to me.[221] Then I was grasped by the binding Silence. It subsided often during the night, but returned. I was afraid after that, and when I felt an inner delight and a loving thirst to receive His Holy Body, the Silence would cease totally. The same Friend of God—and my friend—read the Mass at my altar on that day and would gladly have given me our Lord, but I declined because I had lain there all night without praising God, as was the case whenever He held me in His merciful hands. And I was prepared through the grace of our Lord by his Mass, as usually happened to me whenever I wanted to receive the Eucharistic Body of our Lord. But I did not dare to request what I had previously declined. Now I had great inner yearning for the living God to help me receive Him all the time that he was with me.[222] But I was afraid, for I could not receive Him every day. My Lord, however, is exceedingly generous. In His mercy He cannot withhold Himself from anyone, and so he fulfilled my desires, indeed He gave me more than I could desire. He helped me to receive His Holy Body from his hands eleven times.[223] Every day I felt such lightness in heart and body and had such sweet grace in praising our Lord and in taking sweet delight in all things that I did in the same way that it is always given to me during Advent. About that I have written much. I felt this way especially during all his Masses.

On Friday after St. James' Day I went into choir and began my

Pater Noster.[224] Then the greatest grace overcame me and I knew not how it would end, except that I perceived the grace was so great that I could not finish the *Pater Noster*. My heart was surrounded by such sweet grace and felt so light that I was no longer able to pray. I held the Name *Jesus Christus* within me with sweet loving power and from it I perceived wonderful, sweet fragrances rising up within me.

Also a wonderful desire was given me in the sweetness of grace especially to grasp the pure truth both from God and in God. At that time I had such a feeling and such an understanding of the presence of God and of the Truth, who is the Lord Himself, that if I possessed it all the time, it would be like heaven on earth. Also, in true love it was granted me to yearn for many great, mysterious desires. Then I was answered,

> I have given myself to you and will never withdraw myself from you. It is I alone, the true God who should possess your heart. All your delight is in me and all my delight is in your soul and in your heart. You are my love as I am your love. You do not understand that it is my pure love from which all this comes to you. Suffer me for the sake of my love, because I cannot do without your acceptance of it.[225] It is I alone, the pure Truth, who lives in you and works through you, and I have surrounded you with my mercy. Rejoice that the true God lives in you and that my goodness will never forsake you in time or in eternity. I am your sweet delight on earth and you are my joy in heaven. Compelled by my very great love I have chosen you for myself in order to accomplish in you yet more for my eternal honor here and hereafter. It is I alone, your Lord and your God and your only Love, who accomplish great things in you.

These words and still others that are similar to them were given to me with sweet power, and a sweet fragrance arose from within me, and from this I received wondrous joy. But outwardly all my members were bound and my eyes and mouth were closed shut. This lasted from matins until prime. Then it disappeared with joy so that I could pray, but I became so sick that I could scarcely recover in a week.

When day began to break and the Friend of our Lord came to give me our Lord during Mass, this was revealed to me by the goodness of God: "I am your Lord and your God and I will come today into your soul and into your heart with all my power in the truth of my Holy Sacrament. Your soul delights in me and I delight in her." With a great increase in grace I was given an inner readiness to think about and desire whatever comes to me when receiving our Lord. The great goodness of God instructs me in that when I am not able to control myself externally. When I came to myself again at prime, I was given great delight, indeed, in the works of love of our Lord Jesus Christ, but sorrow too, because I had not recited my *Pater Noster* that day. Then the whole day long I gave myself over to the holy works of love of our Lord in all that I did. On Saturday after that the Friend of our Lord departed from me after Mass.[226] I felt miserable and wretched afterward with a longing for the holy Sacrament and for the many other graces that God had given me by his presence.

On the following Sunday I received our Lord from our chaplain.[227] Toward evening of that day the usual binding Silence came upon me again, as it had previously, and as I have had it ever since— except for the days when I wished to receive our Lord. Since then I have received our Lord twice a week according to the advice of the Friend of our Lord and the merciful help of God. And that pleases me very much, as do all things that we are given by God and from God and with God, because He alone gives all good gifts abundantly. Because of His love, He withholds Himself from no one and from his great richness out of love He gives Himself as a gift. I attest to this before my Lord and my God that He gives Himself with great, powerful gifts and that He is the true friend in need, who can abandon no one and wishes to abandon no one. He is the true Light that enlightens us unto truth. He is the pure Love that teaches us the truth, and He is the boundless Good that preserves us in the truth.

When I had lain down one day at noon, this was said to me, "Get up and praise your Lord and your God!" I received that with great joy and had much grace and joy the whole day through. I went into choir to the place where I usually pray. I had many desires, especially concerning the Friend whom God gave me in His goodness, because of the many matters that concerned him. Then I was told by the ever-faithful God, "My ardent love draws him, my delight impels him, my sweet grace strengthens him, my pure truth teaches him, my truly divine mercy protects him. From him my light shines. Through him my power works. He leads a truly authentic life that upholds my honor."

On Friday in the octave of St. Dominic I lay in the binding Silence during the night and was so sick that I slept little.[228] During matins I fell asleep and it seemed to me as if it were before matins and I had been locked in choir. The choir was brightly illumined. I thought I stood before the tabernacle containing our Lord's body. I wanted to take leave and go out of choir as I usually do. Then I looked around and saw that someone was waiting for me. I took fright but felt such great grace that I could not be afraid. As I came to the holy water font, I saw many people behind the choir stalls dressed in white.[229] I wanted to sprinkle them with water from the font in order to see what they would do. Then they all came running over to me with great joy. I was happy and thought I would say, "Jesus Christ," to see how they would respond to it. And so I said, "Jesus Christ." At that they fell down on their knees with great desire and repeated, "Jesus Christ." From that I gained such great grace and joy that I began to sing the sweet Name of Jesus Christ and they sang with me. And I said, "We should dance." Then they answered, "We should dance and eat and drink with one another." Then it seemed to me as if one of the sisters came and opened up the door to choir. That was disappointing to me and to them because we were interrupted and I would gladly have stayed with them always. Then I awoke and all my sickness had ceased and I was made glad and received great desire to know who they were. I asked my Child Jesus about them. He said, "To you has been shown the joy and the love that reign in heaven."

On the Assumption of the Blessed Virgin Mary I had great divine grace.[230] When I came to table I was told that a really poor man, despised and abandoned by all, had come to our monastery. I learned of this with great joy. I thanked God that He had sent him to us so that we could serve Him in this man. I also felt great delight and desire to bear for my God so dear the kind of great abuse, bitter pain, and wretched suffering this man had borne. Then, at that same time, the Gospel reading about the man who fell among the robbers was being read, how the Samaritan practiced mercy and how our dear Lord said to the master: "Do likewise and you will be saved."[231] I was deeply moved by that. Now my Lord Jesus Christ knows well that I gladly come to the aid of anyone whom I see or know to be suffering —as much as I am able. But whether I have done so perfectly, regrettably, I do not know, only the mercy of God knows. At the same time in a dream I saw that our whole monastery was brightly illumined by the shining sun. When I came to prime, it was told to me that the poor man would die. It seemed to me that he was the sun that I had seen. Now I desired from my Child Jesus that this man enter into eternal life after this life. Then I was told about him, "Let me purify him of sin before that."

On the Sunday after that I came into choir and began my *Pater Noster* because I wanted to receive my Lord.[232] Then I was prevented from receiving grace as on Friday after St. James' Day, about which I have already written. The poor man was already dead four days. It was my primary desire that his soul be given to me that very day. When I was praying, I wanted to pray for him. Then he was taken away from me with great joy, and I offered up no more prayers for him. I could only praise God for the sake of the great grace which he had worked in him. I asked my Child Jesus if he were in heaven. He answered, "Yes, and praise me on account of the great works which I have done with a man of such rough character."

I desired to write down the words that I say as our Lord is elevated at Mass. "Lord, I praise you, true God and true man, and ask you, my Lord Jesus Christ, to forgive us all our sins and to take from us all natural defects by your love and grant us yourself with the full grace by which you accomplish your eternal honor in us now and forever!" I say that when the priest holds Him in his hands. When he elevates Him I say, "I greet you, Lord of the whole world, only Word of the Father in heaven, only true sacrifice and only living flesh and only totally divine and truly human one. Give us love for you, true hope and perfect love, and strong, firm Christian faith in this life and at the hour of death." When he elevates the chalice, I say, "I thank you, Lord Christ that you have changed bread and wine into your Holy Body and Blood, that you, Lord Jesus Christ, have deigned in your love, to be offered to your Father by the priest to your eternal honor, and to console, to help and to sanctify us and all Christians living and dead. Now offer yourself today, Lord, for all the evil that we have done against you and for all the good that we have failed to do. And give yourself to us as a sure help in life and in death, and as true power with which we will be able to withstand all human evil by increasing in your heartfelt love."

On the Birth of the Virgin I went to matins in choir.[233] I wanted to recite my *Pater Noster,* and I began to say it when such great joy

164

and grace came over me that I could not pray. I was bound externally so that I could control myself no longer. Then I turned to those inner desires that I usually have when this happens and which I always recite five times. After that I was answered mercifully: "If I am your love, then you are my love. If your delight is in me then I am in you with all my power and I will never part from your soul and your heart until your soul is in eternal life." I said, "Jesus, you are pure Truth, teach me truth." He answered, "I am the Truth that lives in you and works through you and will accomplish even more through you to my eternal honor." And I said, "Jesus, you are boundless Mercy, have mercy on me and come to my aid." And He said, "I have helped you and I will never withdraw my help from you." He continued in much the same way, not all of which I can write to you.[234]

On the feast of the Angels I experienced the same grace and had the desire to remain with my Lord in all the works of love of His Holy Passion and to receive all the sufferings of my beloved Lord in true love for Him—just as He had suffered them out of true love for us.[235] Then I was told, "My strong love is your consolation, my sweet grace is your strength, my divine delight is your satisfaction, my divine mercy is your help and my pure truth your teaching." And He said many words similar to these, but I can no longer remember them.

One day I was given a great desire to ask Jesus, my Child, about the Emperor Louis, because he was hard-pressed by the king.[236] Then He answered, "I will never forsake him, neither now nor hereafter, because of his love for me, unknown to any but himself and me. Convey that to him from me." I did not do that. I failed to do it out of fear that he would know that it was I.[237] After that, it was revealed to me with great delight and joy that he would overcome his enemies. At the same time, I was told that he was dead.[238] Then I perceived with great joy that the foes he had overcome were the enemies of his soul.

The Friend of our Lord and my friend was with me at that time. With great earnestness he begged me to pray to God for the emperor because he was concerned about what God had done with him since he had suffered such a sudden death.[239] Then I desired to know from Jesus, my Child, how it had gone with him. He answered, "I have given him certainty of eternal life." Then I wished to know how he had deserved it. He said, "He loved me and besides, human judgment is often mistaken." I received that with great joy lasting from Friday until Sunday at matins. Then I went into choir with great joy and realized clearly that I was not able to pray. I sat there with great grace and made many petitions and received answers about which I cannot write. While receiving our Lord I had especially great desire to learn something about the soul of that lord.[240] Then I was told, "Praise me for the sake of the marvels I worked in him during the brief period of time at his death." Then I desired from our Lord that He allow me to pray earnestly for his soul until he be lifted up from me into eternal life.

During the night, I kept vigil a long time and had the same grace before matins that I usually have only after matins, with the words, "Come to me, I want to do good things for you, but you may not say your *Pater Noster*."

On All Saints Day I came into choir after matins.[241] I sat there with great grace and joy and much longing, and many answers were given me about which I cannot write according to the pure truth, because the greater the grace is, the less I am able to ponder it. When, in my petitions, I have asked for something that concerns the living or the dead, then I am so truly and clearly answered that I experience great, wonderful grace. These words were also spoken to me:

> Rejoice that your Lord and God is so near to your soul, because you are my spouse and I am your love. You are my joy and I am your joy. You are my delight and I am your delight. Your dwelling is in me and my dwelling is in you. Suffer me for the sake of my love, and I will reward you with myself and will fulfill all your desires with myself and will give you what no eye has seen nor ear heard and what has never been given to any human heart—I will give you my Holy Divinity for eternal joy.[242]

He said other words similar to these as well.

On the same day I was given great consolation from three souls. The first was a sister of our monastery who had been taken away from me with great joy so that I could pray for her no longer because she had entered eternal life. The second was a woman who belonged to our monastery.[243] I had not been able to think about her before, during, or after her death. One day she was given over to me so that I could think of her and I accepted that with great joy. The third soul was the one from Schlüsselberg for whom I was never able to pray.[244] Concerning him I was shown that he was assured of eternal blessedness. "But he is so deep that you really cannot reach him with your desire." When I came to myself, I was very happy and I read the *Te Deum* as I have usually done ever since.

On St. Martin's Day I was sitting there again with the same grace and much desire for a certain soul, but I was told, "Let my justice remove her sins."[245] Then I desired most urgently to know something about the merciful works that God had accomplished with the Emperor Louis. I was told, "He bore me in his heart; therefore I have surrounded him with my mercy and I will not release him from it until I have prepared him for eternal life." I was asked by a truly spiritual Friend of our Lord to enquire further about the emperor, because a true Friend of God had told him he should have lived longer. I was answered, "That is true. It happened due to the sins of men."

Often I perceived a voice which cried out from within me saying again and again, "I want to go home. Where to? To eternal life!" I was not able to withstand it because of the great grace with which it was given me.

The binding Silence, about which I have previously written and by which I came out of the fast very ill, lasted until the feast of St. Andrew every day without exception.[246]

I had great grace on St. Nicholas' Day.[247] I went into choir with great joy and wanted to receive our Lord, and I said my *Pater Noster* with great delight, especially with the Name *Jesus Christus,* which I repeated often with sweet delight as I usually do in Advent. The priest was delayed in coming at the usual time, but I received great delight and desire for the Holy Sacrament. I wanted to receive Him as the holy Christian faith teaches me: truly the entire divinity and the true humanity, His Body and Blood, not as if He would communicate Himself merely in the Sacrament; rather it seemed to me as if the Lord would come with the priest in human form, just as He had walked upon the earth, true God and true man. So it would be possible for me to enjoy the presence of His whole Body when I received Him in the Holy Sacrament. The arrival of the priest was delayed so long that I began to weep from true distress and the thought that perhaps I myself was to blame. Then I was told, "I had not given myself to you previously because I desired your tears." After that the priest arrived. With what grace the Holy Sacrament was given to me, I have written earlier. So I lived through Advent with the grace and lightness I am given every Advent.

On Christmas Day I awoke before matins with great grace and got up with the great joy that is given to me often on that day. That day and for the whole week I felt great grace and joy.

After that, on the feast of the Circumcision, I came into choir for matins.[248] I began my *Pater Noster* with the sweet Name of Jesus in sweet delight. Then I was bound again with the all-sweetest delight and with powerful, divine grace surrounding my heart and my soul so forcefully that I was incapable of having any desire other than that which was given to me with Jesus and from Jesus. The grace was so powerful and the binding so gentle that I cannot express it in words except to say that I wish everyone could feel it. I was also given many answers concerning all the things for which I had petitioned—as I have written. This happened to me again on the feast of the Three Kings and also on the Purification of our Lady.[249]

About the same time a lay woman died. She was buried secretly in our church, even though the bishop had forbidden it. When I went into the church the next day and wanted to pray, I could utter no word, and I had to leave choir. As often as I tried to pray, I could neither utter any word nor receive our Lord in choir, but when I left choir I could pray well, yes, I prayed whatever I wished. I did this for three weeks. Then one of our superiors came to our monastery to make a visitation. The sisters who know it asked him to command me under obedience to return to choir and to say my prayers there and also to receive our Lord. Then he gave me the command. Now my Lord Jesus Christ knows well that when the command was given I felt a release from great heaviness and received great joy and a feeling of lightness. Immediately, I went into choir and could pray as I liked just as before. And my Lord Jesus Christ knows well that I have felt more affectionate respect for my superiors ever since and greater reverence for their commands than before.

I have already written about the grace and joy and the health which I experience every Advent, all of which lasted until New Year's Day.[250] Then I began to get sick. Toward evening I did not feel so well as before. After Epiphany the binding Silence began, as I have previously written.[251] It came upon me powerfully causing sickness and suffering. On the Monday before Shrove Tuesday my sufferings began with pain from eating and with all the other ills that I have described in connection with the earlier Lent.[252] On Monday after *Laetare* Sunday the Speaking came upon me powerfully and on Tuesday the loud Outcrying.[253] That lasted until the Vigil of Easter.[254] The Outcries were louder and lengthier, and stronger than in other Lents. But in the Speaking—which followed the loud Outcries —I possessed more grace and sweetness than during the earlier Lents, and I had a more mysterious pain than during the other Lents. It was thrust upon me before compline and took hold of me so forcefully that I had no power over my life and I could make no external gesture. I wanted only to survive until morning in order to receive our Lord and then die. I had great desire for that. This happened to me often afterward and I got used to it.

On Saturday after *Laetare* Sunday I was given such a vivid perception of the Holy Passion of my Lord Jesus Christ, it was as if I had seen it right before my own eyes.[255] I have already written about this form earlier Lents when I received our Lord. Then the loud Outcries ceased until compline. I lived through Holy Thursday as in previous years.[256] On the morning of Good Friday I could read the psalter and whatever else I wanted, too, except matins.[257] I had not been able to do that the previous years. Whenever my suffering was about to end, I desired that it would finish me off on that very day in pain and perceptible suffering. But I was not granted more suffering than before. Indeed I was given more grace and sweetness than before.

During Mass I was given two souls about whom I could not previously think, so that I was able at last to think about them. One entered into eternal life. Ever since then I can no longer think about her except to praise God for her. On Holy Saturday the sickness came upon me until nighttime as in other years.[258] Then the most severe pain took hold of me and became so unbearable that I could feel neither inner nor outer grace. I had to go without our Lord on Easter Day.[259] This suffering continued until Friday and then it ceased.[260] Now my Lord Jesus Christ knows well that for me it is a great joy and consolation that the giver and the knower of my whole life, my hidden sufferings, and of all my gifts and graces, is none other than my Lord Jesus Christ. He knows also that His grace and His wonderful gifts fulfill me so immeasurably within that I can experience neither love nor pain from external things. But whatever is contrary to love, truth, and peace, makes me sad.

As I came into choir for matins on Pentecost I was bound.[261] I sat there in great sweet grace about which I cannot write. It was revealed to me in particular that all those who were given to me would never be abandoned by God either here or hereafter. He promised me also that He Himself would be there at my death with His mother and my lord St. John. Now my Lord Jesus Christ knows well that I was so well at the same time that I asked myself how the disciples of our Lord were able to bear the Holy Spirit at all. For three days I was constantly in great grace. Then on Wednesday the illness set in again—about which I have written before—but with the great pain lasting many a day until the eve of the summer solstice.[262] I was sad because I would be without our Lord, for when He came I could not receive Him. Afflicted with this sickness, I fell asleep, but when I awoke I was given the greatest desire for the Eucharistic Body of our Lord with sweet grace indeed. I awoke all who were sleeping near me so that they could help me up for communion. Then the Holy Eucharistic Body of our Lord was brought to me and I received it with great grace. The sickness did not leave me entirely that year, but it always ended in such a way that the Speaking came upon me with great sweet grace. This lasted three days and nights.

On the Assumption of the Blessed Virgin Mary I sat there in the binding Silence with all the grace that I have previously described but with more questions and answers.[263] And with the same grace I sat there on the feast of Mary's birth.[264]

In the octave of St. Augustine I wanted to receive our Lord.[265] During the night I was bound lovingly with a tender sweet bond in the grace of our Lord, and I had no control over myself. Thus I received our Lord because, even though bound tightly, I was not prevented from receiving the Holy Eucharist. Then I lay there until midday without any control over myself.

On the feast of the Exaltation of the Holy Cross I lay there until prime bound in the same way, but with much grace.[266]

On All Saints' Day I sat there again in choir with the grace that I have previously described.[267] I made petitions for the living and the dead, especially because of the troubles that burdened Christianity as a result of the plague. I wanted to know whether the Jews were at fault for this.[268] Then I was told, although there was truth in this, God had permitted the plague because of the great faults and sins of Christendom. I was always granted knowledge on this matter whenever I desired it. Often I have great desire regarding several persons. About them I was told, "I live in them; therefore they live in me." The same was revealed to me about several others: "I will never abandon them either here or hereafter." And also about others, "If they lived for me, then I would do what they wanted." I was asked by a religious, who was worried about his office, whether it was the will of God that he resign it. Then I was answered, "No, because he lives for me in love and humility and in truth."

One day I had great desire again concerning the soul of the Emperor Louis of Bavaria. Then I was told he was in great suffering, "but the degree of his punishment will not deprive him of eternal life for much longer."

Then I also had desire for two souls. I was answered, "As likely as Lucifer is ever to come out of hell, so likely is it that they will come out." Already before that I had not been able to pray for them.

I was asleep on All Souls' Day and it seemed to me as of I had come into a strange place.[269] There I found many sorts of deceased people whom I knew. And with great desire they asked me to pray to God for them. After that I came to a beautiful green place where there were tall trees from which beautiful apples were falling. I saw people whom I knew well and about whom I firmly believe and trust that they enjoy eternal life. Then two others, who were sisters of our monastery, came over to me. They gave me two of the apples. One of them was sour, the other sweet. They asked me to eat them. I took the apples and bit into them. Then I felt such great grace from the apples that I said, "No one on earth could eat both." They said, "If you do not like them, give them back to us." Then I awoke still chewing, and the grace was so sweet and so strong that I could not speak a word and could not take in breath and was really without any of my bodily senses. That lasted a long time with me and after that I read matins without comprehending a word.

On St. Martin's night I dreamed that a bishop was in our monastery with a great retinue.[270] I had great grace and desire for the bishop and for his servants, especially for one of them. I followed them everywhere. The bishop sat among the people and offered them a murky drink from a chalice. I sat next to the bishop and the servant, who was dear to me, sat behind me. To him the bishop said, "Give this one a drink!" Then he offered me a very clear drink in a glass. When I had drunk it, I gave it back to him. Then he said, "Note what the bishop has commanded me and what he has offered you. If you are with him at his death, then he will be with you when you are dying." Then the bishop left with his retinue. I awoke and my heart and my soul were filled completely with grace so sweet that I cannot write about it. And I began with my usual Speaking, in the powerful sweet grace which had been given me from the drink and which I had received from the presence of the bishop and the servant. My Lord knows well that I have ever felt an increase in the sweet joy attending the grace which I had received from eating and drinking. Especially when I said my *Pater Noster* and came to the petition about my lord St. John, then I perceived with the sweetest grace that it had been he who had given me the drink. Three days before the feast of St. Andrew, with sweet grace I was released from all the bonds with which I had been bound for the year.[271] It seemed as if every one of my members was set free. But my Lord Jesus Christ knows well that I cannot speak or write about the powerful and great grace of Advent. My Lord also knows well that much is given me from his merciful Goodness in answer to my prayers and also in a feeling of grace which I cannot describe. Often I refrain from talking about this because of the frequent illness which comes upon me and because of the fear I have of talking about the grace which passes between me and my Lord and God, who is the light of the pure truth, for He knows well that I receive His gifts and grace in real fear because of my great unworthiness.

The Name *Jesus Christus*—the Truth knows this well—blossoms within me during the season of Advent with especially sweet grace and I can do nothing except what is given me with Jesus and from Jesus and in Jesus.

THE *PATER NOSTER*

O Lord, in your highest love and in your greatest and most sweet mercy as they have ever flowed out of your eternal Godhead from heaven to earth, I commend to you in sincerity our souls, in purity our hearts, in true innocence all our lives, and in nothing but truth all our desires and all our intentions. For this, Jesus Christ, your boundless mercy must prepare us and your perfect love compel us so that we attain the sweetest grace and truest love for which you have chosen your most beloved friends in life, in death and in eternity.

I ask you, my Lord, in your pure love to give us a real union with the innermost good which is yourself, O God. And I ask you, my Lord, by the powerful help that you have given us in your sacred human life—with all your works of love—to let us perceive with your visible and invisible presence by a sweet interior movement what true heartfelt love for you is. Let us take delight in nothing but your Holy Passion and in your holy sacraments, and grant us therein true renunciation of all the world, complete disregard for ourselves, and pure recognition of our sins so that we may repent of them and forswear them out of true love. And give us bitter sorrow for all our wasted time in thought, word, and deed and in any neglect of your sweet grace.

Give us, my Lord, constant attentiveness to ourselves in your heartfelt love and a powerful sign of victory over all evil. And give us, my Lord, the truth in which we will know and love you. Give us, too, your boundless mercy by which we grow refined and purified from all our sins so that we appear as pure before the luminous mirror of your divine face as when our soul was poured into our body and our body was lifted up from the waters of baptism.

I ask you, my Lord Jesus Christ, by your perfect grace, to help us always to be guided by your will, be good or ill done to us, so that your powerful might may bind us and your sweet love compel us such that we may have no mere natural life in us, but may you, Jesus Christ, live in us with all your grace; and may we live for you alone in truth. And I ask you to accomplish in us powerfully the sweetest works that you have done out of inner delight in your chosen friends, until we perceive what right love for you is, so that we, when the last moment of our life comes, may perceive with heavenly joy how pure a union there is between yourself and a needy soul whom you have grace with your divinity, to whom you have lowered yourself with all divine nobility, and in whom you have lovingly impressed yourself with divine power, so that—aside from you—the soul is nothing, except in it appears in divine clarity the image of your Holy Trinity.

I ask you, Lord, to pierce us through with the sorrows of your heart so that they may be impressed upon us and become signs of love of your heartfelt love, beyond what you have ever yet given to any heart in true loving desire.

Give us, my Lord, a sweet inner desire from a pure heart for the living food of your Holy Body and a loving thirst to receive you in accord with your innermost mercy; and undertake in us with sweetness a merciful work with full grace, so that we will perceive truly in ourselves the hidden power of your holy sacraments, ever acquiring virtues, ever increasing in grace.

And I ask you, my Lord, to feed us this day in union with the most worthy priest, who receives you today on earth, so that we may be so truly filled with all the graces in the Holy Sacrament that it will be as if we received you presently from his hands and in the same worthiness of desire that he himself possesses. By the grace of your presence may we feel no lack of you because of the sad state of Christianity, and on that account may we never harm by evil the pure Truth, which is you yourself, O God, in whom all truth is seen. And may we appear before your divine face innocent of this sin and of all sins and well adorned with the fullness of all grace. May we be strengthened by your living food so that we increase in fiery love, be surrounded by your boundless mercy against all evil, and be embraced by your pure truth. May all your graces surround us and always be increased in us and nevermore be taken from us until eternal life. May they be for us an eternal reward, an eternal joy, and an eternal delight in you forever. Help us, my Lord, that we may die of pure love and that you may be given to us out of the same love that allowed you to die on the cross out of love for us, so that even while we still live we may become accustomed to eternal joy hereafter with you. Help us, too, to bear all misery with true joy so that after this misery our soul may never more perceive any sadness or fear, and help us never to suffer any lack of you. And from the innermost goodness of your boundless mercy may nothing but you yourself become for us eternal delight and eternal reward by which we will be adorned so as to enjoy your Holy Godhead in purest clarity—just as you give yourself to your most beloved friends.

Now I ask you, my Lord, by the powerful help that you have given us in your sacred humanity and in your holy and efficacious suffering, to attend lovingly and mercifully to all our desires.

I ask you, my Lord, to give us yourself with that intoxicating grace in which you have given yourself to your dearest friends and with your presence deliver us from all evil. What is evil? All, my Lord, that is not you.

And give us the kiss of your eternal peace through the heart and into the soul with the same sweetest sensation that your pure soul in pure loving delight has ever felt or received the sweetest kiss of a pure heart as a pledge of your burning love, as the help of your boundless mercy, as strengthening in pure truth, and as instruction in true Christian belief in life and death, in confirmation of real, true hope.

My Lord, may your glorified, grace-filled humanity, Jesus Christ, be my innermost strength, a purification of my whole life, and an enlightening of all my senses to recognize the real and only truth. My surest way to you, my Lord, on the way of real truth must be for us the true light of your pure life of thirty-three years on earth, your humble deeds, your gentle course of life, your powerful suffering, your love-filled death, your true words.

My Lord, give me a sweet assurance of salvation in the fullness of your grace, a loving end in right disposition, an eternal enjoyment of nothing but your love, where you alone, my Lord are Lord and no one else, and where your honor is our eternal food and your power our eternal joy; where your clear appearance is our eternal guide and where all sadness has an end and all joy is assured by the source of living water. Whence does it flow? From the Father's heart, the Eternal Word, enclosed for love of us in the Virgin's womb in nothing by purity.

Mary, Mother of God, may your purity and your virginal birth cleanse us. May your motherly help and the help of all the saints and all the angels unlock the fount of all mercy from which no one has ever been forbidden to draw. My Lord, may you pour into us yourself and pour your rich gifts over us in full grace! Purify us and cleanse us from all our sins by the Holy Blood of your sacred wounds and quench us, Lord, with the water about which you, Eternal Wisdom and Truth, have said that whoever drinks of it will never thirst again.[272] From this may our souls be quenched quickly with purity. May your loving delight be fulfilled in us and may your praise be increased by us, my Lord, to your eternal joy. Jesus, give us these things by the power of your innermost love, from which all of your eternal blessedness has flowed to us. From the overflowing power of your holy suffering boundless mercy will be given to us with which you will prepare us for your dearest will with all grace. May you adorn us particularly with the grace of true inner and outer peace, with true humility, and with the true shining light of true Christian belief.

And give us, my Lord, a true increase in all your graces until we come to the point where your divine grace will be our eternal joy and our everlasting reward. Amen. *Deo gratias!*

1. Pronouns referring to God or to Jesus will be capitalized throughout to avoid confusion later in the manuscript when Margaret refers to both Jesus and to her spiritual director, Henry of Nördlingen.

2. 6 February 1312. References to dates are not found in the original manuscript but are contained in the critical edition of 1882 by Philip Strauch. They are used here as a point of reference in the narrative.

3. Hyacinthe M. Hanser, O.P., "Marguerite Ebner: une mystique dominicaine du XIV siècle," *Année Dominicaine* (1937), p. 202. Hanser supports the interpretation that Margaret was not very aware or recollected with regard to her spiritual life. "Marguerite, qui avait mené jusque-là une vie assez insouciante, commença à comprendre le vrai sens de la vie religieuse, à s'orienter avec énergie et persévérance vers la perfection."

4. H. Wilms, in footnote 21, p. 282, of his translation explained this passage. "Das längste Leben wird genommen als das verdienstvollste wie im Buch der Weisheit steht: 'Früh vollendet, hat er viele Jahre erreicht.' " (Wis 4:13, *RSV*), "Being prefected in a short time, he fulfilled long years."

5. A.D. 1313.

6. A.D. 1314.

7. "Their" refers to the sisters who were charged with the care of Margaret during her illness.

8. The *Pater Noster* was a prayer form of the time; it consisted of praise of God, petitions, and so on, and was not a commentary on the Lord's Prayer. The "works of love" refer to the wounds of Christ. These are designated as *vulnera* in the Latin edition. Sometimes "works of love" refer to any deed performed by Christ during his earthly ministry. Love is understood as the motive for all of Christ's deeds.

9. "To" the works of love refers to the sacred wounds of Christ; here they are treated as objects of devotion much like the devotion to the Sacred Heart of Jesus or the Most Precious Blood. The Dominican Order celebrated a feast of the Wounds of Christ.

10. The Friends of Our Lord or Friends of God is a reference to a group of spiritual friends outside the monastery.

11. The Poor Souls in purgatory.

12. Emperor Louis IV, the Bavarian.

13. Burgau was besieged from December 1324 to January 1325. Louis was in Lombardy from 1327 to 1330. The verse is Psalm 72:11 (*RSV*), "May all kings fall down before him, all nations serve him."

14. 2 November.

15. Margaret was forced by circumstances to return to her mother's home at Donauwörth during the siege of Burgau.

16. It is not known for certain how many brothers and sisters she had. She mentions one brother specifically.

17. The word *imbiz* may mean lunch or perhaps breakfast here. In the Latin translation the word used is *prandium*.

18. This is a retrospective interpretation of her suffering as a preparation for greater union with God.

19. The "sacred regalia" were the crown, scepter, orb and imperial mantle, all of which were necessary for valid coronation. That Margaret referred to these as sacred hints at the belief that the office of the emperor enjoyed a kind of sacral character. Some theologians held that royal anointing was a sacrament.

20. Ananias, Azarias, and Misael were the companions of the prophet Daniel; their names were changed to Shadrach, Mishach, and Abednago (Dn 1:7).

21. 15 August 1314 to 25 February 1315.

22. "Choir" designates an area of the church used for the singing of the psalms during the office at various times of the day and night. Choir also designates the people who are there singing the office. It is never used in the more modern sense of a church choir. Whenever a sister died, the nuns prayed the psalter from the time of death until her burial, even through the night.

23. *Jesus Christus* refers to the prayer, which is given to Margaret and which also initiates the Speaking.

24. 29 October 1332. The friend is Henry. The date of his arrival at Maria Medingen seems to have been 29 October 1332, as suggested by P. Strauch and H. Wilms. That is the feast of St. Narcissus of Jerusalem (d. 212). The Latin translation sets the date of Henry's arrival as 18 March 1332, the feast of St. Narcissus of Gerona and the feast of St. Narcissus of Augsburg.

25. 2 February 1333.

26. This refers to events in Christ's passion, every detail of which was considered to be a source for meditation.

27. Presumably this is one of the deceased nuns of the monastery of Maria Medingen. It may be the first lay sister, since the answer given is the response to Margaret's question posed to her about the Lord.

28. Henry of Nördlingen wrote of these seals in Letter VII.

29. Septuagesima.

30. Margaret desired to share in the passion of Jesus Christ and to suffer the same wounds inflicted upon him at his crucifixion. Such desire has been traditionally based upon St. Paul's statement that he wished to fill up what was lacking in the sufferings of Christ (cf. Col 1:24–25).

31. 24 March 1334.

32. 27 March 1334.

33. The kiss, the embrace, and the *minnegriff* are all images of union in love.

34. Jn 20:11 (*RSV*), Gospel for Thursday after Easter, 31 March 1334. "But Mary stood weeping outside the tomb, and as she wept she stooped to look into the tomb."

35. H. Wilms theorized that the image of the loving soul portrayed here was her own soul. This is borne out later by a revelation given to Margaret.

36. This ending is reminiscent of the standard conclusion of many sermons by John Tauler.

37. 31 October 1334.

38. Margaret never referred to Henry of Nördlingen directly by name. She always used phrases such as "Friend of God" to speak of him.

39. 1 November 1334.

40. "Our Lady" is a title used for the Blessed Virgin Mary.

41. Margaret confided in her spiritual director and friend, Henry of Nördlingen.

42. 28 February 1335.

43. With this grasp of love (*minnegriff*) Margaret was brought into the mystical life in an extraordinary way.

44. 28 February 1335, Shrove Tuesday.

45. The oil was used in the sacrament of the sick or extreme unction and was considered to have healing power physically as well as spiritually.

46. Jn 16:20 (*RSV*), "Truly, truly, I say to you, you will weep and

lament, but the world will rejoice; you will be sorrowful, but your sorrow will turn into joy."

47. 25 March 1335.

48. The Introit for the Annunciation according to the Dominican rite was based upon Isaiah 45:8: "Drop down dew, you heavens from above and let the clouds rain down the just one. Let the earth be opened and bud forth a savior."

49. 13 and 14 April 1335.

50. 15 April 1335.

51. 17 April 1335.

52. Jn 20:27 (*RSV*), "Then he said to Thomas, 'Put your finger here, and see my hands, and put out your hand, and place it in my side; do not be faithless, but believing.'"

53. 1 Cor 2:9 (*RSV*), "But as it is written, 'What no eye has seen, nor ear heard, nor the heart of man conceived what God has prepared for those who love him.'"

54. Religious orders not specifically placed under interdict were permitted to celebrate Mass and the sacraments in private.

55. Perhaps Dominican nuns helped to educate very young girls. The child was Margaret's niece—another Margaret Ebner.

56. 28 December 1335.

57. 6 January 1336.

58. This emphasizes the importance that suffering compassion with the Crucified Jesus held in Margaret's spirituality. She was unable to conceive of the possibility that there might be some other path to holiness and perfection than through a participation in the sufferings of Jesus Christ.

59. 21 January 1336.

60. 12 February 1336.

61. A "profound inclination" was a liturgical gesture used in private and public prayer. The inclination or bowing was done at the *Gloria Patri*, at the Name of Jesus or the name of Mary. The Brethren of the Order had been taught by St. Dominic to bow before the altar and before the crucifix showing humility to the One who had humbled himself for the salvation of all.

62. 25 March 1336.

63. 29 March 1336.

64. 31 March 1336.

65. This refers to the confused state of affairs caused by the interdict.

66. The *Vexilla regis* was a processional chant. Presumably she had to leave the procession of the sisters in the cloister and go to her place in choir.

67. Here there is a lacuna in the manuscript of 1353.

68. This is a description of the stigmata.

69. Vespers I of Passion Sunday (14 March 1339).

70. 21 March 1339; a processional was a liturgical text sung while the community went in procession through the cloister. The hymn would have been *Gloria, laus, et honor Tibi sit, Rex Christe Redemptor*.

71. 25 March 1339.

72. The term "hours" refers to the liturgical hours of prayer such as prime, terce, sext, and none.

73. 28 March 1339.

74. 13 April 1340.

75. Perhaps she was able to respond by signs to the confessor's questions.

76. 14 April 1340.

77. Margaret wrote *Sanctus ayos*, but it actually should be *Agios, Sanctus*. This is taken from the Reproaches traditionally sung as part of the celebration of the Lord's passion on Good Friday.

78. *Laute ruefen* (loud Outcries) is another mystical phenomenon.

79. This refers to the loud Outcries and is here understood to be a reaction to the swearing. It is unclear whether the swearing was that of a sister, a worker, or a diabolic suggestion.

80. "Shot through the heart" is an indication of the mystical phenomenon known as *sagitta acuta*.

81. The hymn may be *Vexilla regis*, which had been the impetus for Outcries at other times.

82. 1 April 1341.

83. 4 April 1341.

84. There is no hymn appointed for matins on Holy Thursday. It is possible that Margaret was referring to the Lamentations of Jeremiah, which formed a significant and distinctive part of the office.

85. 12 April 1341.

86. 27 May 1341.

87. 9 August 1341.

88. 29 September 1341.
89. This refers to a physical paralysis used analogously to refer to something spiritual as well.
90. 1 Cor 2:9, used again.
91. Henry of Nördlingen.
92. Henry correctly perceived her spiritual and physical condition.
93. 1 November 1341.
94. 2 November 1341.
95. Henry of Nördlingen celebrated the Mass.
96. 4 November 1341.
97. 6 December 1341.
98. The *Te Deum* is an ancient hymn used to praise the Triune God and to give thanks to God on special occasions.
99. Frequent communion was not the practice at that time. As Margaret will imply later, weekly communion was considered to be frequent.
100. 27 March 1342.
101. 29 March 1342.
102. Presumably Margaret could not listen to the *Credo* (Creed) because it mentioned the passion, crucifixion, and death of Jesus.
103. 6 December 1342.
104. 4 March 1343; *Laetare* Sunday was the fourth Sunday of Lent.
105. 13 April 1343.
106. 20 April 1343.
107. Ascension: 22 May 1343; Pentecost: 1 June 1343.
108. 13 November 1343.
109. The "kiss of love" is an image taken from the Song of Songs and interpreted by St. Bernard of Clairvaux in a mystical sense.
110. This passage is reminiscent of the beginning of Margaret's *Pater Noster* in abbreviated form.
111. 30 March 1344.
112. 9 April 1344; 10 April 1344.
113. 23 May 1344.
114. 15–22 August 1344.
115. 9 October 1344.
116. *Totmal* is translated by Wilms as *Totenmale;* by Prestel as *Sterbenmale;* and by Strauch as *Todtenmale.* What is actually meant

by this is unclear. *Totmal* may refer to a birth mark or to a malignancy. It does not seem that it could refer to hypostasis in this instance. Whatever this "sign of death" may have been, clearly all who witnessed it believed that Margaret would soon die.

117. 11 November 1344.

118. Sucking from the breast of Christ and these other images are used to describe an experience of intimacy with Christ. It is wisdom that is received from the breast of Christ. St. John the "Beloved" leaned upon the breast of Christ at the Last Supper, and it is his Gospel which seeks to make known the hidden mysteries revealed solely through the eyes of faith.

119. H. Wilms notes that *wild ain* is a reference to the essence of God.

120. Mt 23:12 (*RSV*), "Whoever exalts himself will be humbled, and whoever humbles himself will be exalted" (cf. Lk 14:11; 18).

121. These are all revelations concerning God's will for Henry of Nördlingen.

122. This is once again an allusion to 1 Cor 2:9.

123. It was customary to rest after the midday meal in addition to the two periods of sleep during the night, which were interrupted by matins. This interruption of sleep was considered to be one of the most difficult demands of the Order's observances.

124. The *Anima Christi* is a prayer often attributed to St. Ignatius of Loyola, but obviously predates him.

> *Anima Christi, sanctifica me.*
> *Corpus Christi, salva me.*
> *Sanguis Christi, inebria me.*
> *Aqua lateris Christi, lava me.*
> *Passio Christi, conforta me.*
> *O bone Jesu, exaudi me.*
> *Intra tua vulnera, absconde me.*
> *Ne permittas me separari a te.*
> *Ab hoste maligno defende me.*
> *In hora mortis meae voca me:*
> *Et iube me venire ad te,*
> *Ut cum sanctis tuis laudem te,*
> *Per infinita saecula saeculorum. Amen.*

125. The *Miserere* is Psalm 50.

126. Here Margaret actually paraphrases the beginning of her *Pater Noster*. Since this text is not identical with the *Pater Noster*, it demonstrates that the wording of Margaret's special prayer was not exact.

127. It was solely at Henry's request that Margaret undertook the task of writing the *Revelations*.

128. 27 December 1344.

129. 28 December 1344.

130. A translation of the text of Margaret's hymn would be:

> Jesus, the way of truth,
> Fount of immense piety,
> Through whom all things live,
> To you be glory and praise.

A hymn very similar to the one mentioned by Margaret appears in *Lateinische Hymnen des Mittelalters*, ed. F. J. More (Herder'sche Verlagshandlung, Freiburg-i-B, 1853), p. 343.

> *Jesu via veritatis*
> *Fons immensae pietatis*
> *Per quem vivunt omnia.*
>
> *Esto meus consolatur*
> *Verbum Patris, vitae datur*
> *In tanta miseria.*

131. There is a lacuna in the original manuscript.

132. Mt 12:50 (*RSV*), "For whoever does the will of my Father in heaven is my brother, and sister, and mother." Margaret has made a rather untheological paraphrase!

133. Lk 1:35 (*RSV*), "And the angel said to her, 'The Holy Spirit will come upon you, and the power of the Most High will over-shadow you; therefore, the child to be born will be called holy, the Son of God.'"

134. Signs of death. See note 116.

135. This incident is termed *mystical lactation*. Margaret uses "heart" as a euphemism for "breast."

136. 26 December 1344.

137. The kiss from the Christ child is perhaps a variant on the "kiss of love."

138. 19 January 1345.

139. 26 March 1345.

140. 23 January–27 March 1345.

141. *Judica* Sunday was the fifth Sunday in Lent. The title comes from the opening words of the Introit of the Mass, "Judica me, Deus" taken from Psalm 43 (42). It was also known as Passion Sunday, which was distinct from Palm Sunday.

142. The Outcry is a mystical phenomenon (*rueffen*).

143. 22 March 1345.

144. 14 March 1345.

145. 15 March 1345.

146. 26 March 1345.

147. 24 March 1345.

148. 25 March 1345.

149. Apparently Margaret's commiseration with the sufferings of Christ created such a distraction to the devotions and worship of the other sisters that she was forbidden to take part in the Triduum services.

150. 27 March 1345.

151. The *Regina Coeli* is an antiphon in honor of the Blessed Virgin Mary and was sung at Eastertide after compline and in procession. Margaret heard the voices of the angels mixed in with the singing of the nuns. Belief in this event is portrayed in the ceiling frescoes of the *Margaretenkappelle* at Maria Medingen.

152. 1 April 1345.

153. 15 August 1345.

154. 29 September 1345.

155. 11 November 1345.

156. 26 November 1345.

157. These are revelations gleaned from her intercessory prayer for the souls in purgatory. It was very difficult for her to pray for some souls. She felt "heavy" when she tried to pray for them at first. Later, she felt "lighter" as it became easier to pray for them. This progression indicated that the soul was drawing nearer and nearer to deliverance from purgatory.

158. Lk 1:35.

159. The "mother of Christendom" is the church.

160. The first one mentioned here is St. John the Baptist, the second is St. John the Evangelist, the "Beloved" disciple.

161. Margaret writes here of the interdict and the confusion as to whether it would be right to receive holy communion under the interdict.

162. 28 August 1345.

163. There is a difference between the interpretation of Strauch and the Latin edition, which sets the date as 6 August, the feast of St. Dominic. From the context it is clear that the "founder" must refer to Hartmann IV Count of Dillingen, who founded the monastery of Maria Medingen. He died 11 December 1258.

164. 30 November 1345.

165. Strauch and Prestel interpret *ewihetag* to mean "New Year's Day." Manuscript *m* replaces this word with "selben tag." It seems that this giving of the name occurred on Christmas 1346. The Latin text used for the beatification process of 1979 also follows this interpretation, even though it would seem logical from a liturgical standpoint that the Name of Jesus would be given to Margaret on the feast of the Circumcision, since that day (1 January) also commemorated the giving of the Name to Jesus.

166. 27 December 1345–3 January 1346.

167. 2 February 1346.

168. 12 February 1346.

169. 29 March 1346.

170. 8 April 1346.

171. The minor hours include prime, terce, sext, and none.

172. 10 April 1346.

173. Margaret was still dreaming here when she related the equation of the living body on the cross with the Eucharist, the Body of Christ.

174. 12 April 1346.

175. 13 April 1346. The first period of sleep followed compline and was interrupted by the singing of matins in the middle of the night.

176. 16 April 1346.

177. 27 April 1346.

178. 4–10 June 1346, 15–22 August 1346, 14 September 1346.

179. The original text of the quote is rhymed imperfectly.

180. 30 November 1346.

181. Communion could not be received more than once per day.

182. 27 December 1346.

183. Rom 14:8 (*RSV*), "If we live, we live to the Lord, and if we die, we die to the Lord; so then, whether we live or whether we die, we are the Lord's."

184. It is unclear from the text whether both the mother and the baptized child were burned, or only the mother.

185. 28 January 1347.

186. 14 February 1347–31 March 1347.

187. 11 March 1347.

188. 12 March 1347.

189. 13 March 1347.

190. 14 March 1347.

191. 2 Cor 13:3 (*RSV*), ". . . since you desire proof that Christ is speaking in me. He is not weak in dealing with you, but is powerful in you."

192. 15 March 1347.

193. Cant 4:11 (*RSV*), "Your lips distil nectar, my bride, honey and milk are under your tongue; the scent of your garments is like the scent of Lebanon." This and other Latin quotes may be interpretative comments added to the manuscript by Henry.

194. Mt 27:46 (*RSV*), " 'Eli, eli, lama sabachthani', that is, 'My God, my God, why hast thou forsaken me?' " and Ps 69:3 (*RSV*), "I am weary with crying; my throat is parched. My eyes grow dim with waiting for my God."

195. This Latin text is unidentified. The note in Strauch taken from *m* expands on the Latin text, "*das ist gesprochen: die erkenntnusse vnd wahrheit dessen sie innen werden in Xo gott dem herrn nach seiner maas als vil als kein mensch der nun lebt vnd davon hat sie seuffzend vnd weinend gebetten demuthigkeit dise wort zu schreiben.*" The Latin text of itself might be rendered into English: "She has undergone a test of these things in Christ to the best of her ability as much as any of the men now living. And at that time she sought, groaning and weeping, that these words be written out of the deepest humility."

196. 16 March 1347.

197. 17 March 1347.

198. 17 March 1347.

199. *De Profundis* is Psalm 130, which contains eight verses. This psalm was recited in the office and at other liturgical events. More important, it was recited every time the sisters processed over the graves of their deceased sisters, who were buried under the interior cloister walk. This psalm, "Out of the depths," was an intercessory prayer for those deceased sisters.

200. 23 March 1347.

201. 23–25 March 1347. *Domine ne longe* Sunday was Palm Sunday.

202. This refers to a period of spiritual aridity.

203. 25 March 1347.

204. 28 March 1347.

205. 29 March 1347.

206. An abbreviated paraphrase of Is 40:3 (*RSV*), "A voice cries: 'In the wilderness prepare the way for the Lord, make straight in the desert a highway for our God.' "

207. A paraphrase of Cant 2:14 (*RSV*), "O my dove, in the clefts of the rock, in the covert of the cliff, let me see your face, let me hear your voice, for your voice is sweet, and your face is comely."

208. This is a direct reference to the *sagitta acuta,* as noted in parentheses in the manuscript of 1353.

209. 30 March 1347.

210. Margaret uses the term "Martyr" to refer to Christ, who gave witness to the truth.

211. Phil 1:23 (*RSV*), "I am hard pressed between the two. My desire is to depart and be with Christ for that is far better."

212. Phil 1:21 (*RSV*), "For to me to live is Christ, and to die is gain."

213. "Augustine went to eat as if to torment and it was the same for Bernard." This is perhaps a note from Henry of Nördlingen and demonstrates the great influence of the example of Augustine and Bernard on the spiritual lives of fourteenth-century religious.

214. 13 February 1347.

215. Ps 120:5 (*RSV*), "Woe to me, that I sojourn in Meshech, that I dwell among the tents of Kedar!"

216. Gal 2:20 (*RSV*), "I have been crucified with Christ; it is no longer I who live, but Christ who lives in me; and the life I now live

in the flesh I live by faith in the Son of God, who loved me and gave himself up for me."

217. 2 Cor 4:16 (*RSV*), "So we do not lose heart. Though our outer nature is wasting away, our inner nature is renewed every day."

218. 31 March 1347.

219. 15–16 July 1347.

220. 24 June 1347.

221. 16 July 1347, "His worthy friend" is Henry of Nördlingen.

222. "He" refers to Henry, not to Christ.

223. By God's help she was able to receive communion from the hands of Henry eleven times during his stay at Maria Medingen.

224. 27 July 1347.

225. *Geraten* is translated as *entrathen* in *m*. An alternative might be, "I cannot ask it of you."

226. 28 July 1347.

227. 29 July 1347.

228. 10 August 1347.

229. Margaret used the word *stuehl* for choir stall throughout. The new choir erected in 1717 is very likely of the same design as the medieval choir at Maria Medingen. If so, there was a large area behind the choir stalls of the prioress, etc., which would have been behind Margaret as she faced the tabernacle.

230. 15 August 1347.

231. Lk 10:30–37.

232. 19 August 1347.

233. 8 September 1347.

234. The word *dir* (you) lends support to the theory that Margaret's letters to Henry were returned to her and were subsequently incorporated into the text of the *Revelations*. This passage may be a vestige of one of the letters, for it seems to be addressed to Henry of Nördlingen.

235. 29 September 1347.

236. Charles IV (1316–78), King of Bohemia, was elected as anti-king to Louis.

237. It is quite probable that Louis and Margaret had met. It is certain that he visited Donauwörth many times during Margaret's childhood. That she knew him personally might explain the great concern she had for the man, not as emperor, but as Louis. Why did

she not want him to know that she was his "spiritual" benefactress? Remember, she also did not want anyone outside the monastery to know what extraordinary graces had been given to her.

238. 11 October 1347.

239. Henry, who had been forced to flee imperial lands because of his support for John XXII, wanted to know the ultimate fate of Louis, who had been the immediate cause of the interdict and its subsequent troubles. Could an excommunicate be saved?

240. Louis IV.

241. 1 November 1347.

242. 1 Cor 2:9.

243. Presumably the second soul mentioned by her was not one of the sisters of the monastery. Perhaps she had been a worker or peasant.

244. Konrad of Schlüsselberg had been one of the most loyal supporters of Emperor Louis.

245. 11 November 1347.

246. 30 November 1347.

247. 6 December 1347.

248. 1 January 1347.

249. 6 January, 2 February 1348.

250. Manuscript *m* records this as the day of the flight into Egypt.

251. Manuscript *m* has "Three Kings' Day."

252. 3 March 1348.

253. 31 March 1348.

254. 19 April 1348.

255. 5 April 1348.

256. 17 April 1348.

257. 18 April 1348.

258. 19 April 1348.

259. 20 April 1348.

260. 25 April 1348.

261. 8 June 1348.

262. 11–23 June 1348.

263. 15 August 1348.

264. 8 September 1348.

265. 4 September 1348.

266. 15 September 1348.

267. 1 November 1348.

268. Margaret refers to the ravages of the Black Death. In his fourth letter, Abbot Ulrich III of Kaishelm asked her to pray because so many of the priests and brothers in his Cistercian monastery had already succumbed to the plague.

269. 2 November 1348.

270. 11 November 1348.

271. 28 November 1348.

272. Jn 4:14 (*RSV*), "But whoever drinks of the water that I shall give him will never thirst; the water that I shall give him will become in him a spring of water welling up to eternal life."

APPENDIX

APPENDIX

FIGURE 1. THE EBNER FAMILY OF DONAUWÖRTH

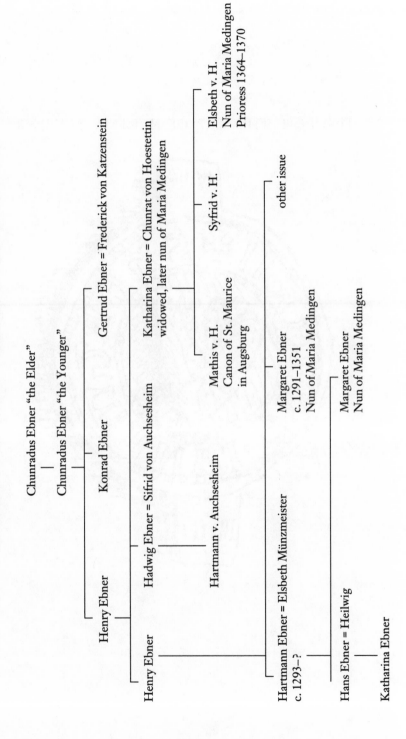

FIGURE 2. THE SEAL OF HARTMANN EBNER

The illustrations of the seals are taken from a study by Anton Michael Seitz, "Verwandschaft, Stammbaum und Wappen der Mystikerin Margareta Ebner von Kloster Maria Medingen," *Jahrbuch des historischen Vereins Dillingen a.d. Donau* 72 (1970): 106–9.

FIGURE 3.
THE SEAL OF MÖDINGEN

FIGURE 4.
THE SEAL OF SCHÄFSTALL

Select Bibliography

————. *Augustana Vindelicorum seu Ordinis Praedicatorum, Confirmationes Cultus ab immemoriabili tempore praestiti servae Dei Margaritae seu Ebnerin.* Vatican City: Typus Polyglottis Vaticanis, MCMLXIII.

————. *Early Documents of the Dominican Sisters.* Vol. II. Summit, N.J.: Dominican Nuns of Summit, 1969.

Une moniale Dominicaine. "Une mystique: Marguerite Ebner." *La Vie Spirituelle.* Vol. 137, (March–April 1983): 209–220.

Bihlmeyer, Karl. "Die Selbstbiographie in der deutschen Mystik des Mittelalters." *Theologische Quartalschrift* 114 (1933): 504–544.

David-Windstosser, M., ed. *Deutsche Mystiker.* Band V. *Frauenmystik im Mittelalter.* Kempten and Munich: Verlag der Jos. Kosel'schen Buchhandlung, 1919.

Dictionaire du Spiritualité. (1980) s.v. "Marguerite Ebner" by Siegfried Ringler, Vol. 10 "M": 338–340.

Dünninger, Josef. "Weihnachtliche Motive in der Mystik der Dominikanerkloster [sic] Maria Medingen und Engelthal," *Bayrische Literaturgeschichte in ausgewählten Beispielen* Band 1: Mittelalter (1965), eds. Eberhard Dünninger and Dorothee Kiesselbach, 337–248.

Gieraths, Gundolf, O.P. "Life in Abundance: Meister Eckhart and the German Dominican Mystics of the 14th Century," *Spirituality Today* 38 Supplement (Autumn 1986): 13–20.

Hanser, Hyacinthe, O.P. "Marguerite Ebner: une mystique domincaine du XIV siecle." *Année Dominicaine* 1937: 202–205.

Hohm [sic], M. Avellina. "Sexto Centenario de la gran Mustica alemana Margarita Ebner." *La Vida Sobrenatural* LII, November–December 1951: 448–451.

Holm, M. Avellina. "Die Mystikerin Margarete Ebner: eine wahrhaft edle deutsche Frau." *Gottesfreunde* June 1951: 20–21.

Jedelhauser, M. Canisia, O.P. "Geschichte des Klosters und der Hofmark Maria Medingen von den Anfängen im 13. Jahrundert bis 1606." *Quellen und Forschungen des Dominikanerordens in Deutschland.* Paulus von Loë, ed. Vol 34. Vechta-in-Oldenburg: Albertus Magnus Verlag, 1936: 9–113.

Kunisch, H. "Margareta Ebner oder das gottgelobte Herz" *Hochland* 36. (1939): 162–166.

Kunze, H. *Studien zu den Nonnenviten des deutschen Mittelalters.* Diss. Hamburg, 1953: 109–166.

Oehl, W. *Deutsche Mystikerbriefe des Mittelalters.* Munich, 1931: 33–343.

Preger, W. *Geschichte der deutschen Mystik im Mittelalter.* Vol. 2, Leipzig, 1881: 277–306.

Prestel, J. *Die Offenbarungen der Margareta Ebner und der Adelheid Langmann.* Weimar, 1939: 5–109.

Pummerer, A. "Margareta Ebner," *Stimmen aus Maria Laach.* Vol. 81, (1911): 1–11; 132–144; 244–257.

Rapp, Francis. "Un combat pour la ferveur et la fidelité," *La Vie Spirituelle.* 36, November–December 1982: 652–665.

Roth, Hyacinth, O.P. "Venerable Margaret Ebner: a possible Dominican Beata." *The Torch.* XX March 1936: 18–19, 28.

Schauenburg, A. *Leben der gottseligen Schwester Margareta Ebner.* Dülmen i.W.: Laumannsche Buchhandlung, 1914.

Schneider, M. Roswitha, O.P. *Die selige Margareta Ebner.* St. Ottilien: EOS Verlag, 1985.

Seitz, Anton Michael. "Verwandschaft, Stammbaum und Wappen der Mystikerin Margaretha Ebner von Kloster Maria Medingen." *Jahrbuch des Historischen Vereins Dillingen an der Donau* 72 (1970).

Siemer, Polykarp, M., O.P. "Geschichte des Dominkanerklosters Sankt Magdalena in Augsburg, 1225–1808," *Quellen und Forschungen zur Geschichte des Dominkanerordens in Deutschland* 33, (1936): 1–318, s.v. Frauenkloster Maria Medingen bei Dillingen: 54.

Stoudt, Debra. "The Vernacular Letters of Heinrich von Nördlingen." *Mystics Quarterly.* (Vol. XII, No. 1, March 1986): 19–25.

Strauch, Philipp. *Margaretha Ebner und Heinrich von Nördlingen.* Freiburg i.B. and Tübingen: Akademische Verlagsbuchhandlung von J.C.B. Mohr, 1882. Reprint. Amsterdam: Verlag P. Schippers N.V., 1966.

SELECT BIBLIOGRAPHY

Theologische Realenzyklopädie. (1982) Band IX. s.v. Ebner M.

Traber, Johannes. *Die Herkunft der selig genannten Dominikanerin Margareta Ebner.* Donauwörth: Historischer Verein Donauwörth, 1910.

Walz, Angelus, O.P. "Gottesfreunde um Margareta Ebner," *Historisches Jahrbuch der Görres-Gesellschaft.* Vol. 72, (1953): 253–265.

Walz, Angelus, O.P. "Margaret Ebner's *Pater Noster.*" *Cross and Crown.* IV. (1952): 227–231, trans. Sr. M. Fulgence, O.P.

Weitlauf, M. "Margaret Ebner." *Bavaria Sancta.* Vol. 3, (1973): 231–267.

Wentzel, Hans. "Eine Wiener Christkindwiege in München und das Jesuskind der Margaretha Ebner." *Pantheon* 18 (1960): 267–283.

Wilms, Hieronymus, O.P. *Das Tugenstreben der Mystikerinnen.* Vechta i.O.: Albertus Magnus Verlag, 1927.

Wilms, Hieronymus, O.P. trans. *Der Seligen Margareta Ebner Offenbarungen und Briefe.* Vechta i.O.: Albertus Magnus Verlag, 1928.

Wilms, Hieronymus, O.P. "Mistica alemana y mistica española, M. Ebner y Teresa de Jesús." *La Vida Sobrenatural.* Vol. XXVII, No. 160, (April 1934): 224–236. Also Vol. XXVIII, No 162, (June 1934): 361–373.

Zoepf, Ludwig. *Die Mystikerin M. Ebner.* Leipzig and Berlin: Verlag B.G. Teubner, 1914.

Zoepfl, Friedrich. *Margareta Ebner.* Meitingen: Kyrios Verlag, 1950.

Zoepfl, Friedrich. "Maria Medingen: Die Geschichte einer Kulturstätte im schwabischen Donautal." *Jahrbuch des Historischen Vereins Dillingen.* LIX/LX (1960).

Index

INDEX

INDEX

Other Volumes in this Series